Brian Re...

Chapel Hill, January 1992

O9-BUD-110

Reforming Products Liability

Reforming Products Liability

W. Kip Viscusi

Harvard University Press
Cambridge, Massachusetts
London, England
1991

Copyright © 1991 by the President and Fellows of Harvard College
All rights reserved
Printed in the United States of America
10 9 8 7 6 5 4 3 2 1

This book is printed on acid-free paper, and its binding materials
have been chosen for strength and durability.

Library of Congress Cataloging in Publication Data

Viscusi, W. Kip.
Reforming products liability / W. Kip Viscusi.
p. cm.
Includes bibliographical references and index.
ISBN 0-674-75323-2
1. Products liability—United States. 2. Products liability—
Economic aspects—United States. I. Title.
KF1296.V57 1991
346.7303'8—dc20
[347.30638]

90-23161
CIP

To William E. Viscusi,
from whom I learned my first
lessons in product safety

Contents

Preface

The liability crisis of the 1980s put products liability reform high on our national agenda. The rapid escalation in insurance premiums prompted a variety of blue-ribbon panels to call for a scaling back of the products liability system. Although many states enacted reform measures, for the most part the impetus behind these changes diminished toward the end of the decade as premiums stabilized.

The ebbing and waning of the public's attention to products liability would be appropriate if the deficiencies in the functioning of the liability regime were cyclical in nature, but the available evidence suggests that the problems are long-term. In the past two decades there has been a tremendous surge in products liability costs in the American economy. These sweeping changes merit greater scrutiny and evaluation than they have received to date. Moreover, there has been no formal attempt to reconcile the increasing prominence of government regulatory agencies with the existing liability regime. Until fundamental issues of institutional responsibility are addressed, the products liability system will continue to function erratically.

The main focus of this book is twofold. First, I provide an economic assessment of products liability law. A well-developed economic literature provides guidelines for the creation of efficient incentives for risk reduction and optimal insurance of accident victims. These findings are well understood in the case of financial losses, but the legal system has done little to apply these insights in the attempt to devise incentives for optimal risk deterrence and insurance of irreplaceable economic goods, such as life and health. Of course, economic theory alone cannot guide our actions. We also have explicit empirical evidence regarding the extent of the economic incentives that must be created to induce efficient behavior and to provide the appropriate level of insurance when it is not feasible to "make the victim whole."

The second principal aim of the book is to present a detailed empirical foundation for assessing the workings of the products liability system. In addition to drawing upon widely available information pertaining to case loads and insurance patterns, I examine two sets of data developed by the Insurance Services Office—the 1977 Product Liability Closed Claims Survey and the insurance industry's ratemaking files for the years 1980–1984. A thorough grounding in empirical foundations enriches our understanding of products liability mechanisms and gives us an appreciation of the insurance problems that have generated much of the impetus for reform.

The intended audience for this book includes all who are interested in the impact of products liability on the American economy and the economic basis for products liability reform. Because I hope to reach readers of varying backgrounds, I have attempted to limit the technical content of the book. In every case, the essential elements of the economic arguments and the empirical evidence are presented. However, many of the technical details lying behind the results are not included. For example, the statistical analyses that generated the findings do not appear, but summary tables that capture the main empirical patterns of interest are included. Since this work draws upon many of my previous publications, I have identified the appropriate works for readers wishing to pursue the more technical aspects of my arguments.

Although I hope the ideas presented here will be taken up in current debates over the law, the task of establishing a sound role for products liability within the context of society's risk management efforts will be a continuing process. This book is not an effort to advocate a specific and immediate legislative agenda. Rather, its main purpose is to provide guiding principles for making the policies needed to better manage the products liability system in the American economy. These principles will be as relevant to insurance crises to come as they are to the debates raging now over the liability crises of the 1980s or the 1970s.

My involvement in the products liability area developed as a natural extension of my research on risk regulation. My initial work focused on the efforts of agencies such as the Occupational Safety and Health Administration and the Consumer Product Safety Commission. In addition, I have been concerned with developing estimates of the appropriate value of life and health from the standpoint of efficient risk regulation. Since the products liability system also creates incentives for risk reduction, it became important to address the respective contributions of various institutions to the regulatory environment. Ideally, we should ensure that the mix of our social programs pertaining to risk fosters society's best interests. My framework for analysis and the criteria I apply to alternative products liability policies parallel the approach I have taken in my studies of other social risk management institutions. This book represents my assessment of how liability can best be reoriented to advance these social objectives.

This research has benefited from the input of a variety of organizations and individuals. At Harvard University Press, Michael Aronson shepherded this manuscript through its various iterations and provided guidance on the overall direction of the book. Much of the readability of the book is due to the editorial efforts of Kate Schmit.

Research support was provided by the National Science Foundation. I am also indebted to the Insurance Services Office for making available to me both their 1977 Product Liability Closed Claims Survey and their ratemaking files for products liability insurance. In each case, I obtained these proprietary data from the Insurance Services Office for use in my scholarly work. Other researchers wishing to use the data for scholarly purposes can request access to the database from the Insurance Services Office. I had no prior association with the Insurance Services Office, and I have had no subsequent association with this group or with any insurance firm that it represents. The Insurance Service Office has issued an extremely comprehensive summary of its 1977 Product Liability Closed Claims Survey, which includes hundreds of tables of information summarizing the results of the survey. This published information is likely to be of substantial benefit to anyone interested in assessing the findings reported here.

I became interested in products liability reform issues primarily through my efforts as an associate reporter for the American Law Institute Project on Enterprise Liability for Personal Injuries. I would particularly like to thank the original head of this project and current assistant attorney general, Richard Stewart, for involving me in it. In addition, I am grateful to Paul Weiler, who is currently the chief reporter for the project, for his continuing feedback on my research in the torts area, including detailed comments on a draft of this book. In a variety of efforts for this project, I was fortunate to be able to collaborate with Alan Schwartz.

Over the past few years I have also been involved in an analysis of the bargaining structure of the litigation process with Lee Lillard of the RAND Corporation. The Institute of Civil Justice at the RAND Corporation provided partial funding for this research. I must also acknowledge the contribution of my other collaborators in the products liability area—Michael J. Moore, Jerome Culp, and Joni Hersch—whose work with me will be cited at various points in the text.

The comments on my papers from participants at a variety of tort liability conferences have helped me refine many of the arguments presented here. These efforts include the conference on tort liability reform held at the University of Virginia Law School and run by Kenneth Abraham; the Stanford Law School conference on liability run by A. Mitchell Polinsky and Carl Shapiro; the Brookings Institution liability conference run by Robert Litan and Clifford Winston; the Brookings Institution liability and innovation conference run by Robert Litan and Peter Huber; the Manhattan Institute tort liability conference run by Walter Olson; and the National Bureau of Economic Research workshop on liability insurance run by Paul Joskow. Seminar participants at Harvard Law School, University of Toronto Law School, and Columbia Law School made a variety of valuable suggestions. Also of great help to me were Peter Schuck's comments on my contribution with Michael Moore for the American Bar Association–American Assembly tort liability conference.

The continued efforts of such groups have helped to provide additional substance to the products liability reform debate. What is needed is not a temporary policy measure but a long-term restructuring of liability law, which will be the result of thoughtful examination and debate of the merits of different tort liability alternatives.

The six years of research supporting this book have drawn on the talents of a series of superb research assistants. I would particularly like to single out the contributions of David Anderson, Mark Dreyfus, Thomas Dunn, Anil Gaba, Oren Lewin, and Sharon Tennyson. Chief responsibility for word processing and all supporting library work for this book was in the hands of Lisa Feinstein, without whose efforts this book would be appearing one year later.

Portions of this book draw upon previously published articles. In almost every case only small portions of the articles appear in the book as they were originally written, because I synthesized and reworked the earlier texts. Nevertheless, I would like to express my appreciation to a variety of publishers for permitting me to utilize portions of these earlier publications: four articles in the *Journal of Legal Studies;* two articles in the *Yale Journal on Regulation;* and individual articles in the *International Review of Law and Economics,* the *American University Law Review,* the *Journal of Products Liability,* and the *American Economic Review.* In addition, I draw upon the findings of a variety of other papers that are cited at the appropriate junctures in the text.

Reforming Products Liability

1

Diagnosing the Liability Crisis

In July 1988, a Beverly Hills oral surgeon, Dr. Andrew Glassman, obtained an out-of-court settlement of $6.3 million for product-related injuries.[1] Dr. Glassman was not a victim of an automobile accident or a hidden chemical hazard. Rather, he suffered an injury to his right hand when he fell off a horse during his polo lesson at the Los Angeles Equestrian Center. He was able to recoup his lost earnings through the generosity of the products liability system.

Dr. Glassman is not the only prizewinner in the tort liability sweep-stakes. A woman in Philadelphia was awarded $1 million after she claimed that a CAT scan caused her to lose her psychic powers. Apparently frivolous claims such as this one are not the exception; some are even embodied in the key cases in the evolution of products liability law. One plaintiff won a case against Fabergé after she and her friend attempted to make a scented candle by pouring perfume over a lit candle.[2] The court ruled that the product was defective for not having a warning alerting users to the flammability hazard.

Seemingly outrageous cases have come to epitomize the malfunctioning of the tort liability system. Unfortunately, they have become symbols of a runaway liability system and dominate public accounts, yet they do not accurately reflect the range of deficiencies of products liability. Product injuries also have a bleaker side. A group of 15,000 Vietnam veterans, for example, sought compensation for ailments that they claimed resulted from their exposure to the herbicide Agent Orange. Proving causality was the main difficulty for the plaintiffs.

Although this case resulted in a record award of $180 million, the payoff of $12,000 per claimant for injuries as severe as terminal cancer and genetic damage does not qualify as a windfall gain.

Victims of fatal product injuries certainly do not profit from an overly generous products liability system. Their families receive compensation usually based on the economic value of lost earnings less the share of these earnings that would have been spent to provide for the deceased. Even apart from the legal fees that must be paid and the chance that no compensation may be received at all, this arrangement is at best a break-even proposition.

The bargain prices that firms are often able to pay for the injuries inflicted by their products represent an economic opportunity that has not been lost on corporations. We cannot reasonably expect manufacturers to make their products completely safe. A risk-free car would have to be built like a tank. Even more feasible increases in safety may not be desirable on balance. Small cars are generally riskier than larger vehicles, but they offer greater fuel efficiency. Because consumers value many attributes of cars and not simply their safety, even consumers would not choose to make them risk-free.

The task of a well-functioning social risk management policy is to strike an appropriate balance between safety and the costs incurred to achieve this safety. Ideally, the social value placed on risk reductions should reflect the value of these improvements to those who will be protected. These financial incentives will then provide the economic impetus for firms to alter the product designs to incorporate all socially desirable safety attributes. If market forces alone are not sufficient to generate these risk reduction incentives, tort liability and government regulation must do so.

Unfortunately, the incentives generated by court awards are often inadequate. A dramatic case in point is that of the Ford Motor Company, which chose to market the Ford Pinto with a gas tank that posed a high risk of explosion upon rear impact.[3] Ford calculated the prospective liability burden, compared this cost with that of altering the design to reduce the risk of injury, and concluded that the design change would be more expensive than the court awards.

The company's decision to forgo the safety improvement on the basis of calculations that put a dollar value on life is not reprehensible. Indeed, a main purpose of products liability law is to encourage firms to confront the tradeoffs that are involved in an explicit manner. The principal deficiency of the Pinto case was the inadequate pricing of the lives that would be lost. The value of a life is greater than the earnings lost to the victim's survivors. If consumers had been aware of the risks of driving a Pinto, their market response would have indicated a willingness to pay for safety that was ten times as great as the levels imposed by a typical products liability award. Notwithstanding the attention-getting headlines of seemingly substantial verdicts, these awards almost invariably provide inadequate incentives for deterring accidents.

These deficiencies in the products liability system have received far too little attention. The ridiculous awards and the million-dollar verdicts dominate the public perception. Not surprisingly, the products liability reform literature has also placed too much emphasis on the excesses and too little on the inadequacies of products liability.

Perspectives on Liability Reform

Three approaches have dominated both academic and policy discussions of products liability reform. The first and largest contingent is the school of tort reform by anecdote. Motels have removed diving boards from their pools. Amusement parks have closed some of their more hazardous rides. Indeed, insurance problems even led to the closing of the well-known Cyclone ride at Coney Island's amusement park, Astroland, for several months.[4] Pharmaceutical companies have discontinued many vaccines and withdrawn contraceptive products. Each of these events can be traced to rising liability costs.

The anecdotal reviews seem not to consider whether these developments are necessarily undesirable. Moreover, they provide no assessment of the magnitude and prevalence of the problems. Even the avalanche of anecdotes included in the most comprehensive attacks on the system do little more than flag a problem that merits closer scrutiny. Anecdotes cannot substitute for analysis.

The second approach is that of tort reform motivated by isolated facts. The anecdotes of the first approach are mirrored in the liability statistics of the second. Counts of million-dollar verdicts continue to escalate. Surely this is evidence that the court system has run amok. However, upon closer examination of verdict trends and the factors that drive verdict levels, such as changes in medical costs, the escalation in million-dollar awards is less disturbing.

Without question the most compelling empirical result has been the tripling of products liability insurance premiums from 1984 to

1986. It was this mushrooming of premium levels that caught the public's attention and led to the widespread consensus that the United States was in the midst of a "products liability crisis."

Although the premium surge served a constructive function in calling public attention to the need for a careful examination of the products liability system, it also raised some suspicions. If the problems were in fact due to a long-term development in the character of products liability law, why was the premium increase so narrowly concentrated? Was there in fact a liability crisis, or was the escalation in the premiums the result of a conspiracy by the insurance industry to secure products liability reform that would be advantageous to them? At a more mundane level, can we attribute this premium surge to the underwriting cycle—a vaguely stated and little-understood financial mechanism that has no obvious link with the structure of liability law? Isolated facts such as the premium surge not only do not imply that there is a legitimate crisis; they also do not indicate the appropriate solution.

These two schools of thought—tort reform by anecdote and tort reform by isolated fact—have dominated current debate. Reform has become a code word for retrenchment. The apparent objective of most reform efforts is simple: costs must be reduced. Unfortunately, a strategy of cost relief will not necessarily make the system more effective or coherent but may instead lead to a grab bag of unrelated reform measures, including a return to a negligence regime, damages caps, and other restrictions on the scope of liability or damages. Only if the problem is, indeed, simply that of excessive cost will such measures be beneficial.

The final school of thought is that of tort reform by legal theory and ideology. This approach is largely responsible for establishing the products liability regime in place today. The belief that firms could play a beneficial role as insurers of the losses of accident victims led the courts to extend the range of contexts in which firms would be liable for injuries. Although insurance is a valid concern, universal insurance of all injuries involving products is not feasible. Automobile companies cannot, for example, compensate every victim of an automobile accident. Eventually some determination must be made regarding when insurance is feasible and what level of compensation the courts should provide. Resolving these issues involves more than legal and economic theory. One must ascertain how the scope of liability changes with different shifts in legal doctrine and whether insurance through products liability is viable. This kind of empirical foundation and comprehensive assessment of the appropriate role of products liability was missing from the proposals for the earlier expansion in products liability and has been absent from the liability reform literature as well.

Even narrowly defined issues such as the correct value of damages to establish incentives for accident deterrence cannot be resolved in the abstract. Deterring property damage is straightforward. Setting damages equal to the financial loss is generally the correct approach.[5] In the case of damage to health or loss of life, focus on financial loss alone will greatly understate the stakes involved. How damages should be set to establish correct incentives can only be ascertained with the aid of empirical analysis.

The perspective of this book differs from the three existing approaches. I view products liability reform not as a response to isolated facts and anecdotes or a matter of legal philosophy and theory alone, but rather as a question of designing an appropriate institutional mechanism to control risks and compensate victims of product-related injuries. The same kinds of criteria that we apply to the regulatory policy structure of the Consumer Product Safety Commission and to the compensation schedules under the workers' compensation system also can be applied to products liability. The task is one of designing social risk policy.

Framing the issue as a policy decision is not sufficient. One must also have some assessment of the merits of alternative courses of action. To provide this empirical foundation, I will explore a variety of new and extensive data bases on the performance of the current products liability system.

Products liability does not have a single mission, but instead has multiple objectives. Chief among these are deterrence and compensation. I will assess the performance of products liability with respect to each of these objectives and develop reference points for judging that performance. The financial loss involved in a product injury typically will not be the correct amount of insurance that should be provided or the amount that is needed to establish adequate deterrence of accidents. In each case a stronger empirical base than has been evidenced in the literature is needed before we can make any judgments whatsoever with respect to the adequacy of products liability.

Even after this foundation has been laid, we will be unable to pinpoint an ideal solution. Inevitably, tradeoffs must be made between providing the right amount of insurance and promoting risk reduction, since no liability structure will be ideal with respect to all objectives. We must have estimates of the magnitudes of these tradeoffs before we can set the optimal course for liability reform. A reform program without an empirical foundation is little more than conjecture and in the usual case says more about the ideological predisposition of the reformer than about the rationales for pursuing a particular program.

If our objective is to establish an appropriate risk policy rather than simply to consider modifications in products liability, then part of our job is to recommend an appropriate institutional division of labor. Perhaps the most striking aspect of the burgeoning of the products liability system is that it has coincided with a major expansion in government's regulation of risk and a tremendous increase in private insurance coverage. Other institutions have assumed the brunt of the responsibility for controlling risk and compensating accident victims. Yet, the number of tort liability cases has increased rather than decreased in recent years. At the very minimum, there is a need to reexamine the products liability system and to coordinate its functions with those of other social institutions with a common focus.

Recent Trends in Products Liability

The widespread perception that there has been a major expansion of the products liability system is correct. Federal products liability lawsuits involving personal injury have increased sixfold from 1975 to 1989. Even if one excludes asbestos litigation, which now makes up over half of all cases in the federal courts, products liability litigation was still greater in the 1980s than in previous decades. The price tag associated with this litigation has also increased, as median verdict levels have nearly doubled from 1980 to 1988; most of this increase can be attributed to the inflation of medical costs.

Examining trends in verdicts and litigation reveals but a small and potentially unrepresentative segment of products liability cases. The overwhelming percentage of claims that are not dropped—95 percent—are settled out of court. Moreover, those cases that go to court do not represent a random sample of all cases. For example, large claims are more likely to be litigated than are small claims.

A closer look at the compensation received by accident victims from out-of-court settlements and court verdicts conveys an impression not at all like the anecdotes of the runaway jury verdicts. If million-dollar awards epitomize the excesses of the current liability regime, one would expect that the generosity of the compensation levels as compared with the size of the economic losses inflicted would be the greatest for cases with losses at the high end. The opposite in fact is the case. Small claims tend to be overcompensated relative to the amount of economic damage, and large claims tend to be undercompensated.

A summary index of the impact of litigation and out-of-court settlements is their net effect on insurance premiums. The surge in premium levels suggests the extent of the increased cost of liability. The popular view is that the insurance crisis is an event of the mid-1980s. Although premiums escalated rapidly at that time, overall there was a greater increase in liability insurance premiums in the decade 1968–1978 than in 1978–1988. The timing of the great escalation in liability costs—in the 1970s and 1980s rather than the 1960s, when strict liability was introduced—suggests that the adoption of strict liability is not the major source of the cost increase. Although the expansion in producers' liability has received the greatest attention in the products liability reform debate to date, other more recent expansions in liability may have been of greater consequence. In particular, the development of the design defect doctrine and the increased prominence of hazard warnings cases coincide more directly with the rise in liability costs.

Compensation to victims is not the whole story, of course. Extensive data drawn from the insurance industry's ratemaking files give us the other side of the coin, the workings of the liability insurance market. The premium surge in the mid-1980s was simply one manifestation of the problem. Before the premium explosion, there was evidence of a shrinking products liability insurance market. The liability crisis was not just a premium surge in the mid-1980s that abated in 1987 and can now be forgotten. Rather, the rise in insurance rates reflected a long-term shift in the impact of products liability that created a temporary explosion in premiums as but one of many effects.

These economic effects are real and quite extensive. Published reports of products liability actions have substantial effects on the stock market price of firms. Rising liability costs have influenced product innovation and product introduction decisions, particularly in markets in which the liability exposure is substantial. And the products liability price tag, which is passed on to the consumer, sometimes reaches staggering levels. Riders on the Philadelphia mass transit system now pay seventeen cents of every fare dollar to cover the insurance costs for injuries to passengers.[6] Similarly, from 15 percent to 25 percent of the purchase of ladders can be traced to legal and liability costs.[7]

One industry that has been particularly hard hit by products liability is the private aircraft industry. American firms produced over 17,000 private planes in 1979. Production decreased to 1,085 by 1987. The leading producer, Cessna, which accounted for 9,000 planes in 1979, ceased production altogether. Beech did little better, as its production dropped from 1,214 to 195 over that period. The cost of liability now averages $100,000 per plane produced. It is so high because aircraft companies are sued in 90 percent of all crashes involving fatalities or serious injury, even though pilot error is responsible for 85 percent of all accidents.[8] The irony is that the suits discourage the production of new planes, which means that the mix of planes in use presents a higher risk than it would if the older planes had been replaced by newer models.

Evidence of economic impacts and changes in product-related decisions does not always indicate an undesirable situation. If firms are marketing overly risky products, then we want the products liability system to establish incentives to ensure an appropriate balancing of risks and costs. Perhaps the principal source of the opposition to liability's expanded role stems from the change in the mix of firms being hit with liability costs. With its focus on manufacturing defects, products liability in the past primarily impinged on the declining firms in an industry. Manufacturing defects were but one component of these firms' overall record of low quality. The same firms also tended to be among the laggards in the industry in terms of innovation and other safety measures.

The adoption of the design defect doctrine shifted the courts' focus, as the courts now became societal risk regulators for product designs. No longer was the impact of liability restricted to the declining firms in an industry. Innovative firms that introduced potentially risky products now faced substantial liability costs. Tort liability had invaded the boardrooms of the Fortune 500.

The shift in the emphasis of products liability to a broad regulatory function not only altered the mix of firms affected but also influenced the overall performance of products liability. Unfortunately, the courts are not regulatory agencies and do not have the expertise to set safety levels, especially since they must act within the narrow perspective of a particular case.

Coupling the design defect doctrine with the application of strict liability criteria, which shifts injury costs from accident victims to producers, has two main repercussions. It extends the range of situations in which courts will serve as regulatory agencies, and it creates new situations in which firms will be serving as insurers for product accidents. Relying on products liability to establish insurance where there was none before is more feasible in isolated cases of manufacturing defects than in cases with a much more substantial time lag, such as those in which damages must be paid for an entire product line.

The most prevalent judicial approach to design defect issues involves the balancing of competing concerns known as the risk-utility test. The risk posed by a product design is balanced against the utility of the product to the consumer. A liability doctrine embodying a balancing mechanism of this sort is a sound approach, but the procedure has not been well specified, and it has been based on an overzealous view of the ability of producers to serve as insurers of the product risks. If we limit firms' responsibility to provide insurance to manufacturing defect cases and restructure the risk-utility test so it will provide more precise guidance both to the courts and affected firms, we can foster safety incentives in an effective manner without imposing infeasible insurance demands on the firm.

The other change coinciding with the surge in the liability burden has been the emergence of a new design defect: the inadequate hazard warning. If plaintiffs cannot demonstrate the product itself was defective, all is not lost. They also have an opportunity to show that the warning was inadequate. Since there are no well-defined criteria for assessing warnings in court cases, the potential for abuse is enormous.

Ideally, warnings should shift more of the responsibility for product safety from the producer to the user. One of the great ironies of the current state of products liability is that hazard warnings have not dampened litigation. Rather, courts' assessment of the adequacy of warnings has simply given firms another test that they can fail and bolstered plaintiffs' chance of success. Responsibility for accidents has shifted from the individual consumer to the producer.

Perhaps the most remarkable aspect of the increased scope of products liability is that it has taken place in the presence of a tremendous expansion in government's regulation of risk beginning in the 1970s. The liability system has done little to recognize the often considerable overlap in the issues addressed by the courts and by regulatory agencies. A better allocation of responsibilities between the two institutions will not only eliminate the overlaps but will also exploit the institutions' special strengths. Regulatory agencies are better suited for establishing economy-wide standards for product design and overall safety.

The surge in the amounts of damages awards is of less consequence than the expansion in liability, but damages too are on the upswing. For the most part, the rise in damages can be traced to medical expenses, which have soared throughout the entire economy. Reform proposals in the damages area do not address these pivotal inflationary forces but instead focus on pain and suffering damages. Awards for nonmonetary losses are an easy target, for they have no clearly articulated legal foundation. Recent economic studies in other contexts have drawn some distinctions as to when pain and suffering awards are appropriate and when they are not and how courts should set pain and suffering damages. Perhaps the greatest need in this area is for greater structure. In providing this discipline we should avoid simplistic solutions such as damages caps, which will affect only a small minority of products liability cases. The primary effect of caps is to penalize victims with large medical expenses, such as those suffering from brain damage or paraplegia. Society's objective should be to foster an appropriate relationship between damages awards and the risk levels. Our objective is to promote the deterrence and compensation functions of liability. The "meat ax" approach of capping or eliminating damages for nonpecuniary losses sacrifices the essential deterrence function.

While most reform efforts have focused on efforts to restrain the liability of firms, one recent development threatens to generate an unprecedented explosion in liability costs. Some courts have considered estimating damages on the basis of the value of life (so-called "hedonic" damages) now used by government agencies in establishing the price society should pay to reduce risks of death. This approach will increase damages awards by a factor of ten. Examination of this concept indicates that it is not voodoo economics. Indeed, it is the correct way to approach deterrence issues. The concept's applicability in the courtroom, however, should be limited to very select instances. The deterrence value of damages is particularly appealing in situations in which punitive damages are awarded. Once the functions of deterrence and insurance are adequately addressed, the constructive role of additional punitive damages substantially diminishes.

Another prominent recent development has been the emergence of mass toxic torts, as thousands of claimants for long-term health effects have sought compensation. Agent Orange, asbestos, and DES are among the cases of this type. In the absence of clear causal links, liability for health effects will not function as a mechanism for controlling risk but will simply serve as a highly imperfect social insurance scheme. Perhaps more than any other example of tort liability, mass toxic torts is an area from which the court system should clearly withdraw and relegate the responsibilities of deterrence and compensation to regulatory agencies and more broadly based social insurance efforts.

The performance of workers' compensation provides mixed lessons for tort liability reform. A striking economic impact of this program is that workers in risky jobs accept lower wages in return for higher workers' compensation benefits. Indeed, workers' compensation in effect pays for itself through savings in wages. The analogy for products liability, in which prices adjust to reflect higher liability costs, is not entirely hypothetical.

Workers' compensation has also had a substantial deterrent effect. Linking firms' accident records to the premiums they must pay has led to much lower risk levels. Death risks for American workers would be 27 percent higher in the absence of these incentives.[9] This economic mechanism will work similarly for any liability cost. Linking liability costs to risks has important deterrence effects and it should receive more attention in liability reform discussions. Focusing on issues of deterrence will reorient products liability toward the objective of controlling risks and away from the objective of compensating victims, which has received excessive emphasis.

Proposals for Reform

The proposals advocated here focus on a fundamental restructuring of both liability rules and damages assessment. The overall objective of products liability should be to foster appropriate incentives for accident deterrence and to provide insurance of accident victims' losses to the extent that doing so is feasible. Retaining strict liability for manufacturing defects is feasible, but in the case of design defects

I advocate a reformulation of the risk-utility test that more closely resembles a formalized negligence standard. In addition, there should be more explicit recognition by the courts of the safety regulations imposed by other branches of government and of the need to avoid overlapping responsibilities.

A sound risk-utility test for judging design defect issues should also reduce ventures by the court into areas such as mass toxic torts. The expansive notion of design defects in these cases, coupled with an overambitious expectation of the degree to which producers can serve as insurers, has diverted the courts from their fundamental mission. The primary task of products liability law is to promote safety incentives in situations not adequately addressed by society's other institutions for risk management and to provide compensation to victims when these safety standards are not met. If these safety levels are acceptable, then courts should not intervene simply to provide insurance. Compensation and insurance of accident victims is a secondary objective that comes into play only once the inadequacy of the risk level has been established.

Hazard warnings should continue to be an important element of products liability cases, but there is a need for a much sounder approach than the current practice of deciding cases on the basis of junk science being propagated by self-proclaimed warnings experts. An ideal outcome would be a national warnings policy with clearly specified criteria for hazard warnings. Other more limited reforms would also be beneficial. Much can be done to improve the scientific validity of the courts' assessments of warnings. The net effect of such reforms should be to encourage consumers to take more responsibility for promoting safety and to encourage firms to provide the information consumers need to make sound safety decisions. Product safety is a shared responsibility, not just a corporate responsibility.

My proposals pertaining to liability standards will reduce the costs imposed by products liability. In contrast, my proposals for scheduling damages and exploring limited use of damages concepts that will create real incentives for deterrence will boost the cost imposed by liability. Proposals with conflicting cost effects are inconsistent only if one views the goal of reform as cost relief, not responsible social risk management.

Some skeptics of reform efforts may doubt whether any reform measures will be effective. Will the courts simply adjust in other ways if, for example, we impose statutory requirements on the manner in which damages are calculated? The evidence regarding the performance of products liability insurance across groups of states with different liability regimes indicates that the structure of liability laws is of enormous consequence for the costs imposed by liability and the feasibility of liability insurance.

The importance of liability structures is reflected in the spirited lobbying efforts on behalf of different reform measures. Attempts to limit the impact of products liability have ranged from detailed blueprints for a new system to more targeted efforts. One highly focused proposal in the Colorado legislature, for example, would eliminate ski resorts' liability in most instances because of the inherent danger in skiing.[10] The attention devoted to legislative initiatives of this kind is a reflection of the economic stakes involved in liability reform.

The crisis atmosphere surrounding the products liability debate has focused public attention on liability reform, but it has distorted our perspective of the problem as well. Our task is not to solve the recurring temporary crises in liability and insurance. Nor should we dismiss the need for liability reform when litigation levels and insurance rates stabilize. Rather, we should be engaged in a long-term effort to make products liability an efficient mechanism for promoting safety, but one that functions in concert with other social institutions for the management of risk.

2

The Dimensions of the
Liability Crisis

The products liability insurance crisis of the mid-1980s has led to a
variety of legal reform efforts. The United States Department of
Justice, the American Law Institute, and the American Bar Association are among the many organizations that are assessing the deficiencies in the tort systems and the needed reforms.[1] The financial
difficulties in the liability insurance industry have provided the impetus for these recent efforts. In particular, a widely held belief that
there has been a dramatic escalation in the burdens imposed by products liability has been the main starting point for reform strategies.
The result has been a series of proposals to reduce these costs—damages caps, restrictions on pain and suffering damages, a return to
negligence doctrine, and similar measures. The dominant perception
is that the producers, rather than the accident victims, are most adversely affected by the crisis; tort liability reform, therefore, should
be directed at diminishing the impact of the crisis on firms.

Although this is a prominent view, it is not altogether obvious that
the surge in products liability insurance premiums indicates a need
to restructure liability rules. Consider the following possible explanations for the crisis.[2] The first hypothesis is that the rise in premiums
does not reflect a long-run escalation of the products liability burdens,
but is simply a consequence of interest rate fluctuations or, more
specifically, the underwriting cycle for the insurance industry. Insurance companies invest the premiums they receive and use both the

principal invested and the interest earned to pay off losses, which often occur many years after the premiums are collected. If interest rates are high, then the premiums that can be charged to cover a given amount of losses will be less, and competition among insurance firms will lower premium rates. Similarly, the decline in interest rates in the mid-1980s forced firms to raise premiums. At approximately the same time, Europeans withdrew from the reinsurance market, because of macroeconomic and international monetary conditions. The premium shift, then, is in part a consequence of broader economic fluctuations that lie outside the domain of tort liability reform.

The second explanation for the hike in premiums is that insurance firms colluded to raise rates in order to justify reform efforts to diminish their future costs. A conspiracy of this kind is perhaps the least plausible explanation, since it requires a degree of coordination among the firms that is difficult to achieve. For example, in 1988, 3,800 companies sold property and casualty insurance in the United States, which is too diffuse a group for a ratemaking conspiracy.[3] Furthermore, a large number of competitors would lead to price competition following liability reform competition that would eliminate the excess profits. The low profits earned by insurance firms in the mid-1980s also suggests that the conspiracy theory is not sound. Elementary economics suggests that firms will, of course, attempt to pursue policies that are in their best financial interest, but coordinating the actions of a large number of firms to raise premiums artificially, a move that would lead to a loss in business, for the purpose of creating an atmosphere conducive to reform seems unlikely.

Moreover, such explanations have an overly simplistic view of what the insurance industry is attempting to accomplish. Clearly, in the short run a reduction in liability costs may be to the advantage of an insurance company that may have written policies for which it will have to pay off losses in the future. Greater certainty in expected liability costs will also make insurance underwriting a less risky proposition. In the long run, however, the insurance industry will profit from a high level of liability since that will increase the amount of coverage it can write. More tort liability generally means more business for the insurance industry. Collusive behavior designed to decrease the amount of insurance business appears implausible. What seems more reasonable is that the insurance industry should have a strong financial interest in pursuing legal reforms to decrease the losses under policies already written and decrease the uncertainty associated with insurance. The predictability of future losses is essential to the ability to write insurance coverage in a reliable manner.

A third explanation for the liability crisis is that it is due to an increase in the level of liability burdens. The higher level could have come either from an increase in the riskiness of the products being marketed or from a change in liability standards. We will investigate each of these factors below.

Finally, a fourth explanation is that the crisis stems not from the increased level of costs but from the greater uncertainty that has been introduced by shifts in liability doctrine. Highly volatile loss patterns limit the insurance industry's ability to write coverage. If a policy runs the risk of leading to substantial and unanticipated insurance payoffs, as in the case of asbestos, then the premiums charged must be raised to cover future contingencies.

At present, there is no consensus regarding the extent to which the different possible causes of higher premiums—the underwriting cycle, conspiracy among insurance companies, increased liability actions, and underwriting uncertainty—have contributed to the products liability crisis. Moreover, how one diagnoses the crisis will influence which reforms one endorses, if indeed it is agreed that the liability system is responsible. The remainder of this chapter explores several factors that affect the functioning of this system.

Accident Rates Decline, But Litigation Soars

If the liability crisis is to be traced to the functioning of products liability, there must have been an increase in products liability litigation or awards. Although comprehensive information is not available for courts at all levels, data are available that permit an assessment of the products liability litigation at the federal court level.

Examination of federal statistics provides an index of trends in products liability but understates the total extent of litigation because it omits the cases that went before state courts. A study of cases by the U.S. General Accounting Office (1989) over three years in five states indicated that 46 percent of all products liability cases were tried in federal courts. As a result, the statistics in the accompanying tables capture just under half of the total products liability litigation.

This emphasis on federal courts may result in a higher rate of growth in the products liability caseload than has been displayed in

Table 2.1. Number of personal injury products liability cases commenced in federal courts, 1975–1989

Year	Total	Airline	Marine	Motor vehicle	Other
1975	2,393	301	46	438	1,608
1976	3,016	160	140	385	2,331
1977	3,366	198	149	372	2,647
1978	3,600	237	139	350	2,874
1979	5,318	699	128	457	4,034
1980	6,876	283	89	535	5,969
1981	8,028	256	69	491	7,212
1982	7,908	374	122	556	6,856
1983	8,026	337	164	574	6,951
1984	7,677	371	133	652	6,521
1985	12,507	278	112	612	11,505
1986	12,459	216	93	656	11,494
1987	14,145	150	99	649	13,247
1988	16,166	185	101	623	15,257
1989	13,408	185	88	662	12,473

Source: Annual Report of the Director of the Administrative Office of the U.S. Courts, 1975–1989, tables "Product Liability Cases Commenced."

state courts because of differences in the case mix.[4] By examining federal caseload trends by type of litigation and, in particular, by isolating the asbestos litigation, we can obtain a better sense of litigation trends more generally. Moreover, the following examination of insurance premium statistics will capture the net impact of all litigation and out-of-court settlements, providing a consistency check on the federal caseload analysis.

Table 2.1 presents statistics on the number of personal injury products liability cases commenced in federal courts from 1975 to 1989.[5] Over this fourteen-year period, there was a considerable escalation in the number of personal injury products liability cases. In 1975 only 2,393 such cases were commenced, whereas by 1989 the number rose to 13,408. For the most part, this increase seems to have occurred outside the transportation area. The number of airline products liability cases has held fairly steady, although the amount fluctuates from year to year depending on random major catastrophes. Similarly, the number of marine-related cases is also fairly stable. Motor vehicle cases rose by roughly 50 percent over the 1975–1989 period, but this increase is nowhere near as great as the nearly sixfold rise in

Table 2.2. Personal injury products liability cases as a percentage of all federal civil cases, 1975–1989

Year	Total	Airline	Marine	Motor vehicle	Other
1975	2.04	0.26	0.04	0.37	1.37
1976	2.31	0.12	0.11	0.29	1.79
1977	2.58	0.15	0.11	0.29	2.03
1978	2.59	0.17	0.10	0.25	2.06
1979	3.44	0.45	0.08	0.30	2.61
1980	4.07	0.17	0.05	0.32	3.53
1981	4.45	0.14	0.04	0.27	4.00
1982	3.84	0.18	0.06	0.27	3.33
1983	3.32	0.14	0.07	0.24	2.87
1984	2.94	0.14	0.05	0.25	2.50
1985	4.57	0.10	0.04	0.22	4.09
1986	4.89	0.08	0.04	0.26	4.51
1987	5.92	0.06	0.04	0.27	5.54
1988	6.75	0.08	0.04	0.26	6.37
1989	5.74	0.08	0.04	0.28	5.34

Source: Annual Report of the Director of the Administrative Office of the U.S. Courts, 1975–1989, tables "Product Liability Cases Commenced" and "Civil Cases Commenced."

products liability cases generally. Although much of the increase stems from the rise in asbestos litigation,[6] litigation other than asbestos has increased greatly as well.

One plausible explanation for the increase in products liability litigation is that there has been an upward trend in litigation more generally. Table 2.2, which shows personal injury products liability cases as a percentage of all federal civil cases, indicates that products liability litigation has become increasingly prominent. Whereas the products liability component of all civil cases was only 2.04 percent in 1975, by 1989 it had risen to 5.74 percent. These two comparison years are not in any way unrepresentative, as they reflect the steady upward trend of litigation of products liability cases generally as well as of all civil suits.

The airline and marine components of liability cases have had a decreasing share, and the motor vehicle share has been relatively flat, if not declining a bit. In contrast, other cases have been escalating considerably, in part because of the now substantial share of asbestos litigation, which comprised 3.52 percent of all civil cases by 1989.[7] Other cases, excluding asbestos and transportation, rose from 1.43 percent to 1.82 percent of all civil cases from 1984 to 1989, indicating increased litigation for other products as well.

What is particularly striking is that both the level of products liability cases as well as their share of all civil litigation jumped in the 1985–1989 period. Since, as we will see below, the liability insurance crisis reached its peak in 1985 and 1986, the rate increases that were observed in the insurance market coincided exactly with the escalation in products liability litigation.

In short, there is evidence at the federal court level of a substantial increase in products liability litigation, both in absolute terms as well as in relation to all civil litigation. Society has become more litigious in recent years, but the litigation increase has not been uniform, as products liability suits have outpaced the rise in other civil litigation. Moreover, as Chapter 5 will document, the level of awards in these cases has risen as well.

With litigation on the rise and court awards escalating as well, a natural inference might be that society is becoming increasingly risky. More specifically, one might conclude that the products we use are presumably more hazardous since they are generating considerably more litigation. Such a conclusion is not borne out by the accident statistics, which indicate that product safety has been improving throughout this century, as have safety records of all types.[8] Indeed, the only accident increase of any kind observed in this century has been the rise in motor vehicle accidents, which coincided with the growth in the use of automobiles throughout the United States. Even in this case, accident rates have declined after one takes into account the changing age structure of the population and the change in the miles driven.[9]

The safety trends over the 1977–1987 decade, which includes the period in which the products liability crisis emerged, all fail to suggest a reason for the explosion in litigation. Total accident rates declined by 20 percent; motor vehicle accidents dropped by 11 percent, work accidents declined by 25 percent, and home accidents declined by 26 percent.[10]

These statistics reflect a more general economic pattern. As society has become wealthier, we have demanded greater safety from our products, and as a result acceptable risk levels have declined. The tort liability crisis cannot be traced to increasing product riskiness, although it no doubt has been influenced in part by increased awareness of classes of risks that formerly were not well understood. Even in the case of asbestos, however, it is noteworthy that exposures to the material in recent years have been dramatically reduced below the levels that were responsible for the wave of asbestos litigation in the courts today.[11]

Although products liability litigation has escalated despite the greater level of safety, one should not then conclude that the additional claims are spurious. Few victims of product-related injuries seek recovery for their injuries through the tort system. Recent changes in the legal environment have expanded the set of claimants who will have favorable prospects of receiving compensation. Whether this expanded liability is desirable is an independent issue, but the fact that this expansion has occurred in tandem with greater product safety does not indicate that it is undesirable.

Society's increased demand for safety has been reflected not only in the safety of the products that are sold but also in the actions of government agencies to promote safety. Beginning in the 1970s, agencies such as the U.S. Environmental Protection Agency, the Consumer Product Safety Commission, the Occupational Safety and Health Administration, and the National Highway Traffic Safety Administration took on the responsibility of promoting safety within their various domains.[12] One would have expected these new efforts to relieve the tort liability system of some of the burdens of promoting safety by establishing an alternative institutional mechanism for addressing safety-related concerns. Instead, what we observe is the opposite result. Safety has improved. Regulation is greatly expanded. Yet demands on the products liability system have also escalated, even though the problems being addressed by the system have diminished. This new regime has shifted the liability standards in a manner that will increase the liability costs on firms, for any given level of safety.

The Surge in Asbestos Litigation

The rise of products liability litigation can be traced in substantial part to the surge in asbestos litigation in the 1980s. The relative share of asbestos suits in the set of all personal injury products liability cases at the federal level is illustrated in Figure 2.1.[13] In 1975 asbestos

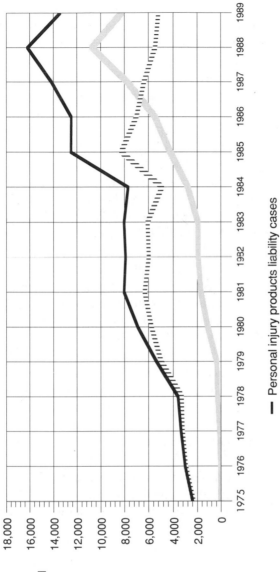

Figure 2.1. The relative shares of asbestos and nonasbestos litigation, 1975–1989

Source: Annual reports of the Director of the Administrative Office of the U.S. Courts, 1975–1989, tables "Product Liability Cases Commenced" and "Civil Cases Commenced"; Dungworth (1988), p. 36

litigation constituted only 2 percent of all products liability litigation. The asbestos share remained negligible through much of the 1970s, but by 1981 it had grown to one-fifth. Between 1986 and 1987 asbestos took the lead in products liability litigation, and by 1989 61 percent of all products liability cases in the federal courts were asbestos-related cases.

Although the surge in asbestos-related cases has been the most pronounced increase, asbestos does not entirely account for the burgeoning case load. As Figure 2.2 shows, the number of cases commenced, both asbestos-related and not, has increased since 1975. The total products liability case load grew at an average annual rate of 13 percent, with the greatest breaks in the trend occurring in 1979 and 1985. The asbestos case load surge also was characterized by two breakpoints, in 1980 and 1984. Until 1977 there were fewer than 100 asbestos cases commenced annually, and by 1989 the number of such cases at the federal level has risen to 8,230.

Although the upward trends for the overall products liability total and for asbestos cases are the most dramatic, litigation over nonasbestos products displayed an increase as well. The number of such suits rose from 2,344 in 1975 to 5,178 in 1989, which is an annual growth rate of 5.8 percent. There was a jump in litigation for nonasbestos products in 1975, which coincided with a rise in insurance premiums in that year. The tailing off of the number of nonasbestos products liability cases in 1986 and 1987 may be a result of tort liability reforms enacted after the emergence of the insurance crisis in the mid-1980s. This stability is also consistent with increased evidence of judgments favoring defendants.[14]

The comparative stability in recent years for nonasbestos cases has not, however, been sufficient to mute the overall increase that has occurred in products liability litigation. Figure 2.3 shows the fraction of products liability cases as a percentage of all civil cases commenced at the federal level. The share of cases over nonasbestos products rose from 2 percent in 1975 to 3.5 percent in 1981, after which it dropped to 2.2 percent by 1989. There appears to have been some stabilization in products liability litigation for nonasbestos products in the 1980s. In contrast, the asbestos share of litigation continues to be on the rise, as it increased from 0.04 percent of all civil cases in 1975 to over 3.5 percent of all civil litigation in 1989. It is the asbestos component of products liability cases that should be the greatest source of alarm for individuals assessing the future role of liability.

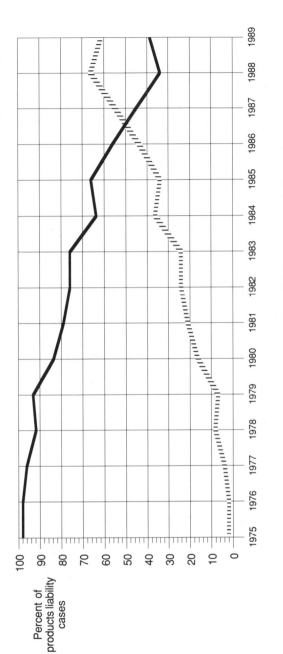

Figure 2.2. Growth in the number of personal injury products liability cases, 1975–1989

Source: Annual reports of the Director of the Administrative Office of the U.S. Courts, 1975–1989, tables "Product Liability Cases Commenced" and "Civil Cases Commenced"; Dungworth (1988), p. 36

— Personal injury products liability cases, excluding asbestos

ıı Asbestos cases

Figure 2.3. Personal injury products liability cases as a percentage of all civil cases, 1975–1989

Source: Annual reports of the Director of the Administrative Office of the U.S. Courts, 1975–1989, tables "Product Liability Cases Commenced" and "Civil Cases Commenced"; Dungworth (1988), p. 36

— Personal injury products liability cases, excluding asbestos

‧‧‧‧ Asbestos cases

Insurance Industry Trends

Although the court statistics examined above suggest a continuing expansion of products liability, federal court statistics have also been used to challenge the notion of a liability crisis. Some observers suggest that the courts are now taking a pro-defendant stance.[15] Beginning in the early 1980s, an increased percentage of decisions in federal court cases favored the defendants. This development does not necessarily imply that the tort crisis is abating. Although these decisions could mark a return to an earlier era, they also may simply suggest that the courts are not pushing the boundaries further in the pro-plaintiff direction. For the decisions of greatest consequence—ground-breaking decisions—there has been a more mixed pattern. The level of pro-plaintiff judgments in ground-breaking decisions exceeds the level of pro-defendant judgments for every year except 1988.[16] The breakthrough cases have continued to favor plaintiffs, although less so than in the past, indicating that on balance the pivotal cases remain pro-plaintiff. The total stock of legal precedents remains pro-plaintiff as well.

Examination of federal court case counts and selected surveys of jury verdicts gives a highly selective and incomplete picture of the nature of products liability activity. It leaves out cases not filed in federal courts as well as the value of out-of-court settlements. A more comprehensive measure of the extent of the change in products liability costs is the trend in insurance premiums. Fortunately, extensive insurance data are available over a long period of time. The insurance premium data, which represent the liability insurance cost to insured firms, reinforce the impression created by case load statistics and extend the time frame for our assessment.

Liability insurance premiums are an instructive index of the change in insurance costs, but they understate the total insurance burden. Many firms have exited the conventional insurance market, with the chief alternative to producing firms being self-insurance. For the general liability premium category, the premium equivalent of self-insurance averaged 30 percent in the 1980s.[17] Firms in some industries have exited the the conventional market in disproportionate numbers; for example, 47 percent of firms in the chemical industry utilize alternative risk-financing vehicles, such as self-insurance and "captive" insurers (an insurance company formed to insure only the parent company's risks).[18] Many major corporations, such as Ford Motor

Co., carry little or no products liability insurance, as they self-insure. In 1986 Ford faced products liability damages claims totaling $4 billion—a substantial liability risk by any standard.[19]

Table 2.3 provides information on general liability insurance coverage in the conventional market, which includes insurance for products as well as other liability risks, such as those associated with property ownership.[20] The decade 1959–1968 was a period of relatively gradual change in terms of the extent of liability insurance increases. The total value of general liability insurance premiums written rose from $0.67 billion to $1.13 billion. Total premiums increased steadily throughout that period, but the overall increase was less than double. Nevertheless, the premium rise exceeded the rate of inflation in every year, meaning that there was a positive real (that is, inflation-adjusted) growth rate, as is indicated by the third column in Table 2.3. This growth was comparable to that of other insurance lines, as general liability insurance constituted almost 5 percent of the total insurance coverage both in 1959 and 1968.

The next decade marked a dramatic acceleration in the products liability burden. The total magnitude of general liability insurance premiums written from 1968 to 1978 rose from $1.13 billion to $6.49 billion. This increase represents over a fivefold increase in the total cost of products liability insurance. During the 1968–1978 period the annual growth rate in general liability insurance was 19.1 percent, with a real growth rate of 8.8 percent. The real growth in premiums consequently outstripped the rate of inflation. The overall share of the general liability insurance among all insurance lines also increased from 4.4 percent in 1968 to 8.0 percent in 1978, marking a relative increase in general liability coverage.

The decade of greatest interest is the period from 1978 to 1988. Although this decade saw the greatest national clamor over the tort liability crisis, the total change in the products liability burden over the course of that decade was actually less than the change in the previous decade. What differs is the distribution of the increase across different years; in other words, the increase is more concentrated in the 1980s than it was in earlier eras.

Overall, net premiums written tripled from their level of $6.61 billion in 1979 to $19.08 billion in 1988. These general liability insurance costs and costs for other forms of liability insurance have formed the basis of assessments that the cost of all expenditures on tort litigation terminating in state and federal courts range from $29 billion to

Table 2.3. Premiums paid for general liability insurance, 1953–1988

Year(s)	Net premiums written ($ thousands)	Annual percent change	Real percent change	Percent of total insurance, all lines
1953	395,685	—	—	4.1
1954	443,085	12.0	11.3	4.5
1955	470,887	6.3	6.7	4.5
1956	518,909	10.2	8.7	4.7
1957	563,030	8.5	5.2	4.7
1958	600,944	6.7	3.9	4.8
1959	668,152	11.2	10.5	4.8
1960	746,194	11.7	10.0	5.1
1961	792,768	6.2	5.2	5.2
1962	820,625	3.5	2.5	5.1
1963	845,410	3.0	1.7	5.0
1964	860,837	1.8	0.5	4.8
1965	880,977	2.3	0.7	4.4
1966	934,078	6.0	3.1	4.3
1967	1,027,964	10.1	7.0	4.4
1968	1,133,043	10.2	6.0	4.4
1969	1,327,593	17.2	11.7	4.6
1970	1,658,245	24.9	19.2	5.1
1971	1,845,236	11.3	6.9	5.2
1972	1,980,290	7.3	4.1	5.1
1973	2,093,521	5.7	−0.5	5.0
1974	2,275,395	8.7	−2.3	5.1
1975	3,085,226	35.6	26.5	6.2
1976	4,251,298	37.8	32.0	8.1
1977	5,845,075	37.5	31.0	8.1
1978	6,490,064	11.0	3.4	8.0
1979	6,612,474	1.9	−9.4	7.3
1980	6,414,678	−3.0	−16.5	6.7
1981	6,046,292	−5.7	−16.0	6.1
1982	5,668,459	−6.2	−12.4	5.5
1983	5,679,295	0.2	−3.0	5.2
1984	6,479,268	14.1	9.8	5.5
1985	11,544,152	78.2	74.6	8.0
1986	19,364,658	67.7	65.8	11.0
1987	20,873,777	7.8	4.2	10.8
1988	19,077,182	−8.6	−12.7	9.4
1958–1968	846,454	6.5	4.6	4.8
1968–1978	2,907,726	19.1	12.6	5.9
1978–1988	10,386,391	11.4	5.3	7.6
1958–1988	4,175,410	11.7	7.4	5.9

Source: Economic Report of the President and A. M. Best Company, Inc., *Best's Aggregates and Averages,* various years. Annual averages and growth rates computed by the author. General liability share of general liability plus malpractice insurance was calculated for the pre-1975 period by multiplying yearly totals by the 1975 general liability share of 0.775.

$36 billion.[21] What is especially remarkable about the recent premium increase was its tremendous concentration. From 1984 to 1985, net premiums written rose from $6.48 billion to $11.54 billion. This increase was then followed by a subsequent rise in net premiums to $19.36 billion in 1986. The tripling in the level of net premiums within a two-year period, as compared with the more general spreading out of the increase in earlier decades, sparked the consensus that there was indeed a crisis in liability insurance.

The ten-year trend for the most recent decade of statistics was not, however, more explosive than the increase in the previous decade. The annual growth rate in premiums was 11.4 percent during 1978–1988. The overall share of all insurance devoted to general liability coverage increased by just under 2 percent in the more recent decade. However, the real increase in premiums during 1978–1988 was under half the value of the increase in the previous decade.

The general picture that emerges is that the explosion in products liability costs has been under way for two decades. It is not simply a mid-1980s phenomenon. This timing coincides with the expansion in tort liability, which has been a gradual process over the past few decades.

The temporal pattern of the insurance premium trends also is suggestive of which liability doctrines have been of greatest consequence. Although premiums rose in the 1960s, the greatest escalation in premiums occurred in the 1970s and 1980s. This timing suggests that it was not the emergence of strict liability and the appearance of §402A of the *Restatement of the Law of Torts* in the 1960s that was most influential. Similarly, the emergence of the design defect doctrine in the 1960 Henningsen decision was not a pivotal event.[22] It was the subsequent development of design defect doctrine and the application of defect tests to hazard warnings that has been responsible for the greatest increase in products liability litigation.[23]

The rather uneven performance of liability insurance in the recent decade, however, merits further discussion. If in fact there was an escalation in the products liability burden being generated over the past decades, why was it that insurance premiums held steady and in fact declined in the early 1980s before escalating quite starkly beginning in 1985?

Two explanations appear most promising. The first is that focusing on premiums alone may be a misleading index of the health of the industry. Premiums reflect the net impact of both the price and quantity of insurance sold. Thus, premiums could hold steady when the cost of insurance has risen and the amount of coverage has declined. Declining coverage could result from a lack of insurance availability. Firms purchased less insurance and in some cases were denied coverage altogether. Evidence with respect to this availability crisis will be presented below and will indicate that there was in fact an affordability problem that is masked by the relatively flat premium statistics over the 1979–1984 period.

Another contributor to premium fluctuations is the influence of changes in interest rates. When interest rates are high, firms can lower premiums because they can earn a substantial return on the premiums before the losses must be paid, which in the case of products liability coverage is typically several years later.

During the early 1980s interest rates were high, and as a result there was substantial price competition among insurance firms.[24] Competition lowered the cost of insurance to insurance purchasers, but, with extreme rate competition in the property and casualty insurance lines, firms began to experience underwriting deficits whereby the losses that would occur under policies exceeded the premiums paid. Firms were still able to make a profit on the insurance despite this deficit through the return they earned on investment income. The ability to maintain a viable insurance operation of the kind in which total losses experienced will eventually exceed premiums hinges on continued high interest rates.

The high interest rates during the early 1980s arose from the Reagan administration's handling of large deficits coupled with a tight monetary policy, policies that led to rates such as the 9.6 percent interest rate on three-month treasury bills in 1984.[25] But, in 1985, interest rates dropped by over 2 percent, and by mid-1985 the insurance industry had reached the stage where investment income failed to offset the underwriting losses. Companies raised the insurance rates, and the softness in the insurance market was eliminated.[26] The insurance industry shifted from a situation of price competition to one in which firms had to rely on higher premiums to ensure the viability of their insurance lines, thus contributing to the dramatic escalation in premiums in 1985. Premiums continued to increase in 1986, not unexpectedly given that interest rates dropped further in that year, as reflected by the 1.5 percent decline in the U.S. Treasury bill rate in 1985–1986. Interest rates held fairly steady in 1987, as did the premium level.

Table 2.4. Average annual rates of return on net income after taxes as percent of net worth, selected industries, 1978–1988

Year	Property/ casualty insurance[a]	Banks	All industries[b]
1978	18.1%	12.9%	14.3%
1979	15.5	14.1	15.9
1980	13.1	13.4	14.4
1981	11.8	13.0	13.8
1982	8.8	12.0	10.9
1983	8.3	12.5	10.7
1984	1.8	12.6	13.5
1985	3.8	13.0	11.6
1986	13.1	12.8	11.6
1987	12.8	11.1	14.4
1988	10.1	12.9	16.2
Average 1978–1988	10.7%	12.8%	13.4%

Source: Insurance Information Institute (1988), p. 25; Insurance Information Institute (1990), p. 19; and calculations by the author.

a. Insurance industry rates of return calculated using GAAP accounting, which is most comparable to procedures in other industries.

b. Median for Fortune 500 U.S. Industrial Corporations.

Although the overall pattern of premiums is consistent with the pattern of interest rates over the past decade as well as the role of price competition during the period of high interest rates, this evidence does not rule out the possibility that the industry experienced a period of substantial profitability throughout this hectic swing in premium levels. The data in Table 2.4 on the rate of return on net worth earned by the property/casualty insurance industry, as compared with other industries, indicate that the crisis did indeed affect the profitability of the insurance industry as well. The two comparison industries of banks and the median for U.S. corporations in the Fortune 500 exhibited relatively steady, two-digit rates of return throughout the past decade, averaging 13 percent over that period. In contrast, the returns experienced in the insurance industry have been quite volatile, reaching as high as 18.1 percent in 1978 and as low as 1.8 percent in 1984. Those years in the early 1980's in which the premium levels were stable because of substantial price competition were not particularly lucrative, as the annual rates of return were below those in the comparison industries and below the overall 1978–1987 average for the property/casualty insurance industry. The escalation of premiums in 1985 did not restore profitability to the industry, and it was only with the premium increase in 1986 that the rates of return were at levels comparable to those experienced in other industries.

Although comparing profitability rates across industries is always a hazardous undertaking,[27] the profitability pattern is consistent with the conclusion that the products liability crisis was a real phenomenon. The crisis was linked both to the emerging products liability burden as well as the temporary fluctuations in interest rates, which in turn generated price competition in the industry. The low profitability of the insurance industry in the early 1980s is not the kind of pattern one would expect if firms were colluding to alter premiums in a profit-maximizing fashion.

Roots of the Insurance Crisis, 1980–1984

A more detailed perspective on the economic conditions underlying the insurance crisis may be gained from a look at the data used by the insurance industry for ratemaking purposes. This information, which is gathered by the Insurance Services Office to advise companies on the risks associated with various kinds of products liability coverage, provides a useful statistical base for analyzing rate trends in detail. The data base of interest here includes information on over 60,000 policies per year over the period 1980–1984, with total premiums for bodily injury and property damage coverage of over $500 million in each year.

It is clear from these statistics that liability insurance costs are not restricted to pharmaceutical companies and other highly publicized producer groups. Indeed, as Appendix A indicates, the image of products liability as a concern of manufacturing firms only is too narrow. The manufacturing sector is, of course, important; it accounts for just under half of products liability insurance sold. However, the construction industry accounts for over one-fifth of all bodily damage coverage and over one-third of all property damage premiums. Many service and retailing industries are also of major consequence. The effects of products liability are economy-wide.

As we have already seen in Table 2.3, overall general liability insurance coverage declined in the early 1980s. The same pattern is evidenced in Table 2.5 for products liability insurance coverage. Premiums for bodily injury insurance dropped by almost 8 percent from 1980 to 1984, and premiums for property damage dropped by over 9 percent. Notwithstanding inflation in the economy, insurance companies were able to maintain stable premiums by engaging in "cash-flow" underwriting. Insurers took losses in excess of premiums in order to reap the investment returns before the losses were paid.[28] The decline in premiums does not enable us to ascertain whether this drop was solely a result of price competition or whether there was also a drop in insurance coverage, but as we explore this issue in greater detail we find that the premium drop is not necessarily an index of good health in the insurance industry. The final noteworthy aspect of the premium levels is that bodily injury coverage tends to be more expensive than property damage coverage; premiums for the former are roughly one and one-half times greater than the latter.

Examination of the claims performance of these policies provides a mixed view. In the case of bodily injury insurance, there was a decline in claims, losses, and loss amounts per claim over the five-year period. The year-to-year pattern is uneven, so we cannot say that there is strong evidence of a declining market, but there is certainly no evidence of an escalation in the personal injury liability burden. What should be emphasized, however, is that there may nevertheless have been an escalation in the liability costs imposed, but these would not be evidenced in an increase in the claims-related variables if insurance firms had cut back their coverage over that time period. Once again, the key to understanding whether there is a products liability crisis hinges on whether there has been a change in insurance coverage. In the absence of such a decline in coverage, the comparatively steady premium levels provide no evidence of an emerging liability crisis.

The pattern of claims-related variables for property damage is more in line with what one would expect if a products liability crisis existed. Claims rose by 23 percent, losses rose by 33 percent, and loss per claim amounts rose by 8 percent over the five-year period. One would have expected some increase in the loss amounts and loss per claim amounts simply as a result of inflation. Indeed, if the loss per claim amounts had simply kept pace with inflation, then they should have risen by 31 percent, as opposed to the 8 percent increase that actually occurred. Once again, the pattern is one of an insurance market that is failing to exhibit the expected growth. The decline in

Table 2.5. Nationwide statistics for products liability insurance, 1980–1984

Year	Premiums paid (% change)	Number of claims (% change)	Losses paid (% change)	Average loss/claim (% change)	Loss ratio (% change)
A. Bodily injury					
1980	$361,171,432	20,242	$318,763,939	$15,748	0.883
	(—)	(—)	(—)	(—)	(—)
1981	323,268,398	21,216	272,578,237	12,848	0.843
	(−10.49)	(4.81)	(−14.49)	(−18.42)	(−4.46)
1982	280,081,272	19,173	263,649,183	13,720	0.939
	(−13.36)	(−9.63)	(−3.50)	(6.79)	(11.39)
1983	284,954,194	20,233	293,908,122	14,526	1.031
	(1.74)	(5.53)	(11.73)	(5.88)	(9.82)
1984	333,272,327	18,533	278,155,904	15,009	0.835
	(16.96)	(−8.40)	(−5.36)	(3.32)	(−19.08)
Average					
1980–1984	$316,549,525	19,879	$285,291,077	$14,370	0.906
	(−7.72)	(−8.44)	(−12.74)	(−4.69)	(−5.43)
B. Property damage					
1980	$244,653,743	14,969	$119,221,880	$7,965	0.487
	(—)	(—)	(—)	(—)	(—)
1981	240,392,829	18,441	159,563,140	8,653	0.664
	(−1.742)	(23.19)	(33.84)	(8.64)	(36.21)
1982	213,560,024	18,682	160,078,318	8,569	0.750
	(−11.16)	(1.31)	(0.32)	(−0.97)	(12.93)
1983	212,447,719	19,571	163,003,830	8,329	0.767
	(−0.52)	(4.76)	(1.83)	(−2.80)	(2.36)
1984	222,216,604	18,360	158,438,124	8,630	0.713
	(4.60)	(−6.19)	(−2.80)	(3.61)	(−7.07)
Average					
1980–1984	$226,654,184	18,005	$152,061,058	$8,429	0.676
	(−9.17)	(22.65)	(32.89)	(8.35)	(46.31)

the inflation-adjusted amount of losses per claim indicates that there was also a change in the composition of the risks being insured.

The loss ratio, or the ratio of losses to premiums, is the key index of insurance industry profitability. A loss ratio below 1.0 is essential for insurance to be viable. If 20 percent of premiums goes to various insurance-related expenses such as marketing, operations, claims settlement costs, and normal profits, one might expect that firms should find it difficult to maintain loss ratios below 1.0, unless the lag before losses must be paid is great.[29] Loss ratios for individual policies and even for large industry groups exhibit enormous volatility, as the statistics in Appendix A indicate. Here we will focus on the national averages, which are more stable.

What we find is that, particularly in the case of bodily injury coverage, loss ratios are quite high, averaging 0.91 during 1980–1984 and reaching a high of 1.03 in 1983. The 1983 value indicates that, after excluding all administrative costs as well as interest earned on premiums, the insurance industry paid out more in losses than it took in through premiums. This situation cannot be viable in the long run if interest rates decline. In the 1985–1986 period an interest rate drop did occur, and a dramatic escalation in premiums resulted.

The loss ratios for property damage coverage are lower than those for bodily injury, but they experienced a much more dramatic rate of change, an increase of 46 percent, over the five-year period. Overall, there is a substantial narrowing of the loss ratios for the two sets of coverage; the loss ratio for bodily injury coverage exceeded that for property damage coverage by 0.39 in 1985 but the gap was reduced to 0.13 by 1984. This narrowing is exactly what one would expect in a competitive market. If the distribution of losses over time of all types of coverage is the same, then in a competitive market firms should equalize the loss ratios across different kinds of coverage to ensure their equal profitability. The narrowing of the loss ratios reflects this economic effect.

Overall, the data in Table 2.5 are not as alarming as the statistics considered earlier. The liability crisis did not stem from escalating claims and losses, as these were apparently kept under control by restrictions in coverage. The loss ratios reached alarmingly high levels that could not be sustained in the long run, and the declining premium amounts indicated an underlying difficulty with the products liability insurance market more generally. In particular, in a situation in which the economy was expanding (GNP increased by 47 percent over the 1980–1984 period),[30] premiums declined by almost 10 percent. Relative to the pattern displayed by the economy at large, which is the basis for what is to be insured by the industry, premiums should have increased by roughly 60 percent more than they did over the 1980–1984 period. The comparative stability of this situation is in fact a signal of a market that is in turmoil.

Although the products liability crisis in terms of premium levels emerged in 1985–1986, a preview of the crisis with respect to availability occurred earlier. A rational insurance firm will deny products liability coverage when risks cannot be effectively pooled and spread or when risks are highly unpredictable. Although no precise measure exists of how often coverage was denied, and indeed one might not even wish to pose the question in exactly this manner since one would want to know whether it was denied at a particular price, we can establish the extent to which firms chose to exit the market for products liability insurance.

One would expect an increase over time in the exposure level (that is, the level of risks covered) associated with a particular policy. The exposure level is typically the dollar volume of product sales insured, and in a growing economy exposure levels should rise if the level of insurance is constant. Instead, some industries experienced a drop in exposure levels, some a rise. Because exposure units are not always comparable across all industries (sometimes physical units are used in place of dollar units insured), I chose to analyze which industries increased their insurance coverage and which did not.

Table 2.6 breaks down the data on exposure levels in 1980–1984. Results for both bodily injury and property damage coverage are provided, for both monoline coverage (coverage for products liability alone) and multiline coverage (products liability coverage that is part of a broader insurance policy). The patterns in Table 2.6 are quite consistent with a belief that there was a crisis in insurance availability in the early 1980s. Whereas one would have expected dramatic increases in insurance levels, in many cases there were none. For overall bodily injury coverage, 41 percent of all industries representing 44 percent of all premiums experienced a decrease in exposure levels over that period. This pattern is especially striking in the case of multiline bodily injury coverage, for which 67 percent of all industries and 75 percent of all premiums reflected a decrease in exposure levels. There appears to have been less of a problem with respect to property damage, as only 19 percent of all industries and 21 percent

Table 2.6. Changes in products liability insurance exposure levels, 1980–1984

Type of insurance	Percent of industries with 5-year percent change in exposure		Percent of total 1980 premiums with 5-year percent change in exposure	
	< 0	≥ 0	< 0	≥ 0
Bodily injury, multiline	66.8	33.3	74.6	25.4
Bodily injury, monoline	20.9	79.1	31.1	68.9
Bodily injury, total	41.3	58.7	43.7	56.3
Property damage, multiline	37.1	62.9	30.6	69.4
Property damage, monoline	64.9	35.1	72.8	27.2
Property damage, total	18.9	81.1	20.9	79.1

of all premiums experienced a decrease in exposure, which is roughly half of the decrease amount observed in the insurance of bodily injury. Nevertheless, in the case of monoline products liability coverage of property damage, 65 percent of all industries and 73 percent of all premiums experienced a decrease in exposure.

In a period in which there was substantial growth in the dollar value of the GNP one would have expected the level of exposure to increase dramatically as well, since exposure levels are usually tied to the dollar value of sales. Instead, large drops in the level of exposure were experienced in substantial segments of the market and, for some classes of coverage, in the majority of industries and for the majority of premiums involved. These drops represent a striking departure from what should have been expected in a normally functioning insurance market. They suggest that the relative stability and slight declines of premiums should not be viewed as a sign of health. We do not have an insurance market in which premium stability has been maintained solely through price competition. Rather, there has been an important and dramatic decrease in the quantity of insurance purchased in many sectors, indicating a true availability problem in this market.

To see how changes in exposure come about, consider the data in Table 2.7 for a single industry. Exposure units plummeted from 2.2 million in 1980 to 31,565 in 1984. The shrink in the market was accompanied by a dramatic increase in the price of coverage, as the premium per exposure unit ratio rose from $0.08 to $0.38 over that

Table 2.7. Profile of an industry with decreased insurance exposure levels: oil, gasoline, or kerosene refining

	1980	1984
Exposure units	2,213,549	31,565
Premium/exposure	$0.08	$0.38
Loss/exposure	$0.01	$2.70
Loss ratio	0.10	7.00

period. This change in the price of insurance also reflected an increase in the losses, as the loss per exposure unit rose even more—from $0.01 to $2.7. Indeed, whereas this industry formerly was a relatively attractive insurance market, with a loss ratio of 0.1 in 1980, by 1984 loss levels exceeded premiums by a ratio of 7 to 1. What these results suggest is that the decline in exposure levels is often the result of a complex change in prices of insurance as well as the mix of policies that are bought within an industry.

Nation-wide, premiums held fairly steady or declined in the early 1980s, but this trend represented a substantial drop in the real value of the insurance market. Perhaps the main evidence with respect to price competition is how prices changed in relation to losses. The surge in loss ratios in 1982 and 1983 reflect a failure of insurance prices to keep pace with the losses, which is the pattern one would expect with greater price competition. In a market in which demand for insurance was expanding because of the growing GNP, and the price of insurance as measured by the inverse of the loss ratio was not rising on a national basis, one would have expected there to be a dramatic increase in insurance premiums. The fact that there was not such an increase suggests that there was an insurance availability problem.

Other Economic Effects of Products Liability

Since products liability costs are a real expenditure to firms, the economic ramifications of products liability lawsuits may be extensive. Most fundamentally, the value of a firm may be reduced by such actions, leading to a decrease in the stock price of the firm. These costs in turn will affect incentives to innovate and the desirability of product safety improvements.

One manifestation of the economic impact of liability suits is their

Table 2.8. Selected characteristics of products liability lawsuits

Firm name (Date of *Wall Street Journal* article)	Description	Abnormal return on event date (% change)	Estimated change in dollar value of firm ($ millions)
Beech Aircraft (7-30-71)	Several suits allege that four Beech models had defective fuel tanks, leading to numerous crash deaths.	−27.4	−23.0
Johnson & Johnson (4-7-83)	Individual sues over adverse reaction to Zomax.	−0.6	−43.8
Eli Lilly (8-3-82)	Nader group and others file federal suit seeking ban of Oraflex as an imminent hazard.	−4.0	−176.4
McDonnell Douglas (3-7-77)	Shareholder sues company and executives alleging awareness of DC-10 defects leading to crash.	−2.0	−19.6
Northwest Industries (2-27-78)	Michigan seeks $119.2 million in damages and $60 million for gross negligence in suit claiming that a feed mixup led to PBB hazards and destruction of 2 million farm animals.	−1.4	−11.4
Pullman Inc. (6-15-79)	New York City seeks $112.3 million in damages for defects in subway cars. Pullman directors meet to discuss allegations of bribery to get N.Y.C. officials to accept faulty railroad equipment.	−3.9	−16.4
A. H. Robins (3-19-75)	A. H. Robins discloses that it has been named in 186 products liability suits over Dalkon Shield. Deductible on its insurance is raised to $4 million.	−6.2	−18.3
A. H. Robins (2-19-76)	Dalkon Shield suits naming A. H. Robins rise to 547, seeking total of $444 million.	−15.7	−49.2

Table 2.8. (continued)

Firm name (Date of *Wall Street Journal* article)	Description	Abnormal return on event date (% change)	Estimated change in dollar value of firm ($ millions)
A. H. Robins (8-2-76)	Dalkon Shield suit filed in W.Va. federal court claiming $2.7 million in damages for "loss of right to natural childbirth."	−1.9	−6.1
Rockwell Intl. (6-15-79)	Rockwell Intl. involved in Pullman suit since it designed and mounted undercarriage of subway cars.	−0.2	−2.6
Syntex Corp. (8-15-85)	Syntex will contest five dioxin suits in Missouri seeking $2.4 billion in damages.	−0.9	−27.2

Source: Viscusi and Hersch (1990).

effect on the stock market prices of firms. Any products liability action of course involves many stages, but from the standpoint of investors what is important is the information that is disseminated to potential purchasers of the stock. In this regard coverage in the *Wall Street Journal,* which is a main source of information for analyzing stock market repercussions of various economic phenomena, is the prime indicator. Table 2.8 summarizes the estimated stock market effects for eleven different products liability events reported in the *Wall Street Journal.* The dollar values of the stock market losses range from $2.64 million in the case of a suit against Rockwell International over allegedly defective New York subway cars to a high of $176.35 million for a suit against Eli Lilly seeking a ban of Oraflex. These estimates reflect only the loss on the day of the newspaper coverage; there may have been additional losses associated with each of the events. For example, Beech Aircraft's troubles were but one part of the private plane industry's mounting liability problems after 1971. By 1990, Beech and Cessna Aircraft discontinued making planes that cost under $100,000, and Piper was mired in a severe sales slump.[31] Overall, there was a 90 percent decline in the sales of small American planes and jets from 1979 to 1989.

Although the total liability burden for all planes ever sold per new plane produced averages $100,000, the prospective liability costs associated with each new plane produced is much less. A fundamental misperception by the industry has been the assumption that the liability costs for planes already sold can be recouped in today's marketplace. The price of planes sold in an earlier liability era did not fully reflect their ultimate liability costs. Firms should treat these unanticipated liability costs as sunk costs. Efforts to price new planes to cover past liability costs cannot succeed, because current consumers do not benefit from a liability price tag that includes not only their own prospective liability costs but also a share of earlier liability awards. As a result, substantial inroads have been made in the market by foreign competitors not encumbered by these past costs or the mistaken notion that they can be shifted to today's consumers.

The effects of liability on the pharmaceutical industry have also been devastating. A. H. Robins eventually was forced to reorganize under federal bankruptcy law and set up a fund of almost $3 billion to pay for the liability claims arising from the Dalkon Shield intrauterine device.[32]

A more complete analysis of product risk events indicates that cost effects on firms are greater for products liability suits than for regulatory actions. In addition, when dollar amounts of losses or potential losses are named in the article, generally the stock market effects are less than the amounts of damages that are claimed. This is to be expected for several reasons. Dollar amounts of awards are generally less than the total value of claims. In addition, there is some probability that the plaintiff will not win the suit. Even if the firm loses the case, costs will often be shared with the insurance company. Other information about the case may also have already been taken into account by investors, and these estimates in all likelihood reflect lower bounds on the impact.

Liability problems will not always lead to bankruptcy, exit from the market, or stock market repercussions. Nevertheless, the economic impact of liability costs is real, increasing, and substantial.

The Design Defect Doctrine and Hazard Warnings

I have presented evidence from a variety of sources to show that the products liability crisis is neither imaginary nor a contrivance of the insurance industry. Litigation has risen dramatically. The insurance industry was able to mute some of the effects of this escalation in suits because rising interest rates in the early 1980s increased the return on premiums. In addition, the shrinking market for products liability insurance masked much of the explosion in the costs of coverage. The dominant pattern in the early 1980s was one of a disappearing insurance market. This phenomenon prompted many public accounts of a crisis in availability, which were often accompanied by case studies of, for example, day care centers or municipal playgrounds that were denied liability coverage.

Once interest rates began to decline in the mid-1980s, it became essential for insurance companies to raise the price of insurance. The escalation in premiums that took place did not mark the advent of a liability crisis, but simply a different manifestation of an ongoing crisis. In particular, a crisis in availability was experienced in the first half of the 1980s, and a crisis in terms of escalating prices emerged in 1985. Both problems were generated by the same underlying phenomenon, the dramatic growth in the liability burden.

This escalation in the cost of liability and the level of litigation more generally was not a phenomenon restricted to the 1980s, but has been the result of a longer-term shift in the role of products liability in American society. It has had a profound effect on the products liability insurance market, which is but the most visible symptom of the widespread economic ramifications of a changing tort liability system. Although the greatest surge in litigation has been for asbestos-related claims, other products liability litigation has risen as well. This evidence in no way implies that earlier liability regimes were superior to the more costly liability regime now in place. The fundamental shift in the impact of liability suggests, however, that a careful reexamination of its functions is warranted.

The timing of the expansion in insurance premiums is also instructive. Although premiums rose in the 1960s, the greatest expansion occurred in the 1970s; increases continued, but not so dramatically, in the 1980s. This pattern indicates that the expansion in the product defect doctrine and the emergence of hazard warnings cases, rather than the adoption of strict liability, are at the root of the products liability crisis. Focusing on these aspects of the shifting structure of liability gives this volume a different slant from those of most tort reform proposals, which generally emphasize the strict liability doctrine for manufacturing defects as well. The following discussion will indicate that not only are the design defect doctrine and hazard warnings doctrine principal contributors to the surge in liability costs, but they are also fundamentally flawed.

3

The Litigation Process

Easily the most neglected aspect of the products liability reform debate is the way decisions are made within the litigation context. Observers marvel at the escalation of verdict awards and the rise in the
number of cases and view these as symptoms of a flawed legal process
without looking at the behavior behind the statistics. Similarly, legal
reformers call for caps on pain and suffering awards or abolition of
strict liability without making any effort to explore how the reforms
would affect the behavior of plaintiffs and defendants.

This inattention can be ascribed more generally to the long-standing view of litigation as the outcome of noneconomic influences. Do
injured parties file lawsuits simply because they seek justice, or, at a
more mundane level, because they are mad at the injuring party? Or
is their motivation the prospect of economic gain? Defendants have
long been believed to have economic motives in mind, but even they,
especially large corporate defendants, are often assumed to be stub-
born or intransigent rather than simply acting in their best economic
interests.

The substantial recent literature in law and economics indicates
that these caricatures have been overly simplistic.[1] In particular, one
can explain a great deal of the behavior of plaintiffs and defendants
as well as the character of litigation outcomes by treating litigation
behavior as the result of economic maximizing. In the simplest version, plaintiffs are seen as pursuing those actions that are in their
best economic interests, which are those actions that provide the high-

est expected payoff. Defending firms and insurance companies are assumed to be similarly motivated, except that their objective is to minimize their expected losses. Moreover, should one wish to do so, the equivalent monetary value that individuals place on other concerns, such as achieving a just outcome, can also be incorporated in the analysis. By framing litigation behavior as the result of conscious economic decisions, one can analyze which shifts in the litigation environment will alter the probability that cases will be dropped or settled out of court. In addition, one can assess how these influences affect the magnitude of out-of-court settlements and the mix of cases decided in court.

The Overall Structure of Products Liability Litigation

The data to be used in this and several subsequent chapters are drawn from the Insurance Services Offices (ISO) Product Liability Closed Claim Survey.[2] The ISO, an insurance industry group, obtained very extensive data from twenty-three insurance companies on products liability claims closed between the latter half of 1976 and mid-1977. Although not a random sample of all claims (it leaves out, for example, those not covered by insurance), the sample was broadly representative and included claims from all fifty states.

The ISO survey took place after the modern products liability doctrines had been established in the courts, but it precedes the closing of many of the mass tort cases, those concerning asbestos, DES, the Dalkon Shield, and Agent Orange.[3] The focus of the analysis undertaken here will be on claims involving some bodily injury loss. In all, 10,784 claims with complete data on the key variables of interest were examined.[4]

The survey followed the upsurge in products liability lawsuits in the 1970s. The number of such cases filed in U.S. District Courts tripled from 1974 to 1977.[5] The growth has continued since then, but at a slower rate. Changes in the level of compensation over time also do not appear to have diminished the pertinence of the ISO data. Adjusting for inflation, the level of compensation for claims included in the survey is of the same general magnitude as that reflected in a more recent, small-scale survey of products liability claims involving large losses.[6] The advantage of the ISO data is that it represents by far the largest and most extensive survey of products liability claims.

Table 3.1 lists some of the characteristics of the claims surveyed and breaks down the data by disposition status. Roughly four-fifths of the claims were settled out of court. Few claims proceeded to a court verdict—only about 4 percent. The average bodily injury loss—consisting of lost earnings, medical expenses, and other economic losses—was almost $14,000, or roughly double that in current dollars. What is most striking is the wide variation in victims' loss levels. The standard deviation is almost ten times the mean loss level, and the bodily injury payments made by defendants also show a large deviation. Bodily injury payments are generally about three-fourths the losses. The sample of claimants averaged thirty-five years in age and consisted of an almost equal number of men and women.

The cases that proceeded to a court verdict are the more severe accidents, and they differ in character as well. They tend to involve a disproportionate share of accidents that occur on the job or that involve a fatality.

The success of a claim may hinge on whether the product violated Occupational Safety and Health Administration regulations or Consumer Product Safety Commission regulations. If either set of regulations was said to have been violated, the regulation measure assumed a value of one. The law gives an advantage to plaintiffs who can show that the manufacturer did not adhere to legal standards. The plaintiff can introduce the violation as evidence of failure to adhere to the required negligence or strict liability standards, although firms may be able to show a good reason for violating the rule.[7] Still, on balance, the pressure of regulatory violations generally gives plaintiffs a substantial advantage, which we explore in greater detail in Chapter 6. Two other characteristics distinguish those cases that went to court from the others: the presence of collateral private insurance payments and the time in years between the date of the injury's occurrence and the date the claim was closed. Cases involving collateral payments may be more likely to be litigated because of the difficulty in assigning liability in these cases, many of which involve complex subrogation actions. As one might expect, the time lag before a claim was closed was greater for cases that went to a court verdict, which were in dispute for four years as opposed to 1.5—1.6 years for other cases.

The survey also showed a discrepancy in the legal criteria applied in different products liability cases. Of the four possibilities—absolute liability, strict liability, negligence, or breach of warranty—absolute liability principles were involved in very few claims—only 2 percent—and cases that relied on the other three criteria were divided fairly evenly.

Strict liability, which holds producers responsible for product defects even when there is no negligence, became prevalent in the past three decades because of a belief that existing theories of liability were not adequate.[8] The oft-stated rationale for imposing liability without fault is that manufacturers are better able to assume risks and can spread the cost over all consumers. A similar argument could be made for other changes in the law, such as the broadening of the concept of what constitutes a defect. Increasing the firm's responsibility for accidents would increase the incentive for manufacturers to supply safe products in a world of costly litigation, and establishing a more lenient test of liability would overcome some of the difficulties plaintiffs often have in proving negligence. The principal criterion under strict liability is the existence of a product defect coupled with an unreasonable danger posed by the defect. Some states do, however, permit comparative negligence defenses even in strict liability cases. To the extent strict liability principles increase the chance of a plaintiff's victory, one should observe a positive incremental effect of this doctrine on the prospects of products liability claims.

Although widely accepted, the principle of strict liability has not been adopted universally. Four states (Massachusetts, North Carolina, Virginia, and Wyoming) have not yet officially adopted strict liability rules. Just over 5 percent of all claims are filed in these states, and this fraction exhibits little difference by stage of disposition.

Absolute liability permits no defenses to be used to lessen the burden of strict liability.[9] Because most jurisdictions allow some weakened version of the usual defenses (for example, contributory negligence), this liability theory in all likelihood will continue to play only a minor role.

The negligence principle pertains when the manufacturer knew or should have known of the defect in the product that created the risk. To prove liability on the basis of negligence the defendant is "required to exercise the care of a reasonable person under the circumstances."[10] The combination of these tests makes it usually more difficult for a plaintiff to recover under a charge of negligence than under strict liability, where the plaintiff need only show a causal relationship between a product defect and his injuries.

The difference between the two principal liability doctrines—strict

Table 3.1. Sample characteristics of ISO products liability claims (mean and standard deviation)

	Full sample	Cases settled out of court	Cases that reached court verdicts
Bodily injury loss ($)	13,723.00	13,483.66	46,157.06
	(119,925.48)	(128,582.96)	(154,677.77)
Bodily injury payment ($)	9,995.01	11,707.22	24,782.03
	(72,042.79)	(79,380.92)	(88,945.48)
Claim is dropped (0–1)	.191	.0	.0
	(.393)	(.0)	(.0)
Claim is settled out of court (0–1)	.768	1.0	.0
	(.422)	(.0)	(.0)
Court verdict won by plaintiff (0–1)	.015	.0	.366
	(.121)	(.0)	(.482)
Age of injured party (years)	35.415	35.531	35.616
	(15.673)	(15.765)	(15.452)
Injured party sex (male = 1)	.517	.507	.614
	(.500)	(.500)	(.487)
Injury occurred on the job (0–1)	.134	.118	.262
	(.341)	(.323)	(.440)

Regulatory violation claimed (0–1)	.156 (.363)	.166 (.372)	.202 (.402)
Fatal injury (0–1)	.037 (.189)	.032 (.177)	.129 (.335)
Collateral payment received (0–1)	.197 (.398)	.174 (.379)	.333 (.472)
Lag before claim closed (years)	1.544 (1.934)	1.594 (1.992)	3.881 (2.256)
Absolute liability (0–1)	.018 (.120)	.019 (.131)	.012 (.068)
Strict liability (0–1)	.299 (.429)	.302 (.447)	.321 (.396)
Negligence (0–1)	.350 (.442)	.341 (.459)	.321 (.376)
Warranty-based claim (0–1)	.322 (.434)	.335 (.459)	.303 (.373)
State without strict liability (0–1)	.057 (.231)	.056 (.231)	.051 (.219)
N	10,784	8,286	435

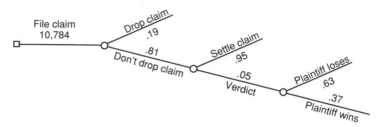

Figure 3.1. The disposition of products liability claims in the ISO survey

liability and negligence—can be seen in the context of the following example. Suppose that the manufacturing process for coffeemakers is imperfect, the result being that appliances pose the risk of electric shock. Under a strict liability rule, the firm will be responsible for all resulting injuries. Under a negligence standard, however, the firm will be responsible only if it did not exercise reasonable care in the manufacturing process. Adoption of strict liability consequently broadens the range of circumstances under which the firm must compensate accident victims.

The final liability principle is breach of express or implied warranty that the product is generally fit for normal use.[11] An implied warranty results simply from the sale of the product—a specific intent to establish a safety-related guarantee is not a requirement. These provisions are in some respects similar to strict liability in that the manufacturer does not have to be at fault. In addition, contributory negligence is not a defense to a claim of breach of warranty.

Figure 3.1 sketches the stages in the disposition of the products liability claims sampled. Of the over 10,000 claims filed, about one-fifth are dropped. Most claims proceed either to settlement or to a verdict. Of the claims not dropped, 95 percent lead to an out-of-court settlement either before or during the trial. A high out-of-court settlement rate would be expected if litigation costs are high, as they often are in products liability cases. Overall, about three-fourths of all products liability claims filed ultimately lead to an out-of-court settlement. A very small fraction of total claims—about 4 percent—eventually go to a jury for a verdict, and, of this group, the plaintiff wins over one-third of the cases.

It is instructive to compare this record with that of medical malpractice suits.[12] In all, 43 percent of medical malpractice claims are dropped, which is over double the amount for products liability. Of those not dropped, 88 percent lead to an out-of-court settlement. Although the reliance on out-of-court settlements for malpractice is great, it is even greater for products liability cases, where 95 percent of all claims not dropped are settled out of court. The success rate of plaintiffs in products liability verdicts is 37 percent, which exceeds the 28 percent success rate in medical malpractice cases.

Compared with medical malpractice claims, there appears to be a substantially greater chance for making a successful claim for products liability.[13] This difference may stem from the greater ability an injured party has to identify a product defect, which can be monitored much more closely both before and after the accident than can a physician's practices. For example, a patient's condition before treatment cannot be readily monitored on a retrospective basis, whereas it is possible to ascertain the nature of any systematic defects in an entire product line even if the specific item that caused an injury is no longer available. Moreover, the nature of a doctor's actions, other than his or her general mode of treatment, is often difficult to observe. Did the patient die because the doctor failed to exercise the proper care or because the patient was in ill health? Claims resulting from product risks are less concerned with the degree of care exercised by the manufacturer but instead focus on whether the result of these actions—the product—is defective. The law also makes it easier for a physician to claim to have acted in good faith than it does for a manufacturer. A final contributing factor is that the town doctor is likely to be treated with reverence, whereas the out-of-state producer represents a more inviting target for a large liability award.

The nodes of the tree diagram in Figure 3.1 sketch my overall approach for structuring discussion of the ISO data. The final stage of analysis is that of court verdicts. By that stage, all the major litigation decisions—whether to drop a claim, pursue a claim, or to settle a claim—have been completed and the suit will be governed by the characteristics of the case and legal doctrine. Thus, at this final stage the main actor is a legal institution rather than the parties of the case.

The plaintiff's probability of success as well as the expected court award will in turn have an effect on earlier actions. The main mechanisms affecting individual behavior are anticipatory. In particular, plaintiffs' prospects in court will influence their willingness to settle out of court and their incentive to drop a claim. Similarly, the expected losses that firms face will govern their behavior regarding litigation. Since firms are often engaged in multiple suits involving a particular class of products, the effects of a single verdict may involve more than the stakes in a particular case. Highly publicized court awards may lure other plaintiffs' attorneys into pursuing claims that they would not have otherwise litigated now that the stakes are higher.

The node in the decision tree preceding the verdict of the court is the decision whether to settle or to go to court. Unless there is a disparity in the parties' beliefs about the prospects of a claim in court, it is generally in their joint interest to settle out of court to avoid the litigation costs. The high settlement rate of 95 percent of all claims that are not dropped reflects these economic incentives. An even earlier decision regards dropping the case altogether. If the litigation costs are too high, parties may simply choose not to pursue claims with a low expected return. Many claims are dropped because the injured party was seeking compensation from more than one source. For example, a worker injured on the job may file a workers' compensation claim and may also file a products liability claim against the manufacturer of the equipment involved in the accident. Similarly, a plaintiff may bring suit against more than one defendant and, as the claims are resolved, it may become apparent that one of the products liability claims is inappropriate. Put somewhat differently, a plaintiff may obtain information over time indicating that the expected payoff is not worth the trouble or cost of pursuing the claim.

Court Verdicts

Although the pattern of court verdicts will be dictated by the nature of the legal regime for a particular class of cases, the disposition of any group of cases, such as those in the ISO survey, is affected by the mix of the cases that are litigated. Court cases do not arise randomly. Rather, they reflect the expectations that prospective plaintiffs and defendants have of winning, and these expectations are based on the outcomes of other cases that have recently gone to trial. Consider the extreme case in which parties have identical beliefs regarding the plaintiffs' probability of success and the economic payoffs they will receive. In this instance, the only cases that will be tried will be those which, because of some random factors, fail to be settled out of court. Settlement is in the economic interest of both the claimants and the defendants because all parties will lose the value of the litigation costs by not settling. The joint payoffs of out-of-court settlements are consequently greater, but the parties must reach agreement on how to divide the gains from saving the litigation costs.

Under conditions of complete symmetry, the parties will have identical beliefs regarding the plaintiff's prospects of success. Moreover, the expected court award to the plaintiff will equal the cost of losing the case to the defendant, thus ruling out adverse effects on other cases. Under these conditions, those cases that do reach trial should consequently be evenly divided between those in which plaintiffs and defendants are successful. All the aspects of the liability structure that are of consequence will have already been taken into account at the settlement stage, and cases reaching the courts will be chance occurrences.[14]

Actual litigation patterns do not exhibit such randomness, however.[15] Plaintiffs win only 37 percent of the cases that are decided in a court verdict.[16] If one only examined court verdicts, one might conclude that the legal regime is fairly hostile to plaintiffs. By examining only the final stage of litigation, one neglects the fact that 95 percent of all the claims that were not dropped were settled for a positive amount. In particular, in terms of the overall outcomes, 19 percent of the claims are dropped, and 3 percent of total claims result in verdicts against the plaintiff, but the overwhelming majority of claims result in positive payments.[17]

Once a claim has reached court, its outcome rests on the factors leading to the injury, the nature of the arguments presented, and the legal doctrine governing the suit. The size of the loss has no statistically significant impact on the prospects of a claim, for juries do not appear to be swayed by large and catastrophic losses.

Chief among the influences that do matter is the liability doctrine used in the case. Many aspects of the legal environment have changed over the past three decades. The concept of product defect, especially as it relates to design and warning defects, has undergone major revision. The classes of available defenses based on a plaintiff's misuse of a product and assumption of risk have been narrowed, and the evidentiary burdens placed on individual plaintiffs, especially on proof of causation, have been reduced.

Claims based on strict liability criteria are much more likely to succeed in court. Statistical analysis indicates that the applicability of strict liability increases a claimant's chance of success by 20 percent.[18] This substantial differential suggests that, for this class of cases, the parties do not fully incorporate the influence of strict liability at the settlement stage. The influence of case selection is not so complete as to eliminate the advantage that strict liability cases have.

Cases based on the more traditional negligence doctrine also tend to fare relatively well, although not as well as claims based on strict liability.[19] The weakest basis for claims is implied or express warranties.

The locale of the injury also proves to be of substantial consequence. Individuals who are injured as part of their job have less success in filing a products claim. This disadvantage is expected since one would expect that workers' compensation would be the more appropriate remedy, particularly to the extent that it is the employer rather than the producer of equipment at the firm that is more responsible for the injury.

The pattern of verdict awards is also of interest. Table 3.2 summarizes the award levels as a function of the loss amounts. Large loss claims tend to be undercompensated, and lower loss claims tend to be overcompensated. This overcompensation represents overpayment for monetary damages alone; part of the award may reflect compensation for pain and suffering, loss of consortium, and other nonmonetary losses. Overall, the ratio of court awards to the value of claims is 1.74, which indicates that there is net compensation for nonmonetary losses—a phenomenon that will be explored in much greater detail in Chapter 5.

These results contradict the views propagated by the popular press and in much of the debate over products liability reform. The cases involving large losses for the most part tend to be undercompensated. These cases are not high-profit outliers that make the products liability system lucrative for plaintiffs. Rather, the small claims tend to fare best. Although some "undercompensation" of large claims is due in part to the fact that large claims may be systematically overstated, this pattern holds up for a variety of sets of data and tort liability litigation contexts.

An intriguing statistic in Table 3.2 is the average success rate of cases in different loss ranges. Although the pattern is somewhat uneven because of the small sample size in some of the groupings, the general pattern is that losses of $100,000 or less tend to be associated with higher success rates, whereas claims with losses in excess of $100,000 have lower success rates. This pattern reflects the workings of the contingency fee system. Lawyers who take on a case for a fixed percentage of the payment, such as one-third of the award, will be

Table 3.2. Losses and payments for cases settled by court verdicts

Loss range (dollars)	Mean loss (dollars)	Mean payment (dollars)	Mean replacement ratio	Fraction of claims in group	Average success rate in loss range
1–10,000	1,432.05	27,767.38	19.39	.67	.37
10,001–25,000	17,213.44	78,493.28	4.56	.16	.41
25,001–50,000	39,677.78	108,320.33	2.73	.06	.38
50,001–100,000	63,447.04	107,225.50	1.69	.04	.43
100,001–200,000	124,872.17	194,800.60	1.56	.03	.33
200,001–500,000	259,189.18	575,400.00	2.22	.03	.21
500,001–1,000,000	602,272.72	265,000.00	.44	.01	.17
Over 1,000,000	2,250,000.00	112,500.00	.05	.01	.33
Overall	38,877.23	67,799.88	1.74	1.01	.37

willing to take on much weaker cases involving large payments. As a result, the larger cases may be more dubious than the smaller cases.[20]

The factors driving court awards follow many of the expected patterns. Higher levels of losses increase the size of court awards overall, but less than proportionally. For low levels of losses, court awards increase on a one-for-one basis with the size of the losses, but the responsiveness declines substantially thereafter. At the mean loss level of all litigated cases, a 100 percent increase in losses will lead to a 39 percent increase in the size of the court award.

Of particular interest is the differing effect of the components of the loss on the size of the court award.[21] Medical expenses have the greatest effect, as 42 percent of any increase in medical expenses will be transmitted into the court award. For wage losses, however, the rate of transmittal of claims into payments is only 13 percent, and for miscellaneous losses it drops to 7 percent. It may be that juries view medical expenses with more favor than other forms of losses. These losses also may be less prone to misrepresentation.

Claims Settled Out of Court

The lion's share of all claims that are not dropped are settled out of court. Although the decision to settle will be influenced by one's prospects in court, what is involved is a game between the plaintiff and defendant, where the parties attempt to arrive at a settlement to their best advantage.

Consider the extreme points of the bargaining range. From the standpoint of the plaintiff, it is never in the plaintiff's interest to settle for an amount lower than the value of what the plaintiff will obtain if he or she had proceeded to a court verdict. Thus, the bottom line from the standpoint of the plaintiff is the expected payoff of going to court less any litigation costs. Estimates of the award must, of course, take into account appropriate deductions for the delay in receiving the payment.

In addition, the value of the payoff must be adjusted to take into account the plaintiff's risk aversion. Plaintiffs want to avoid the chance of receiving no compensation at all. Although the average payoff for a class of claims will be most instrumental, the degree of uncertainty that a particular suit will be successful also matters. In terms of the impact on the likelihood of settlement, the uncertainty regarding the court award has approximately half the effect of the expected payoff.[22] This uncertainty creates an incentive for plaintiffs to settle their claims out of court rather than risk not receiving any court award.

The other end of the bargaining range is governed by how much companies are willing to spend to avoid the prospect of litigation. The prospective costs to the firm include the expected losses imposed by the case plus any associated litigation costs. Because of the multiple lawsuits involving the firm and the chance that an adverse verdict will set off a wave of litigation against it, the losses associated with a litigated claim often exceed the dollar payoff that must be made to the particular claimant.[23]

For a bargain to be feasible, the most the companies would be willing to offer to settle a case must be greater than the minimum amount plaintiffs are willing to accept. Litigation costs, which boost the maximum offer amount and lower the minimum acceptance amount, create a substantial motivation for bargaining. One factor that might undermine a successful bargain would be overoptimistic beliefs on the part of plaintiffs relative to the beliefs of defendants. Given that the great majority of cases are settled out of court, however, this factor seems not to be a dominant influence.

Where the parties will end up within this bargaining range depends solely on the nature of the bargaining game. The situation is not unlike one of buying a new car. The car dealer generally has a minimum price that can be charged and still make a reasonable profit on the sale of the car. Similarly, the purchaser may have a limit on what he or she is willing to pay for the vehicle. These amounts seldom coincide, and buyer and seller usually engage in a ritualistic bargaining process before arriving at a price in the intermediate range, with the dealer typically making several visits to the manager to get approval for the unprecedented deal that is being offered. How good the resulting deal is depends on the bargaining skill of the parties, the softness of the car market, and similar factors.

The size of out-of-court settlements for products liability cases likewise depends on bargaining skills and a variety of other influences. There are no formulas that dictate bargaining outcomes, except that there is some discipline on the bargaining range imposed by the fact that each party has an expectation with respect to the likely consequences of bringing the case to trial. Another important difference between selling a car and settling a claim is that the car dealer often is under pressure to clear the lot, but defendants have little incentive to spend their money quickly. Also, there are administrative costs to maintaining files and continuing negotiations. A company may be eager to settle small cases to avoid these costs, which may account for the rather large overpayment of small claims. In cases involving considerable awards, however, delay is often in the interest of the defendants. Particularly when it is possible that the plaintiff may die, defendants may drag their feet, for the plaintiff's death will reduce the expected medical bills and the lost earnings of the accident victim.

Plaintiffs are clearly disadvantaged by a long bargaining period. They are unable to draw on the expected value of the liability award to meet their medical bills and living costs while they wait for an award. These factors suggest that plaintiffs are partly at the mercy of large corporate defendants. An influence in the reverse direction is the shift in liability rules, which has tilted the balance in favor of plaintiffs. One judge, for example, acknowledged the satisfaction he receives from raiding corporate defendants' deep pockets:

> I may not always congratulate myself at the end of the day on the brilliance of my legal reasoning, but when I do such things as allow a paraplegic to collect a few hundred thousand dollars from the Michelin Tire Company—thanks to a one-car crash of unexplainable cause—I at least sleep well at night. Michelin will somehow survive (and if they don't, only the French will care), but my disabled constituent won't make it the rest of her life without Michelin's money.[24]

Given the shifts in liability doctrine in favor of plaintiffs and the ability for a single adverse judgment to set off a wave of cases, one would expect companies to want to settle cases without the adverse publicity of a trial.

Upon close inspection and statistical analysis, neither extreme view—that the plaintiffs are favored or that the defendants are—turns out to be correct. Indeed, in the case of products liability claims settled out of court, one obtains the surprising result that there is a fifty-fifty split between the maximum amount that companies are willing to offer and the minimum amount plaintiffs will accept.[25] This finding indicates that the bargaining power of the two parties is identical. Neither party should be viewed as the victim of a bargaining process that is dominated by the other party.

The settlement amounts resulting from this bargaining behavior follow the same general pattern as do court verdicts. As indicated in Table 3.3, overall payments equal losses, but small loss claims are overcompensated and large loss claims are undercompensated. Com-

Table 3.3. Losses and payments for cases settled out of court

Loss range (dollars)	Mean loss (dollars)	Mean payment (dollars)	Mean replacement ratio	Fraction of claims in group
1–10,000	581.87	4,125.49	7.09	.92
10,001–25,000	15,179.35	46,904.18	3.09	.03
25,001–50,000	34,619.06	67,853.36	1.96	.02
50,001–100,000	74,425.40	192,017.54	2.58	.01
100,001–200,000	138,727.35	83,236.41	.60	.01
200,001–500,000	285,341.18	165,497.89	.58	.01
500,001–1,000,000	667,798.76	287,153.47	.43	.00
Over 1,000,000	2,157,243.50	560,833.33	.26	.00
Overall	12,184.06	12,191.28	1.00	1.00

panies may be willing to overcompensate small claims in recognition of the pain and suffering the claimant may have experienced and to avoid prospective litigation and administrative costs. It is striking that the preponderance of all claims settled out of court tend to be for fairly small losses, those under $10,000.

The responsiveness of the size of out-of-court settlements relative to increases in the size of the loss is roughly 50 percent. Thus, a 10 percent increase in the size of the loss will generate a 5 percent increase in the size of the out-of-court settlement. There should be some reduction below a one-to-one relationship because of the probability that the plaintiff would lose in court. In addition, as in the case of court verdicts, claims for very large losses may be overstated.[26]

A well-founded economic model of the litigation process would predict that a higher prospect of plaintiff success and a higher expected court award will each raise the maximum amount that defendants are willing to offer plaintiffs and the minimum amount that plaintiffs require to settle a case out of court. There is solid statistical evidence bolstering each of these predictions, indicating that there is very strong support for viewing behavior at the settlement stage as being responsive to what would have ultimately happened had the claim been taken to court.

The settlement amount is influenced not only by the size of the loss but also by characteristics of the case. Factors that increase the prospects of plaintiff success will raise the amount that companies offer and the amount that plaintiffs require, thus boosting the settlement level. These include regulatory violations pertaining to the product injury, the applicability of a strict liability doctrine, and past occurrences of similar accidents involving the product. Factors that reduce the amount of the settlement are the occurrence of the injury on the job, company claims that there is no product defect, and reliance on a breach of warranty doctrine rather than strict liability or negligence.

Perhaps the most remarkable aspect of the pattern of claims outcomes is how far one can push a model of economic behavior for explaining the settlements reached. Moreover, not only does the economic framework structure the behavior of claimants and defendants in a systematic manner, but it also enables us to address issues such as the relative bargaining power of the two parties. Without an economic assessment of such issues, one's views on such issues would typically be driven by one's ideological alignment in the tort liability reform debate.

Cases That Are Dropped

Cases that are not settled out of court are either litigated or dropped by the plaintiffs. Dropped cases in many respects are similar to situations involving injuries for which no claim is filed. In particular, the stakes of pursuing the claim are not sufficiently worthwhile to make it profitable for the claimant to continue.

Dropped claims are not always those for which there is no chance of securing any recovery. Claimants able to obtain collateral insurance benefits, for example, are more likely to drop a case. In addition, a claimant engaged in multiple lawsuits may drop a case against a defendant only tangentially involved in the liability action. Even though it may be dropped, the initial claim may not have been frivolous. Rather, as the claim progresses through the legal system the plaintiff learns more about the prospects of the claim or about other opportunities for reimbursement and consequently may choose not to pursue this particular action.

Unlike settlement decisions, which reflect the beliefs of opposing parties, the decision to drop is ruled largely by the plaintiff's own perspective of the ultimate worth of the case. As the size of the loss increases, the frequency of dropping claims declines because the greater stakes make pursuing the claim worthwhile. Similarly, claims in which a violation of a U.S. regulatory standard is alleged by the plaintiff are also less likely to be dropped because plaintiffs have a greater chance of demonstrating liability in this instance.

Two key factors that boost a plaintiff's incentives to drop a claim are whether the injury was job-related, in which case workers' compensation typically will be a more appropriate remedy, and whether the plaintiff has received collateral insurance benefits, which may indicate that some other compensation remedy is more appropriate. Drop decisions are not driven by whimsical factors, but instead are governed by the stakes that the parties have in the litigation actions.

As in the case of out-of-court settlements, a plaintiff's risk aversion also appears to be consequential but not instrumental. Although the average loss level and its likely effect on future payoffs will usually determine the decision to drop a claim, the uncertainty with respect to the level of the expected payoff has about half the effect on the claims-dropping decision as does the expected award itself. Risk aversion on the part of plaintiffs who are reluctant to pursue claims with highly uncertain prospects does have a dampening effect on litigation behavior, but the expected reward is the more decisive factor.

Using Economic Models to Assess Reform Proposals

Products liability reforms will have far-reaching effects that can be best understood by applying the economic model of decisionmaking outlined in this chapter. Consider, for example, two proposals for reform—a damages cap and abolition of strict liability with a return to a negligence standard. The effect of each of these measures will be quite different at the final stage of behavior considered—court verdicts. In particular, changes in the liability rule will primarily affect the probability that the plaintiff will win. The presence of the damages cap will not affect the propensity of plaintiffs to win but will lower the magnitude of the award.

The impact of these measures will extend beyond their effect on court verdicts, however. Out-of-court settlements will generally equal the expected court award plus adjustments for litigation costs and differences in the bargaining power of the two parties. Both the damages cap and the change in liability doctrine will influence the expected court award, so they will have a similar effect on earlier stages of the litigation process.[27] Each will decrease the settlement amount and will have an uncertain effect on the likelihood of settlement. In addition, the mix of cases that are litigated may change, depending on how these shifts alter the relative perceived expected payoffs for each of the parties.

Finally, a reduction in the expected court awards will increase plaintiffs' incentives to drop a case, thus altering not only the mix of cases that are litigated but also the mix of cases that are settled out of court.

Products liability reforms consequently will not only influence court outcomes but also will affect the mix of cases going to court, the character of out-of-court settlements, the likelihood of out-of-court settlements, the mix of cases settled, and the likelihood of cases being dropped. These diverse impacts arise because the parties anticipate the subsequent economic returns in the litigation process and they act upon these beliefs in a systematic manner.

Analysis of litigation behavior provides a view of products liability litigation that is at odds with the public's perceptions, which are based on the substantial publicity given to large damage awards in litigated cases. The great majority of claims are settled out of court (98 percent of all claims receiving payment), and the amount of the bodily injury payment is often comparable to the size of the reported loss. The responsiveness of the bodily injury loss with respect to the bodily injury payment is substantially below a one-to-one relationship for the average loss, and this response declines as the size of the loss increases.

The most fundamental implications of the data examined here support the applicability of economic models of the litigation process. The decision to drop a products liability claim, for example, is negatively related to the size of the loss and to defendants' violations of government regulations. That is to be expected; these factors raise the expected court award (that is, the probability of winning multiplied by the size of the award). Similarly, factors that diminish the claim's prospects, such as an injury being job-related, increase the likelihood that the claim is dropped.

The decision to settle a claim out of court is also governed by economic factors. Chief among these influences is the party's bargaining power. Defending firms and claimants each wield the same bargaining power in the settlement process. Neither side enjoys a disproportionate share of the bargaining gains.

As predicted by several economic models, there is a negative relationship between the size of the stakes and the likelihood of settlement. The amounts that firms will offer and plaintiffs will accept each increase with the likelihood of plaintiff victory and the expected verdict. Firms have a stake in the court outcome that extends beyond the immediate court award and litigation expenses to embrace factors such as lost sales and future liability burdens. In subsequent chapters we will explore these residual effects in greater detail, along with the implications of various reform measures for the tort liability regime.

4

The Design Defect Test

Before considering how the tort liability system should set criteria for product design, let us first think about how product design decisions are made within the context of a perfectly functioning product market. If market forces are fully effective, then product safety will be at its most efficient level—the objective of tort liability. Moreover, examination of the nature of the market will also highlight the chief ways in which markets may fail, thus indicating why products liability law and hazard warnings are necessary.

Firms typically have a variety of designs for a product from which to choose. They also have the option of not marketing the product at all. Suppose that products differ only on the basis of two attributes, their cost and their risk. One can then narrow the set of choices to the cheapest versions of the products that achieve various levels of safety. A firm will always choose to produce the safer product if it can do so at less cost. The main tradeoff from the standpoint of the firm is how much extra cost it should incur to improve product safety.

The simple answer that all products should be completely safe is certainly not correct. Cars would be safer if they were built like tanks and if they did not go fast, but this improved safety would come at a cost, not the least of which would be decreased fuel efficiency. The National Highway Traffic Safety Administration (1990) estimates that the move to smaller, more fuel-efficient cars has led to 1,300 additional fatalities annually.

Firms do not make arbitrary judgments regarding how far they should push in providing product safety. That judgment is actually made by consumers through the prices they are willing to pay for the extra safety. If consumers are informed of the risks posed by alternative product designs and if they make rational decisions, then the prices consumers are willing to pay for products will fully reflect the value to them of the added safety. Safety does have a value and, as we will see in Chapter 5, this value is quite high, but it is nonetheless finite.

We demonstrate our willingness to make such tradeoffs in our daily risk-taking decisions. All forms of transportation are hazardous, but we value our mobility. Exercise poses a variety of risks, but lethargy imposes risks as well. Many of the foods we eat and the water we drink create some risk of cancer. These risks have not paralyzed our ability to make choices, because we learn to make tradeoffs between the risks and benefits.

A consumer who is fully informed of the health consequences of a product will similarly take these risks into account when deciding whether to purchase it, or whether to pay a higher price for greater safety. Price incentives may be quite substantial, and they apply to the cost of labor as well as the cost of products. My estimates for the labor market, for example, indicate that firms pay workers an extra $100 billion per year in higher wages for risk, in addition to what they pay for workers' compensation.

The higher price of safer products in turn will establish an incentive for the producer to sell safer variants of the product. In choosing the product design, the producer will be guided by how much more consumers are willing to pay for greater safety. The producer will continue to increase the level of safety until the extra payment received from consumers no longer offsets the added costs.

This kind of calculation is not crass or otherwise inappropriate. Indeed, if consumers are fully cognizant of the risks they face, it will lead to the correct level of safety. The key ingredient of the market mechanism is that it is consumers' preferences for safety that in effect establish the price of safety and how much safety will be provided. The firm is simply responding to what consumers demand.

If this market ideal was generally applicable, there would be no need for social risk management institutions such as products liability or regulatory agencies. Unfortunately, market mechanisms are not perfect; there may, for example, be too few sellers of a product for the market to be competitive.

For the most part, however, the chief inadequacy of the market is inadequate risk information. Knowledge of the risks posed by products is seldom perfect, and the usual assumption underlying products liability law is that consumers are unaware of the risks they face.

This approach of equating imperfect knowledge of risks with underestimation of risk is not borne out in studies of risk perception, however. Several different situations can be distinguished. The first consists of situations of ignorance, in which individuals have no knowledge whatsoever of product hazards. Risks that are hidden from the consumer and that come as a surprise are in this category. Cancer risks that asbestos posed to the World War II shipyard workers are likely to be of this type, as are many hidden chemical hazards. If there is no awareness of the risks whatsoever, then there will be no safety incentive provided by the price mechanism. Firms will simply choose the least expensive variant of the product. Products liability can potentially remedy this inadequacy by imposing costs on the producer when it chooses risk levels that are not efficient. Thus, the rationale for liability is that it replaces incentives that are missing when the market is not functioning perfectly.

A more prevalent situation is that in which there is some individual awareness of the risk, but this knowledge is not perfect. Individual risk perceptions diverge from actual risk levels, and these discrepancies vary in different hazard contexts. For example, individuals display a tendency to overestimate low-probability events and underestimate larger risks.[1] For example, people greatly overestimate the chance of being struck by lightning or being killed in a tornado, whereas the more common risks we face, such as the overall chance of dying from heart disease, stroke, or cancer, are substantially underestimated. Similarly, most product risks tend to be comparatively small, and in the typical case in which there is some (imperfect) awareness of the risk, individuals are likely to overestimate these risk levels. Incentives for safety generated for firms will consequently be too great, rather than too small.

A second manner in which risk perception biases vary systematically is with respect to how much publicity the risk has received. Risks that have been the subject of widespread publicity tend to be overestimated. This accounts in part for the high risk assessments for events such as tornadoes and earthquakes, which are covered extensively in the press but which affect a small number of people. Similarly, the dramatic reactions to two recent incidents—the poisoning of Tylenol capsules and the discovery of traces of cyanide on two Chilean grapes in Philadelphia—indicates the potential for strong and possibly alarmist responses to small risks. In much the same vein, the widespread cancellation of trips to Europe after isolated terrorist attacks were reported also represents an overreaction to low-probability events.

One product risk that has been given extensive publicity is the potential danger of cigarette smoking. The possible health hazards have been the target of annual reports by the Surgeon General and have been identified on product labels and in widespread media coverage. Here again the result has been overestimation of the risk: individuals believe that getting lung cancer from smoking cigarettes is almost a fifty-fifty proposition, thus overestimating the actual lung cancer risk level by a factor of 4 to 8.[2] If risks are highly publicized and are overestimated, there is no need for additional intervention through tort liability.

A third class of biases pertains to the character of the risk. The extent and probability of harm are not the only matters of consequence. How the injury is inflicted is also important in our perception of risk, perhaps because we draw upon information that we have about different classes of injuries. Events that are vivid and dramatic, such as being killed in an explosion, tend to be associated with high risk assessments. Similarly, risks identified as possible causes of cancer also tend to be associated with substantial risk perceptions.[3] An effect that goes in the opposite direction is that risks that are substantially within an individual's control tend to be underestimated. The overwhelming majority of drivers consider themselves to be average or below average in riskiness, for example; very few drivers believe they have more than the average risk of having an accident.

The fact that risk information is imperfect is not necessarily a justification for the existence of tort liability. One must examine individuals' perceptions of product risks to determine if the result of these perceptual biases will be inadequate levels of safety.

A Case Study of Risk-Utility Tradeoffs

Questions concerning appropriate product design have become particularly prominent with respect to the potentially chilling effect of products liability on innovation. In an earlier era, when the main focus of products liability was on manufacturing defects, there was little interaction between product design choices and tort liability. The increased role of the courts in assessing whether a product is defective has in effect turned decentralized court decisions into a form of national product risk regulation. As a result, the aspects of a particular case are used to judge the efficacy of a product design for an entire product market.

Tort liability can potentially augment the financial incentives for safety that are missing if consumers undervalue the risk. The purpose of products liability is to fill the gaps left by market imperfections and to replicate the incentives that would have been generated had markets been functioning perfectly.

Much of the concern regarding the potentially adverse effect of tort liability on innovation has stemmed from a series of case studies, most of which have involved the pharmaceutical industry. Whereas thirteen companies produced vaccines for five serious childhood diseases in 1981, within a decade the number had dwindled to three.[4] Liability costs for childhood vaccines are likely to be particularly high because they are administered infrequently and because the low risk per vaccination is coupled with administration to an extremely large population. In partial recognition of these concerns, the National Childhood Vaccine Injury Act of 1986 established an administrative compensation mechanism to reduce the litigation costs associated with vaccine-related claims.

Products used for contraception and during pregnancy have also been the target of substantial products liability actions. After spending $1.5 million in a single year to defend itself in four different lawsuits against its Copper-7 contraceptive device, which had annual sales of only $11 million, G. D. Searle and Company discontinued the product. The National Academy of Sciences (1990), noting that tort liability had put the United States a decade behind Europe in the development of contraceptive devices, recently concluded that the products liability system must be overhauled.

A similar example is Bendectin, the only prescription drug the Food and Drug Administration (FDA) had approved for treating the nausea experienced by many pregnant women. Court cases alleged that birth defects of children born to mothers who took Bendectin were attributable to the drug, although the causal link had never been established. The absence of precise scientific evidence against Bendectin does not necessarily imply that the drug is risk-free. Establishing teratogenicity with any statistical precision is an inherently difficult task. Our degree of expertise in determining whether a substance causes cancer is, for example, much greater than our ability to estimate a substance's link to birth defects. After its review of the scientific evidence, the FDA concluded that the drug posed potential risks, as do virtually all pharmaceutical products, but that the drug should remain on the market.[5]

Despite these official reassurances, Bendectin's manufacturer, Merrell Dow Pharmaceuticals, incurred $18 million per year in legal costs for Bendectin cases—a burden almost as great as the $20 million annual sales. The most striking aspect of these statistics is that these expenditures were incurred before the company had ever lost a case. Not surprisingly, Merrell Dow discontinued the product.[6]

Other classes of innovative drugs may also be affected. George Frazza, general counsel of Johnson & Johnson, observed that strict liability "encourages timidity" because of the uncertainty over what will be found to be a defect.[7] If his company developed an AIDS vaccine, he would advise withholding it until Congress passes protective legislation.

Not all these stories are necessarily an indication that the effects of products liability are adverse. A well-functioning products liability system should lead to the discontinuation of existing product lines that are overly risky. Some new products should also be discouraged. Ideally, there should also be a constructive effect on the introduction of safer new products. There are competing effects in terms of discouraging innovations that are risky and encouraging product innovations that enhance safety. Products liability should alter the character of innovation rather than the overall level of innovation.

Unfortunately, uncertainty over prospective liability costs discourages investments in new designs that will have an uncertain payoff. If the design defect test in the courts is not well specified, the potential liability that firms face will be difficult to predict.

Ascertaining whether products liability has an adverse effect on innovation requires a more comprehensive assessment than the case studies of the pharmaceutical industry allow. Toward this end we may look to two national surveys undertaken by the Conference Board (1987, 1988), a private, business-oriented group. The first of these surveys of risk managers, in 1986, indicated that liability had a mixture of both beneficial and adverse effects on innovation. Some firms undertook actions designed to promote product safety: over one-third of the respondents added or improved their product labels and warnings, and an additional one-third of the firms altered the design of their products to make them safer; and one-fifth of the firms making these changes reported a decrease in the accident rate. There was also evidence of a discouraging effect on innovation: almost one-sixth of all the firms indicated that they had decided not to invest in a new product or service because of products liability. Almost half of all the firms reported that some price increases had resulted from products liability costs, but these were generally minor.

A more extensive study by the Conference Board (1988) in 1987 also indicated that there were competing effects on innovation. Products liability led to improvement in the safety of products for 35 percent of the firms, a redesign of product lines in 33 percent of the cases, and improved product usage and warnings in 47 percent of all cases. Moreover, the expectation of liability costs had an additional effect: improving product safety in 29 percent of the cases, leading to product warnings in 21 percent of the cases, and leading to a redesign of the product line in 13 percent. Thus, both actual and prospective liability costs are of consequence in fostering safety incentives.

The flip side of these effects is that products liability also led to the discontinuation of product lines in 36 percent of the cases and decisions against introducing new products in 30 percent of the cases. Moreover, a number of firms closed production plants (8 percent) or laid off some of their work force (15 percent) in response to actual liability costs.

Although products liability costs are clearly of consequence in influencing design choices, we would also like to know the incidence of these costs and their magnitude. In particular, is it the innovators and the leaders in the industry that are being hardest hit by the liability burden, or is it the less innovative firms in the industry that are forced to reconsider speculative and highly risky designs? A quantitative perspective on these issues is provided by the statistics in Table 4.1, which are based on products liability premiums and product sales for firms and industries with or without various kinds of patents.[8] Only a small segment of the American economy is truly innovative in the sense of having product patents or process patents that are of significance. On average, over the 1980–1984 period, the products liability burden is fairly similar for firms with and without patents. Since we are concerned with product design defects, the firms of greatest interest here are those with significant product patents. Lia-

Table 4.1. Products liability premiums/sales index (mean and standard error of mean)

	Percent of firms	1980–1984 average	1980	1981	1982	1983	1984	1985	1986	1987	1988
Firms with significant product patents	18.09	5.74 (0.73)	6.39 (1.27)	5.66 (1.22)	3.95 (1.30)	5.74 (2.93)	7.08 (4.87)	12.28	20.32	20.56	17.27
Firms without significant product patents	81.91	5.45 (0.35)	5.15 (0.56)	5.44 (0.66)	5.21 (0.80)	5.80 (1.05)	9.17 (2.25)	15.90	26.31	26.63	22.37
Firms with significant process patents	16.27	4.88 (0.55)	3.75 (0.66)	5.24 (1.12)	4.54 (1.20)	6.99 (2.26)	9.95 (4.31)	17.26	23.39	23.67	19.88
Firms without significant process patents	83.73	5.62 (0.37)	5.65 (0.59)	5.53 (0.66)	5.06 (0.80)	5.50 (1.11)	8.45 (2.31)	14.66	24.26	24.55	20.62

Source: Viscusi and Moore (1991).

Note: The premiums/sales index is the ratio of the average products liability premiums/policy in the ISO sample divided by an index of sales for this industry. This sales index equals the average value of sales (in millions) per firm in the industry. Figures for 1980–1984 are calculated from the data; figures for 1985–1988 are projected levels based on actual sales amounts and patent levels, coupled with projected premium amounts. Patent data by individual firm are from the Profit Impact of Marketing Strategies data base; sales data and data on the number of firms by three-digit industry classification are from the U.S. Department of Commerce; and data on liability premiums per policy are from ISO. The PIMS and ISO data bases consist of proprietary, computerized survey data.

bility costs for these firms have been increasing at a slower rate than for the noninnovative segment of the market. Although the projected rates for 1985–1988 are more speculative, they indicate a continuing rise in the liability burden, for both innovative and noninnovative firms.

More detailed statistical analysis of the data indicates that except in very high levels of liability, the net effect of products liability is to foster innovation rather than deter it. Once the liability level in an industry becomes too great, however, the dampening effect takes hold. In subsequent sections we will explore the manner in which design defects are resolved by tort liability and examine how products liability can promote safety in an efficient manner. The aim is to strike an appropriate balance between fostering constructive product innovations and promoting the enhancement of product safety.

Risk-Utility Analysis

The major developments in products liability law over the past three decades have been the adoption of strict liability, the development of the concept of a design defect, and the assessment that inadequate warnings may be considered a design defect.[9] These developments are not unrelated, for the major test for defective designs is a strict liability concept. In particular, the general approach now used to determine liability for product defects is the risk-utility test (or what is sometimes referred to as a danger-utility test) developed by Dean Wade.[10]

The emergence of the design defect test coincided with the expansion in liability costs and litigation in the 1970s and 1980s. The design defect doctrine may have enormous consequences for firms. If firms can be held liable only for manufacturing defects, then only random manufacturing errors will generate liability claims. But if firms are liable for design defects also, the cost of all risks associated with an entire product line can potentially be charged to the producer. Liability then depends on whether the product was too risky to be marketed or whether it should have been designed differently. Proving either of these claims involves risk-utility analysis. The risk-utility test calls for a balancing of the risks associated with the product design against the utility of the design. In the case of a design change, for example, one must inquire whether the costs associated with an improved and safer design are warranted given the level of risk reduction that will be achieved.

Risk-utility analysis is instrumental in three different liability contexts.[11] First, courts have applied it to changes in the physical design of the product, ascertaining for example whether a particular safety guard or other modification is warranted.[12] Second, the risk-utility test has been used to assess one major class of design change—hazard warnings.[13] Warnings alter the risk by providing information to consumers rather than by changing the product's physical attributes. The third and most controversial area to which the courts have extended risk-utility analysis is the more fundamental question of whether the product should be marketed at all.[14]

Unfortunately, the increased use of the risk-utility approach has not been accompanied by a sound articulation of the procedures that courts should follow in undertaking the analysis.[15] Little guidance is available for interpreting a risk-utility test, other than the list of seven factors articulated by Dean Wade (1973) in his seminal article. These factors alone, however, do not touch all the bases. Some critics have called for the abandonment of the risk-utility approach, saying the test functions more as a metaphor than as a precise legal doctrine that can be implemented by the courts.[16]

Nevertheless, the risk-utility test has been widely used to determine whether firms should be held strictly liable for accidents caused by their products.[17] Although the seven factors are insufficient, they do highlight the importance of tradeoffs. Achieving improvements in safety requires additional expenditures of funds, and one must strike an appropriate balance between these additional expenditures and the safety gains they will produce. The interests of consumers, manufacturers, and the general public are all of consequence.[18]

Risk-utility analysis has been applied mainly to the engineering aspects of product design. For example, Honda motorcycles have been subject to litigation over the adequacy of crash bars and whether they would have passed a risk-utility test.[19] In addition, risk-utility analysis has also been applied in court cases involving products as diverse as pharmaceuticals[20] and construction materials.[21]

The risk-utility doctrine has obvious advantages over other approaches, such as a consumer expectations test, in which no balancing of cost versus gain need be required.[22] Under a consumer expectations test, risks that consumers do not expect are not taken into account. Furthermore, if the costs of alternative designs are substantial, a product should not necessarily be declared "defective" even if consumers' expectations are not met, since consumers might well have continued to purchase the good even if they had known of the defect. Consumers may be disappointed when cars driven into a lake do not float, but a failure to meet these expectations does not imply that the product is defective.[23]

Ultimately, some judgment regarding product risks and benefits must be made. The important question is whether the producer has selected the efficient level of safety, not the level consumers expect. The courts should eliminate the consumer expectations test and focus instead on the market for which the product has been designed.

The risks and benefits of concern in products liability, as laid out by Wade, are as follows:

(1) The usefulness and desirability of the product—its utility to the user and to the public as a whole.

(2) The safety aspects of the product—the likelihood that it will cause injury, and the probable seriousness of the injury.

(3) The availability of a substitute product which would meet the same need and not be as unsafe.

(4) The manufacturer's ability to eliminate the unsafe character of the product without impairing its usefulness or making it too expensive to maintain its utility.

(5) The user's ability to avoid danger by the exercise of care in the use of the product.

(6) The user's anticipated awareness of the dangers inherent in the product and their availability, because of the general public knowledge of the obvious condition of the product, or of the existence of suitable warnings or instructions.

(7) The feasibility, on the part of the manufacturer, of spreading the loss by setting the price of the product or carrying liability insurance.[24]

Although Wade should be given credit for stressing the importance of making safety tradeoffs and raising many relevant factors, the risk-utility test is not fully operational. Wade does not propose a definitive test. How is the performance of a product with respect to the seven factors to be measured and, once measured, how are these values to be aggregated to assess whether the product passes or fails the test? There are no formal procedures of this type. In almost all cases, a product that meets one criterion fails another. Under what circumstances are opposing effects offsetting? Do all factors receive equal

Table 4.2. Two approaches to implementing a risk-utility test

Factor	Attributes for evaluation	Product safety policy to be evaluated
1. Usefulness and desirability of product	Consumer benefit	
2. Safety of product	Risks to consumer	
3. Availability of substitute products		Product ban
4. Feasibility of altering design	Costs of product changes	Product modification
5. User's ability to exercise care		Shift of responsibility to consumer
6. Risk awareness and warnings	Expected and unexpected injury costs	Warnings
7. Loss spreading	Insurance costs	

weight? How many dimensions must a product fail on before it is found to be defective?

The factors do not constitute a checklist of pertinent considerations or a series of tests that should be undertaken. Rather, they are a little, but not enough, of both. Table 4.2 summarizes the distinction. Some of the factors pertain to evaluations of attributes of the product and the market in which it will be sold (factors 1, 2, 4, 6, and 7); others pertain to quite different kinds of judgments, whereby one tests the desirability of the current product relative to the following alternatives: a product ban (factor 3), alteration of the product's characteristics (factor 4), reliance on the consumer, not the producer, to avoid injury (factor 5), and alteration of the product through provision of warnings (factor 6).

Even if the factors had been fully articulated, it would not be sensible to combine all these criteria into a single test. Consider each of the factors in turn. In evaluating the first, the utility of the product, one must be careful to avoid the pitfall of imposing one's own notion of value on others. This possibility is evidenced in *O'Brien v. Muskin*: "The evaluation of the utility of a product also involves the relative need for that product; some products are essentials, while others are luxuries." The fallacy in such statements is that essentials provide utility whereas luxuries do not. From an economic standpoint, arbitrary judgments such as this are inappropriate. The usefulness and desirability of a product will be reflected in the price that consumers are willing to pay for it.[25] The real measure of value is individual willingness to pay, not some arbitrary notion of usefulness. In a democratic society, courts should not be engaged in deciding for the public that some products (such as recreation equipment) are not useful or essential. We can rely on effective markets, when they exist, to establish the appropriate values. Thus, the value of the product to consumers is the sum of their total willingness to pay for the product. This value will generally exceed the total amount that consumers actually spend on the product. The difference between the price consumers are willing to pay and the price they actually do pay is their net benefit from the purchase. Economists call this magnitude the "consumer's surplus."

The second factor, the frequency and severity of likely injury from the product, is clearly important, as are changes in the frequencies or severity that can be achieved through actions by either the manufacturer or the user.

Third, the availability of substitute products is probably very difficult to assess precisely on a practical basis. It is not a separate attribute for evaluation, since the determination of the utility of the product to the consumer (factor 1) will have already taken substitutes into account. Measures of consumer willingness to pay are already conditional on the current set of substitute products. The availability of substitutes does, however, suggest a test that can be applied to a product. If a product were to be found to be inherently too risky to be marketed, the attractiveness of the available substitutes would determine the desirability of keeping the product on the market.

The fourth factor, manufacturer's ability to alter the product, may be evaluated in two ways. The current product may pass a risk-benefit test, but there may be alternative product designs that are superior in that regard. Has the firm's choice across product variants been optimal? What are the costs and benefits associated with these modifications? The issue is not whether safer product alternatives are available, but whether from a total risk-utility perspective the best product has been selected. If consumers are cognizant of the risks, a competitive market will ensure that the product mix is optimal, so courts need not make any assessments on this matter.

The fifth factor introduces the issue of the cheapest cost avoider. The user's ability to exercise precautions is clearly relevant, particularly if he or she can reduce the risk more efficiently than can the firm. Even if that is the case, the firm may bear a responsibility to provide the information needed to motivate the precautionary behavior.

The sixth factor should really be viewed as a prerequisite of efficient market operation. Risk awareness is crucial for efficient product choice and for precautionary behavior, and warnings are potentially central in this regard. If consumers are fully cognizant of the risks and purchase a product voluntarily, then the presumption should be that the product passes a risk-utility test.

The Producer as Insurer

The seventh factor raised by Wade is whether it is feasible for the producer to act as the insurer. The expected costs of accidents could be borne by the producer, which would compensate the victims. The producer would then shift this cost, at least in part, to consumers of the product through higher prices.[26] In effect, when the consumer bought the product he or she would also be purchasing an insurance policy for it. Although the insurance objective may be a valid but subsidiary objective in some products liability contexts, it does not establish an appropriate general basis for liability.

First, and most important, strict liability is not tantamount to absolute liability.[27] The intent of tort law is not to make the producer the insurer of all product-related injuries. If that were the case, compensation would be divorced from causality. Under absolute liability, for example, car manufacturers would have to pay for all damaged cars and all lost earnings and medical bills of those involved in car accidents. A more moderate alternative would be to have the insurance function become pertinent only when a product "caused" the accident. The extent to which a party "causes" an accident, however, depends on whether that party could have made additional efforts or safety expenditures that were relatively more productive than the other party's and also justified in relation to their costs.

A different class of problems with a broad insurance role for products liability is that the courts are relatively inefficient insurers compared with firms whose main business is insurance.[28] Whereas administrative costs of insurance consume roughly 20 percent of the premium dollar, the standard contingency fees when injured parties take producers to court are much larger. The estimated share of compensation devoted to plaintiffs' legal fees and expenses is 39 percent for asbestos and 30 percent for other tort actions.[29] Moreover, the net compensation received by victims is less than half of *total* litigation costs. Of the $29 to $36 billion in national tort liability expenditures in 1985, plaintiff compensation after deducting litigation costs for both sides is only $14 billion to $16 billion.[30]

The dollars that plaintiffs receive also do not arrive promptly and with certainty. Court actions often involve long delays and a probability that the claimant will receive no reward at all.

A general disadvantage of comprehensive product risk insurance is a problem known as "moral hazard." The presence of insurance may alter the behavior of the insured. The producer cannot monitor how the products are used, and it cannot monitor all of the other consumption and personal activities that the individual engages in that will affect his health over the years. This is one reason why the government has established the Consumer Product Safety Commission and other regulatory agencies as opposed to simply relying upon the courts to handle consumer losses.[31] The analogy to workers' compensation breaks down in the consumer products context. Whereas the employer can monitor workers at the workplace, the producer cannot monitor the consumer's behavior.

It is also not feasible for any organization to act as the insurer in situations in which risks of different items in a product line are highly correlated with one another. The insurance approach may be feasible when, for example, random manufacturing defects cause injuries. If, however, major insurance costs are associated with an entire product line, affecting all consumers of a prescription drug, for example, insurance arrangements will not be viable. The main difficulty is that if one product is defective, they all will be. All of the risks are correlated, so there will be no offsetting risk in the insurer's portfolio. In general, insurance companies write policies for uncorrelated risks and pool the various risks of different policies in their portfolio of risks. The average losses from year to year will be fairly smooth and will be in line with the premiums paid. In contrast, as the experience in the asbestos industry has shown us, highly correlated risks do not lead to risk spreading but instead may lead to the shutdown of the industry. It is noteworthy that in a major case in which the court articulated the risk-spreading objective of products liability (*Beshada v. Johns-Manville Products Corp.*, 90 N.J. 191, 447 A.2d 539, 1982), the scale of the risk made risk spreading infeasible.

Another difficulty with having the producer act as the insurer arises when it is not evident whether the product caused the injury. In many cases, the scientific evidence is so imprecise that the linkage between the product and the risk remains uncertain even on an average prospective basis. We often cannot even assign probabilities reliably to possible product risks. After the fact, causality may be difficult to determine because of the highly varied set of activities and personal habits of individuals over their lifetimes. When there are multiple causes and long time lags involved, it is difficult to establish a meaningful basis for assessing what the appropriate insurance should be.

A pivotal limitation of having the producer act as the insurer is the often long time lags between purchase and injury, in which case the notion of loss spreading is inappropriate. The idea of insurance is to have the purchaser of the product, in effect, buy his or her insurance through a premium paid at the time of purchase. If, however, there is a lag of two or three decades before the adverse health outcomes become known, the amount that would have to be added to the price to fund all past liabilities would greatly exceed the value of the insurance to current consumers of the product. Thus, the insurance analogy breaks down. Even if the scale of the health risks involved were not substantial, this huge discrepancy in timing undermines any attempt to establish a meaningful linkage between the benefit of insurance and payment of a premium.

The emergence of the risk-spreading objective for the risk-utility test and strict liability more generally is in part a product of the historical context. When these doctrines were introduced, federal social insurance efforts were not well established. Moreover, private health insurance coverage was not nearly as extensive as it is today.[32] With the substantial expansion of health insurance as a benefit of employment, the insurance gap that tort liability fills is not as great. Indeed, concern has shifted to the possibility of overinsurance, for individuals may have multiple forms of recovery for the same accident.

A final limitation of having producers act as insurers is that in effect each risk will be insured separately. From an insurance standpoint, this is less efficient than comprehensive coverage.[33]

Although providing insurance is a laudable objective, doing so may not always be economically desirable. The insurance objective may come into play as an additional dividend of compensating the occasional victim of a manufacturing defect. Design defects involving large-scale risks or deferred health risks are not adequately addressed by utilizing products liability as an insurance mechanism.

Table 4.3. Benefit and cost measures for purchasers, producers, and society

	Purchaser	Private	Social
Measures of benefit			
Consumer willingness to pay for product	X	X	X
Profits		X	X
Taxes			X
Benefits to other parties			X
Measures of cost			
Purchase cost	X	X	X
Unexpected injury cost	X	X	X
Costs to other parties			X

Alternative Risk-Utility Measures

Table 4.3 summarizes three alternatives to Wade's risk-utility analysis. From an economic standpoint, more than one risk-utility test is needed because the components of the test differ depending on the context. I propose that the risk-utility test should be extended to three separate measures, to be evaluated in sequence.

First, the purchaser's risk-utility index should be considered. In particular, this index can be used to ascertain whether on balance it is sensible for the individual to purchase a particular product. Given the available knowledge of the product's risks of accident or illness at the time the product was produced, on balance do the expected benefits received by the consumer outweigh the expected injury costs?

In effect, the objective of this test is to ascertain whether the producer would have marketed the product on the basis of a benefit-cost test rather than on the basis of the product's profitability. The informational standard to be used in making such judgments is what the producer should have known about the risk. There may be things the firm should have known but did not, particularly if it undertook no research or did not monitor product-related accident reports. The test should not, however, assume that firms had advanced knowledge that was not available and that they should not have acquired in the normal course of their operations. Thus, the imposition of retroactive liability on asbestos producers in the *Beshada* case is not consistent with this test. The issue is not whether in retrospect a product should have been marketed but whether a firm making a socially oriented product risk decision is behaving in the correct manner given the state of knowledge at that time. In effect, firms should be given a "state of the risk information" defense.

Under the private risk-utility measure, one broadens the analysis of costs and benefits to include effects on the producer. In particular, the producer earns a profit from the sale of the goods, and the overall net gain to both parties—the consumer and producer—must be considered when analyzing the desirability of design changes and warnings. The benefits and costs to the producer are ignored in Wade's formulation, except through the vague reference to eliminating a product's risk without making it too expensive.

The private risk-utility test should consequently be twofold. Firms should not market products that do not pass the first test—that the expected benefits of the product exceed the expected injury costs—even if substantial profits would accrue to the corporation. Products must pass a threshold test of being an attractive purchase on an expected value basis for the average consumer, based on the best knowledge of those risks at the time the product was purchased. This test involves no comparison with alternative designs.

The specific product design must also pass a second test, one that takes into account the profits to the producer. It is the second test that serves as the standard measure of economic efficiency in economic analysis. Our objective should be to establish the product mix to maximize this net surplus accruing to both the producer and the consumer, subject to the first test being met.

The third test extends the measure beyond the parties involved in the transaction; it is a social benefit-cost test. If the product has adverse effects on parties other than the purchaser, then these should be taken into account. One should also be cognizant of the favorable effects as well. If one includes the costs of product risks to society (such as increased medical costs borne by society at large), one should also recognize the benefits to society from product risks (such as reduced pension costs and social security costs) and the broader economic benefits from making the product in the first place.

One could also envision situations in which a product passes a social test but does not pass a private test. If, however, a product fails an earlier test in the sequence, its good performance on a social risk-utility basis should not overrule that failure. The most fundamental purpose of products liability law is to protect the consumer, not to advance objectives such as employment at the consumer's expense.

Although there may be situations in which the court must make societal assessments, I will treat the third test primarily as a government regulation test rather than as a liability test for use in the courts.

A market that is fully efficient allows only those products that satisfy each of the three tests. All products would be attractive to consumers (pass the purchaser risk-utility test) and have positive private and social utility as well. Indeed, if all social repercussions are fully recognized by the producer and the user, social welfare is maximized by an efficient market.

Each test examines a different set of factors. The purchaser's risk-utility measure concerns the average consumer, not the individual consumer involved in a particular liability case. A more stringent criterion would require that every consumer who purchases the product must reap expected benefits in excess of the expected costs of purchase. Such a test would be appropriate if the firm could in fact distinguish the merits of the good to each consumer purchasing it and then charge a person-specific price to reflect these differences. Clearly, such fine tuning and discriminatory pricing is not feasible.

The emphasis on the value to the entire product market calls into question whether the courts are the appropriate forum for cost-benefit judgments. The knowledge of a particular plaintiff is irrelevant to the broader judgment of whether a product design was appropriate for an entire market. Class actions are better suited to arriving at such judgments, but ideally regulatory agencies should have that responsibility.

The purchaser's risk-utility measure entails a set of three factors. The first is the value of the product to the consumer, which is the consumer's willingness to pay for the product. The determination of the value to the consumer is not a mystical issue that turns on an external observer's assessment of what is valuable and what is not. Rather, economists have a well-established methodology for approaching this issue.[34] The other two factors are costs, namely, the purchase price of the product and the cost of an unexpected injury. Thus, one must subtract from what consumers would be willing to pay the amount that they actually do pay to obtain a net willingness-to-pay figure. Only the unexpected costs should be subtracted since all expected losses associated with the product will already have been internalized through the price that consumers are willing to pay for the product. If consumers on balance overestimate the risk associated with the product or have accurate perceptions, then there are no unexpected injury costs to be taken into account. Only when consumers underestimate the risks will there be an unanticipated cost that must be recognized. The issue then becomes whether these unanticipated costs outweigh the net difference between consumers' willingness to pay and the purchase price of the product.[35]

In comparing the purchaser's risk-utility measure and the overall private risk-utility measure listed in Table 4.3, there is only one change in the calculation: profits to the firm have been added. The overall net benefit of the product reduces to the sum of the consumers' surplus and the producers' profits, less the unexpected injury costs.[36]

Once we extend the risk-utility measure to include the benefits and costs to society, three main additions are needed. The first is a tax component. Excise taxes represent a net gain to society above the cost of producing the product, and this financial contribution should be recognized. Second, there may be benefits to other parties from the production of the good, such as the workers who make the product. The third class of effects pertains to the costs imposed on third parties.

These risk-utility measures together function as a more tightly specified negligence standard. Did the producer exercise an appropriate degree of care for the consumer's welfare in the design of the product? Two distinctions between the negligence standard and the tests proposed here are most salient. First, the question being posed in a negligence case is one of fault. Did the producer have knowledge of the risk and fail to act upon this knowledge in a responsible manner? In the risk-utility analysis, a firm need not know the risk or have "constructive knowledge" of the risk or be inflicting an intentional harm.[37] Rather, the issue is simply whether the product design passes a particular test of desirability, assuming that the defendant had knowledge of the risk.

A second distinction is that the insurance and risk-spreading objective does not arise under negligence, but it is a component of strict liability and risk-utility analysis, as Wade and others view the approach. This objective is not part of the formulation I have outlined.

On the Threshold of Marketability

Easily the most controversial aspect of risk-utility analysis has been its extension by *O'Brien v. Muskin* to decide whether a product should be marketed at all. Traditionally, the focus of risk-utility analysis has been on design defects and on hazard warnings. In *O'Brien v. Muskin*, the court indicated that it is appropriate to apply risk-utility analysis to ascertain whether the risks of a product are so great relative to its utility that the product should not be sold at all.[38] Such categorical applications of risk-utility analysis have been increasing in recent years.[39]

The threshold marketability test is really a consumer protection standard. Firms need not be protected through a separate test; if firms are losing money on the sales of a product, then they can voluntarily choose not to market it. Alternatively, if firms are making substantial profits, but consumer well-being is being harmed by the product because of unanticipated risks, then firms should not be permitted to reap these gains at consumers' expense. Unless a product passes the minimal threshold of promoting consumers' overall interests, it should not be marketed. When considering changes in the product, however, as in the case of warnings and design changes, one should recognize the profits of the firm, subject to the constraint that the product not make consumers worse off.

Because an informed market will only accept products that necessarily pass a risk-utility test, courts and legal scholars have generally excluded from the "potentially defective" category products whose risks are well known.[40] Alcoholic beverages have common and obvious dangers, and it is not appropriate for courts to apply a risk-utility analysis concerning whether these products should be marketed. Similarly, courts have ruled that handguns likewise have obvious risks so it is not an appropriate use of risk-utility analysis to assess whether the risks of this product outweigh their utility.[41] Finally, tobacco also poses well-known risks. As the *Restatement of the Law of Torts* observes, to the extent that one assesses whether tobacco has a product defect, it will be with respect to whether the product is "good" tobacco or whether the product has been tainted in some manner.[42] In the absence of such a defect, tobacco would pass a risk-utility test because of the well-known nature of the risks, which have been formalized in a series of hazard warnings and widely disseminated by the Surgeon General of the United States.[43] Risk-utility analysis is more helpful for deciding the marketing threshold when the risks are not well known, an excellent case in point being the rabies vaccine.[44]

One might question whether only those products that are found to be defective because of the absence of a warning should be held to the threshold liability test, since it is only products for which decisions are not informed or rational that would not be weeded out by market mechanisms. This restriction would not be appropriate for several reasons. First, it may not be feasible to provide effective hazard warnings. It may be too costly to warn, but that does not necessarily imply that there are no informational inadequacies. Second, the requirements that are placed on hazard warnings are less stringent than those that we have placed on a market to show that it is fully effective. One would want to tighten the warnings requirements if a firm's ability to pass the hazard warnings test implied that it would be exempt from liability. Consumers must receive, fully understand, and act upon a warning for the market to be efficient. Because of the limitations at each of these stages, even a well-designed warning may not be effective in informing consumers. Third, and perhaps most important, the tests are different and must be applied sequentially. The warnings test specified above is based on the private risk-utility measure of the product after the warnings have been given as compared with the private measure of the product before the warnings have been given. In contrast, the threshold marketing test is based on the purchaser's risk-utility measure, which excludes profits from consideration. Warnings may not enhance a product, either because of inadequacies of consumer choice or the extreme costliness of warnings, but a product nevertheless may not be in the consumers' best interests.

Who Decides?

A recurring question asks who should carry out the risk-utility test. One can pose this question narrowly, as did Dean Wade, and ask whether it should be the judge or the jury. In some instances, it has been decided that this is a question of law and policy—not issues of fact—and as a result the court has the discretion of whether to submit the issue to the jury.[45] One can also raise a more fundamental question: which set of institutions—the courts, regulatory agencies, or the Congress—is best able to make the risk-utility judgments?

If regulatory requirements exist and lead to an efficient level of safety for a product, then a risk-utility test in the courts is extraneous. In effect, the analyses supporting the regulations would have already provided the answers to the risk-utility test in that they have shown that the resulting guidelines are efficient.

To reduce institutional overlapping and avoid giving firms conflicting guidelines for their products, an effort should be made to take advantage of the regulatory arena when assessing the desirability of judicial intervention. Ultimately, most if not all of the major design and warning regulations may be turned over to regulatory agencies since these issues hinge on overall market performance as opposed to the idiosyncratic issues involved in a particular case before a particular court. Whether or not we reach that stage depends on whether the federal regulatory agencies continue to expand the scope and competency of their efforts. Until a complete shifting of responsibilities has been achieved, there should at least be greater recognition of the interdependence of these institutions and the commonality of their functions.

Although much of the information required to undertake a risk-utility assessment is routinely calculated as part of government agencies' regulatory analyses, it is not generally feasible to carry out the same calculations for every design defect case. This does not mean the risk-utility standard is reduced to a simple "metaphor." Rather, it provides a checklist that a court can use to frame the options before it. In the case of a product design change, for example, the evaluative task appears feasible. The courts must ask whether the improved safety benefits resulting from a change are justified given the added costs that they will generate, where these costs will be reflected both in higher consumer prices and lost profits to the firm. A subjective assessment of these options, or qualitative measures of their importance, may be the best that is achievable. Nevertheless, it is useful to have guidelines regarding the set of pertinent concerns and how they should be combined.

Proposals for Restructuring the Product Defect Test

The feasibility of having the courts carry out design defect tests may be much less when broader product risk issues are at stake. Assessing the desirability of a particular design feature, such as a machine guard, requires only that one compare the costs of the design change with the reduced injury costs, where these costs are evaluated using the deterrence values for injury outlined in Chapter 5.

In the case of the threshold decision of a product's marketability, matters are quite different. A sound analysis requires that one examine all of the fairly complex concerns outlined in Table 4.3. These components comprise pertinent economic considerations that must all be recognized, and there is no meaningful way to simplify the task. Even under a best-case scenario, carrying out such a comprehensive product evaluation would pose a serious challenge to the ability of any jury. Moreover, the society-wide assessments that must be made as to whether a product should be marketed at all seem better suited to institutions with resources of staff and expertise that juries lack—Congress and regulatory agencies. If the domain of tort liability were restricted to design defect cases involving particular design components, excluding questions of whether a class of products is inherently too risky, the scope of the courts' evaluations would be greatly simplified.

Products that are unavoidably risky, such as handguns, diving boards, and above-ground swimming pools, would not, however, be completely exempt from court review. These products would also have to be accompanied by appropriate hazard warnings to make consumers aware of the risk, if it was not apparent.

Distinguishing which product modifications involve design components rather than fundamental changes in the character of the product may appear to be infeasible, but application of the risk-utility framework above can resolve this issue. In particular, a design change that will significantly affect the consumer's demand for the product for reasons other than the greater safety it offers would be addressed by social institutions other than the courts.

The intent of this proposal is to engage the courts in a manner that recognizes two types of error. It may be that some products that should be banned will not be addressed by other social institutions (a type-II error). However, a greater danger seems to be that the courts will erroneously judge products too risky to be marketed on the basis of a narrow and, in all likelihood, incompletely informed assessment of the factors involved in a particular case (a type-I error).

Strict liability would continue to pertain to manufacturing defect cases, because the risk-spreading role of liability insurance is feasible for such cases. A risk-utility test restructured along the lines I have suggested will serve as the design defect test. In the case of specific design features, the courts would apply this test to assess the desirability of particular safety improvements. Compliance of the current design with a specific regulatory standard would, however, be exculpatory. Responsibility for carrying out the risk-utility test to assess the threshold marketability issue would lie with Congress and regulatory agencies. Firms would, however, be subject to court review of the adequacy of the warnings for unavoidably dangerous products.

The principal objective of these proposals is to reallocate the institutional division of labor to focus the efforts of the courts on those product risk issues to which they are best suited. Subsequent chapters will explore the regulatory compliance defense and hazard warnings proposals in greater detail.

The overall scope of my design defect test proposals would be modest rather than revolutionary. The courts would abandon the consumer expectations test, decrease the emphasis on the producer's role as insurer, restructure the risk-utility test, and roll back the recent extensions of the risk-utility measure to include the threshold marketability issue.

The fact that these reform proposals are incremental in character does not reflect a substantial satisfaction with the current liability regime. Major shortcomings in the liability regime do exist, and the task of determining which design changes are warranted will remain intrinsically difficult. The problem is that there are no ideal remedies.

The risk-utility test developed by Dean Wade has become increasingly prevalent in products liability cases in large part because it reflects the kind of balancing of consumer and producer interests that is necessary to form a reliable economic judgment regarding the inadequacy of a product. Safety improvements to a product and hazard warnings should be assessed on the basis of the impacts they will have on both consumers and producers.

The original emphasis of risk-utility analysis on the need for balanced decisions with respect to products liability was a correct and fundamental one. Moreover, many traditional factors that have been considered are legitimate, but they did not provide a framework for comprehensive and consistent risk-utility judgments. The intent of this chapter has been to develop a series of economic formulations of the risk-utility test that would establish a sounder basis for a products liability defect doctrine.

Making product design judgments will, however, remain a task that can be carried out more effectively by institutions better suited than the courts to addressing these societal risk issues. Subsequent chapters will elaborate on these proposals for an appropriate division of labor.

5

The Explosive Mathematics
of Damages

After the space shuttle *Challenger* disaster, the families of four astronauts killed in the rocket explosion received annuities from the federal government for $7.7 million, or almost $2 million per fatality.[1] Survivors of a civilian NASA employee killed in the crash, Judith Resnik, settled with the rocket manufacturer, Morton Thiokol, for an amount in the $2 million to $3.5 million range.

Million-dollar awards are not limited to highly publicized national tragedies. The proliferation of substantial products liability awards has made six-digit payoffs from a products liability suit much more frequent than comparable payoffs from state-run lotteries. The leading money winner in the products liability sweepstakes in 1987 received $95 million.[2] The general impression created in the media is that not only are liability suits on the rise, but the awards being won have escalated as well.

Products liability reform proposals often include various constraints on the awards for the reason that damages amounts set the prices that drive liability costs. Although there have been few criticisms of the determination of economic losses, noneconomic losses have come under considerable fire. This criticism has arisen not necessarily because of arguments over the idea of compensating for pain and suffering. The main shortcoming is the absence of clear criteria for determining the *level* of compensation.

Uncertainty over the prospective level of pain and suffering damages often has dramatic incentive effects. In 1990 the Coca-Cola Co.

introduced its "MagiCans" promotion for Coke. MagiCans did not contain Coke, but instead were designed so that a prize popped up when they were opened. To prevent consumers from identifying the lucky cans, the bottom of the MagiCan contained heavily chlorinated water, and some consumers mistakenly drank the water.[3] Since some of these cans were "defective" (that is, the prize did not pop up, or the chlorinated water leaked into the prize chamber and was consumed), Coca-Cola would be strictly liable for harm done because of the defect. The principal open issue is what damages a jury would award to those who took a sip of the foul-tasting water.

By almost any reasonable injury standard, such damages should be negligible. What juries will do in practice, however, is highly uncertain. Rather than subject itself to the risks of runaway jury awards, Coke abandoned the MagiCans campaign in which it had invested $100 million. Since Coke estimated that 8,700 cans would be defective, their economic investment per potentially defective can was $12,000. In comparison, the actual pain and suffering costs appear trivial—except when the potentially capricious impact of juries is taken into account. In this situation, there were no well-defined limits as to what juries could reasonably do.

Although there have been calls for constraining these escalating and random awards levels, recent developments show tort liability heading in the opposite direction. The concept of so-called hedonic damages, for compensating individuals for their lost enjoyment of life, has been adopted in some cases. If generally accepted, these damages could easily increase awards by a factor of ten, to levels that would dwarf the "jackpot" awards in the news today.

Before assessing which products liability reforms, if any, will rationalize procedures for determining damages, we will begin with an exploration of the criteria that should be used in setting damages. We will then examine recent trends in damages awards, including compensation for noneconomic damages. As we examine some of the newer damages concepts that have been developed, the main issue to keep in mind is not so much how we can calculate value-of-life figures but rather under what circumstances it makes sense to do so. The Ford Pinto case best illustrates the potential merits of this approach.

The principal reform decisions hinge on a selection of the pertinent objectives that should be served by compensation for personal injury. Once there is agreement on these objectives, designing the appropriate products liability reform strategy becomes straightforward.

The Insurance Value and the Deterrence Value of Damages

Setting damages in personal injury cases is complicated primarily by the fact that the losses are not merely financial. In a standard textbook case of property losses, tort liability functions quite effectively.[4] Optimal compensation replaces the victim's property loss and setting compensation levels is quite straightforward. Moreover, either a strict liability or a negligence regime can produce efficient levels of accident deterrence, provided of course that contributory negligence on the part of the accident victim is also recognized.

In contrast, personal injury cases are much more problematic, for they must confront the irreplaceable character of life and health. Whereas one can easily pay for the repair of a car, the appropriate "reimbursement" for health losses is less obvious. Consider the losses suffered by an accident victim who loses the use of both legs. In property loss cases, compensation is set as the amount that should make one "whole," but no monetary transfer may restore a paraplegic to the level of well-being associated with good health.[5]

When we try to set a dollar amount to describe what has been lost when a person is injured or killed, we use terminology such as the "value of life," but this is somewhat confusing. There is no unique value of life; the appropriate value depends on whether our concern is with accident prevention or compensation.[6]

We will distinguish two different measures of damages—the insurance value and the deterrence value. Consider first the value of compensation from the standpoint of insurance. The appropriate reference point here is not the insurance amount that individuals actually do select, perhaps on the basis of limited understanding of the risk. Rather, the insurance value is the amount of insurance people would select if economic markets were perfect.[7] With perfect markets, risk-averse individuals will fully insure property losses. The optimal insurance for adverse impacts on health is indeterminate. Until we know more about the nature of the injury, we cannot know the extent to which we should restore the pre-accident level of welfare.

The optimal level of insurance is driven by how the accident affects one's ability to derive benefits from additional expenditures. In the extreme case of death, the appropriate bequest will seldom restore the victim's entire lifetime wealth level, since the victim will not be able to benefit from this wealth. The accident victim will typically wish to leave a bequest, but for less than total lifetime wealth. Much the same result holds for the typical on-the-job injury. Workers faced with perfect insurance for disabilities would select insurance that provides for only about 85 percent earnings replacement.[8]

There may, however, be situations in which the accident may boost the well-being one can derive from additional consumption expenditures. One can, for example, envision circumstances under which expenses for computers and televisions might enhance one's well-being more after a disabling accident than before. Typically, the most important expenditures of this type are already subsumed under the medical expense damages component of awards. For example, the cost of vans and the expenditures needed to adapt one's residence after an accident generally are treated as medical and rehabilitation expenditures.

The second approach to valuing personal injury might best be termed the deterrence value. Consider a situation in which the accident victim is facing a small risk. Specifically, suppose that this risk equals the average hazard posed by a typical job—an annual risk of death of 1/10,000. Suppose that this worker is willing to face this risk for an additional wage premium of $500 per year. The presence of the risk and the required wage offset establishes the risk-dollar trade-off for the individual, thus establishing the price for bearing risk.

In this case, the price per unit risk is quite substantial. In particular, $500 compensation for each 1/10,000 risk of death implies a total compensation level per statistical death of $5 million. Viewed somewhat differently, if 10,000 workers each faced an annual risk of death of one chance in 10,000 and were compensated at $500 each for facing the risk, then the total risk compensation for the one expected death would be $5 million dollars. This $5 million figure establishes the value of life set by the individual bearing the risk. From the standpoint of the accident victim it provides the appropriate measure of the deterrence price that should be charged so that the producers inflicting the accident will fully reflect the interests of those exposed to the risk.

Making the producer pay the $500 to each individual who must bear the risk will foster effective safety incentives. The firm will be faced with a choice of either compensating those exposed to the risk or making a financial expenditure to enhance safety. This compensation mechanism will lead producers to take an efficient degree of care.

This market scenario requires that individuals make conscious choices with respect to product risk. Individuals must have some awareness of the risk in advance and be compensated either through higher wages or lower prices. In contrast, tort liability ideally should address situations in which there is believed to be some shortcoming of the market, either because of a lack of voluntary trade or a failure to fully appreciate the risks that are present. In these situations, the compensation will not be paid in small increments in advance, but instead will be paid after the fact in a lump sum to the particular accident victim.

In terms of creating safety incentives, it matters little whether we pay 10,000 individuals exposed to the accident $500 each or we pay the particular accident victim $5 million. In each case, the firm's price tag for risk is identical and the same safety incentives will be created.

The impact on the insurance objective differs, however, depending on whether the single accident victim's survivors receive a payoff of $5 million or each of the 10,000 individuals exposed to the risk receives $500. The premium before the accident, or the *ex ante* compensation for the risk, in effect makes all potential accident victims whole from the standpoint of their expected welfare. When compensation is provided after the fact, however, there is not the same link to the accident victim's welfare. A $5 million award to one's survivors will not restore the well-being of the deceased. The main justification for such compensation must be deterrence rather than insurance.

The choice of the appropriate compensation mechanism can be seen by considering the different decision contexts outlined in Table 5.1. For three different situations, we will assess different approaches to determining compensation—the insurance value, the deterrence value, or some compromise between the insurance and deterrence values.

Missing from this list of potential approaches is a compensation measure based strictly on justice. For the purposes of this discussion, we will assume that it has been decided, for reasons of equity, to pay compensation to the accident victim. Justice is also at issue when deciding the amount of compensation that will be paid. For example, it may appear to be unjust to give equal compensation to two accident victims who experience the same financial loss but one of whom experiences substantial pain and permanent disfigurement. Such notions of justice, however, may simply reflect underlying concerns with deterrence. The main reason we view compensating these individuals the same amount as inequitable is that we would like to establish

Table 5.1. Effects of different compensation mechanisms

Producer's safety decision	Insurance value	Deterrence value	Insurance/deterrence mix
No safety investments	Optimal insurance, inadequate incentives	Overinsurance, adequate incentives	Overinsurance, inadequate incentives
Moderate safety investments	Optimal insurance, possibly adequate safety incentives	Overinsurance, excessive incentives	Overinsurance, possibly adequate safety incentives
Safety investments just below efficient standard of care	Optimal insurance, excessive incentives	Overinsurance, excessive incentives	Overinsurance, excessive incentives

incentives so that responsible parties will have additional incentives to avoid accidents that impose additional nonmonetary damages.

Consider the first situation in Table 5.1. The firm makes no effort whatsoever to make a particular product safe. Setting compensation according to the appropriate insurance value will provide an optimal level of insurance, as it will in all other situations listed in Table 5.1, but insurance-based compensation will not generate adequate incentives to promote product safety. Higher compensation levels based on the deterrence value of compensation will remedy the incentive problem, but because the deterrence amount is paid to a single accident victim, too much insurance will be provided.

To retain the deterrence incentives but avoid overinsurance, one might envision mechanisms in which the deterrence value of compensation was paid not to the victim but instead was paid as a fine to the government. However, this approach would immediately be undermined by out-of-court settlements. Firms will attempt to limit their losses and plaintiffs will seek a share of the fine by settling out of court for their compensable losses as well as a portion of the fine.

The best that can be achieved is a balance between the competing objectives of compensation and insurance. We must sacrifice some of our deterrence objective to limit the degree of overinsurance. The more sensitive the safety decision is to financial incentives and the greater the ability of the accident victim to reap welfare benefits from additional expenditures, the closer the compensation level should be to the deterrence value.

The second situation considered in Table 5.1 is that in which the firm makes moderate safety investments, but these investments are not sufficient to raise the safety level to the standard of care required under products liability law. In this situation, insurance values of compensation will probably generate inadequate safety incentives, unless the safety level selected is already close to the appropriate amount. Compensation equal to the deterrence value will provide excessive safety incentives, since the firm is already engaged in the process of promoting safety. The ideal will typically be some compromise between the insurance and deterrence values.

In the final situation, the firm has made safety investments that are substantial, but they fall just below the level required under the efficient standard of care. In that instance, even the insurance value of compensation may provide for excessive financial incentives for safety, since the firm might already have been so close to providing the efficient product risk level that only a minor additional financial incentive was needed.

The insurance value of compensation establishes an appropriate level of compensation and can serve as the floor for ascertaining the appropriate compensation levels. As the level of safety selected by the producer departs by an increasing amount from the optimal standard of care, it will be more appropriate to shift the level of compensation from the insurance value to the deterrence value. Even when no safety precautions are currently being taken, however, one would generally want to set a compensation level a bit below the deterrence amount to avoid overinsurance.

Although recognizing the deterrence value of accidents may raise one cost component of awards, this change in damages valuation procedures will also make it possible to eliminate the need for punitive damages. The three main functions of punitive damages are deterrence, retribution, and compensation.

All of the damages amounts discussed above will provide sufficient compensation to ensure efficient insurance given the character of the injury. The deterrence goal is met also, because the value-of-life numbers are based on the amounts needed to create efficient incentives to avoid accidents. Moreover, since the deterrence values reflect the terms of trade (that is, the risk-dollar tradeoff) required by the individual bearing the risk, no additional compensation or retribution is needed. In particular, these same numbers are the amounts workers must be compensated for accepting risks. If the accident victim is willing to accept compensation based on the deterrence values in the context of the labor market, there is no justification for charging a higher price in a different context.

The principal exception to these guidelines pertains to high risks of accident. These deterrence values are based on the usual case of the unlikely accident. The law will treat firms that market products having a fifty-fifty chance of killing customers in quite a different manner. It should also be noted, however, that the market will treat these risks differently as well. The selling price for bearing risk will also be higher in this instance. The underlying methodology remains correct, but the deterrence values differ. Society may have additional interest in discouraging large risks.

Eliminating punitive damages will remove a major source of uncertainty in the current liability system but will not greatly affect the total compensation victims receive.[9] A computerized case search identified 108 products liability cases from 1970 to 1989 in which punitive damages were awarded and for which the final award actually received by the plaintiff could be ascertained. The total punitive damages awarded by the courts in these cases was $250.2 million, or about $2.5 million per case. However, plaintiffs received only $71.7 million, or 29 percent of the original punitive award. Courts often reduce punitive damages on appeal, and defendants may negotiate a reduction in this amount in return for prompt payment of the damages amount.

The appropriate level of compensation consequently hinges on whether one wants damages to provide insurance and create accident deterrence or whether one wishes to focus on only a single objective. One might view compensation as a means of providing insurance, and it is the task of liability standards to address the incentives issue. These functions cannot be divorced, however, since the damages amounts set the price tag firms pay for risky products.

A preferable long-run solution is to avoid these tradeoffs altogether by establishing a division of labor among different social institutions. A main theme of Chapter 6 is that regulatory agencies are better suited to promoting deterrence than is the tort liability system. Recognizing the expertise of other institutions in controlling risks will partially address the difficult tradeoff problems involved.

Inflation and the Increase in Verdict Awards

A frequently cited index of the need for tort liability reform is the rise in million-dollar verdict awards. Although data are not available for the products liability component of these awards, the tally for all personal injury cases indicates a large number of seven-digit awards. There were 7 million-dollar verdicts in 1970, 115 million-dollar verdicts in 1980, and 474 million-dollar verdicts in 1988.[10] These counts also include, for example, medical malpractice awards, so that the number of products liability cases resulting in million-dollar verdicts is considerably less. Moreover, at the end of the litigation process, recipients of jury verdicts in excess of $1 million ultimately receive less than half of the original award.[11] Furthermore, there may also be many million-dollar settlements out of court that are not included in the tallies.

Awards of the kind received by the *Challenger* astronauts' families should not necessarily be considered windfall gains. Suppose an accident victim will either be permanently disabled or will incur medical expenses for forty years. A million-dollar award averages only $25,000 per year.[12] This is not only a modest amount of earnings when compared with full earnings lost, but it also represents a small fraction of what medical expenses could be if constant supervision or expensive procedures were required. A brain-damaged victim requiring eight hours a day of nursing care at a cost of $10 per hour will incur expenses exceeding $1 million over forty years.

The rapid increase in the number of million-dollar awards does not, however, imply that the tort liability system has become more generous or that the damage standards have been liberalized. Inflation accounts for much of the increase. A $1 million award in 1987 had the same purchasing power as an award of $341,500 in 1970.[13] To buy what $1 bought in 1971 required an expenditure of $1.79 in 1979 and $2.80 in 1987. Since prices have roughly tripled over the past two decades, the $300,000 verdicts of the early 1970s became the million-dollar verdicts of today without any change in their real economic value.

The contribution of inflation to products liability awards can be seen more clearly by examining the statistics in Table 5.2. Included in the table is information regarding the median and average verdict levels for products liability cases from 1971 through 1988. Post-trial adjustments stemming, for example, from inadequate insurance by

Table 5.2. Products liability verdict awards, 1971–1988

Year	Midpoint verdict award	Annual percent change	Real percent change	Average verdict award	Annual percent change	Real percent change
1971	$71,500	—	—	$195,020	—	—
1972	106,000	+48.3	+43.6	223,659	+14.7	+11.1
1973	72,500	−31.6	−35.6	237,462	+6.2	−0.1
1974	100,000	+37.9	+24.3	345,783	+45.6	+31.2
1975	121,475	+21.5	+11.3	393,580	+13.8	+4.3
1976	100,000	−17.7	−22.2	366,081	−7.0	−12.1
1977	125,000	+25.0	+17.4	430,948	+17.7	+10.5
1978	137,000	+9.6	+1.9	1,657,187	+284.5	+257.4
1979	190,000	+38.7	+24.5	761,009	−54.1	−58.8
1980	225,000	+18.4	+4.4	563,438	−26.0	−34.7
1981	340,000	+51.1	+36.9	800,586	+42.1	+28.7
1982	300,000	−11.8	−16.9	850,700	+6.3	+0.1
1983	300,000	0.0	−3.1	1,245,646	+46.4	+41.9
1984	300,000	0.0	−4.1	1,467,435	+17.8	+12.9
1985	450,000	+50.0	+44.7	1,091,005	−25.7	−28.3
1986	678,826	+50.8	+48.1	1,161,522	+6.5	+4.6
1987	430,000	−36.7	−38.9	1,325,443	+14.1	+10.0
1988	405,000	−5.8	−9.5	1,535,944	+15.9	+11.3
Annual growth rates						
1971–1979		+12.99	+5.04		+18.55	+10.21
1979–1988		+8.77	+3.03		+8.12	+2.41
1971–1988		+10.74	+3.97		+12.91	+6.01

Source: Jury Verdict Research (1990), p. 31. Real percent change figures were calculated by the author.

defendants reduce the actual amount received from a jury award by an average of over one-fourth.[14]

Still, the surge in awards has been considerable. Median verdict levels increased from $71,500 in 1971 to $405,000 in 1988. Similarly, average verdict levels increased from $195,020 in 1971 to $1,535,944 in 1988. These increases far outstripped inflation. For both the median verdict levels and the average verdict amounts, Table 5.2 reports the annual percentage change as well as the real percent change, which is the difference between the percent change in verdict levels and the percent change in the consumer price index. In most of the years considered in the table, the size of the verdict increase exceeds inflation.

These patterns are borne out in the growth rates calculated at the

Table 5.3. Increases in wages and medical prices as compared with increases in the Consumer Price Index (CPI)

	CPI price increase	Wage increase[a]	Wage increase − interest rate[c]	Present value of $1 wages for 30 years	Present value adjusted for base wage shift
1971	4.4	7.2	2.9	48.2	48.2
1979	11.3	7.9	−2.1	22.1	39.2
1987	3.7	2.4	−3.4	18.6	49.1

	CPI price increase	Medical price increase[b]	Medical price increase − interest rate[c]	Present value of $1 medical expenses for 30 years	Present value adjusted for base price shift
1971	4.4	6.2	1.9	40.7	40.7
1979	11.3	9.2	−0.8	26.6	49.7
1987	3.7	6.6	0.8	34.0	122.6

a. Percent change in private hourly earnings for private nonagricultural workers, *Economic Report of the President* (1989), p. 358.

b. Calculated from data in ibid., p. 373.

c. Interest rate statistics are based on three-month Treasury bill rates; ibid., p. 390.

bottom of Table 5.2. Both the median verdict amount and the average verdict amount exhibited annual rates of change from 1971 to 1988 of 10–13 percent. Although most of the increase is attributable to inflation, there was nevertheless a 4–6 percent real (inflation-adjusted) increase. Most of the verdict growth rate is attributable to rising prices, but verdict levels have risen faster than the overall rate of price inflation.

The composition of the changes in prices and wages may account for some of this discrepancy. The two main components of economic loss are the present value of lost earnings and the present value of medical expenses associated with the injury. The performance of each of these components has differed markedly over the past two decades, and this difference has led to an increase in the relative importance of medical expenses.

The statistics in Table 5.3 illustrate the key relationships. As the first two columns at the top indicate, rates of wage increase in the economy exceeded rates of price increase in 1971, but following the oil price shock of the 1970s and continuing through the budget deficit era of the 1980s the rate of wage increase has been less than the rate of inflation.[15] Accelerating wages have not outstripped inflation so that increases in the lost earnings component of awards cannot account for the rapid increase in verdict levels found in Table 5.2.

The pattern for medical expenses is quite different. The substantial demands placed on our medical sector have led to annual medical price inflation rates of 6 percent or above for two decades. These rates have consistently exceeded overall rates of inflation except during the aberrational energy crisis years. In 1987, for example, medical price inflation was almost 3 percent higher than the overall rate of price increase.

Small swings in inflation rates of 1 to 2 percent become magnified when one calculates the present value of the lost earnings or medical expenses in a damages calculation. The main measure that governs the long-term losses is the relationship between the rate of growth in the earnings or medical expenditure and the rate of interest, since it is the rate of interest that is used to convert future losses into their present financial value. The third column of statistics in Table 5.3 gives the spread between the rate of wage increase and the rate of interest. Subsequent to 1981 the rate of wage increase was below the rate of interest by 2–3 percent. In contrast, medical price increases have maintained comparability with the rate of interest.

Modest differences with respect to the rate of interest can have enormous effects on present value calculations that extrapolate losses over a longer time horizon. The figures in the fourth column of the top panel of statistics in Table 5.3 indicate the present value to a worker of losing $1 in wages on a continuing basis over the next thirty years. These calculations assume the rate of wage increase relative to the rate of interest is the rate given in the third column in Table 5.3.[16] For 1971, when the rate of wage increase exceeded the rate of interest, the value of $1 earnings lost was more than $30 over a thirty-year period because the worker's wage would have risen over time, outpacing interest rates. As a result, the total present value of the loss is $48.20. If, however, an individual were to lose $1 in wages over a thirty-year period beginning in 1987, the present value of the earnings loss would be only $18.60, because the rate of wage increase has dropped considerably relative to the rate of interest.

The total earnings award levels in 1987 will not necessarily be lower than those in 1971, however. Inflation over the past two decades has boosted the base earnings level used in the calculation. Whereas workers were formerly making an average of $3.45 per hour in 1971, by 1987 average hourly wages had risen to $8.98 per hour. Even with a decline in the rate of wage increase relative to the rate of interest, this rise in the base level of wages used to project future earnings losses will offset the dampening of the earnings growth rate. Adjusting for this shift in wage levels, the value in 1971 dollars of a $1 earnings loss over a thirty-year period is $48.20, and the value in 1987 of an earnings loss with the same purchasing power as $1 of wages in 1971 is $49.10. The striking result is that there has been virtually no change whatsoever in the level of the earnings component of damages awards.

The situation for medical price increases is quite different. If medical price inflation were to just keep pace with the rate of interest, then the present value of $1 in medical expenses over a thirty-year period would be $30. Over the past decade the present value of $1 in wage losses had dropped to below $30. In contrast, the present value of $1 of medical losses over a thirty-year period in 1987 was $34. Thus, projecting $1 of loss in any given year over a thirty year period leads to a bigger present value of loss for medical expenses than for wage expenses.

Compounding this difference is the fact that the base level of medical expenses has been rising considerably from year to year. The same medical services that cost $1 to provide in 1971 cost over $3 in 1987. The result of this shift in medical prices is that the present value over a thirty-year period of $1 in medical expenses in 1971 dollars rose from $40.70 in 1971 to $122.60 in 1987. Although the quality of medical services has no doubt also improved, much of this increase is attributable to the increased demands on our health care system made possible by Medicare, Medicaid, and extensive health insurance coverage for American workers.

Table 5.3 indicates that it is unlikely that the main contributor to the surge in products liability awards stems from a rise in earnings, as earnings losses have been relatively flat. Medical price increases have, however, outstripped inflation and the medical loss component of awards has skyrocketed. For the standardized thirty-year loss calculation presented, the medical component tripled whereas the wage loss component was stable. The inflation of medical prices, which has outstripped the overall rate of inflation in the economy, contributes to the escalation of products liability awards noted in Table 5.2.[17]

Noneconomic Damages

It has often been speculated that one of the reasons for larger court awards has been a rise in the amounts awarded for noneconomic loss, chiefly pain and suffering. Although the principles used for establishing pain and suffering compensation have not changed, the absence of any well-defined criteria for setting compensation levels has led many observers to speculate that there has been an escalation of pain and suffering awards.

In addition to income and medical losses, accident victims incur a welfare loss associated with adverse health effects. The "pain and suffering" designation is usually used to refer to these nonmonetary losses. Spouses also may suffer a loss of consortium after a fatality.

Court awards address each of these loss components. The objective of compensation for financial losses is well defined—to restore the victim to "a position substantially equivalent in a pecuniary way to that which he would have occupied had no tort been committed."[18] But for pain and suffering, compensation is "intended to give to the injured person some pecuniary return for what he has suffered or is likely to suffer. There is no scale by which the detriment caused by suffering can be measured and hence there can be only a rough correspondence between the amount awarded as damages and the extent of the suffering."[19] Although pain and suffering is a legitimate component of compensation, there is no well-specified measure of what it is or how much of the welfare loss it is intended to replace.

The most that legal scholars have offered are somewhat negative guidelines that indicate what pain and suffering is not. The appropriate pain and suffering award is not the market value of a certain loss of this type.[20] One should not, for example, pose the question in terms of how much the accident victim would require to accept the certainty of a particular loss, such as hemiplegia.[21]

The most widely used set of quantitative guidelines is the approach suggested by Melvin Belli, who urges that plaintiffs' lawyers ask the jury to assess the pain and suffering for a small time interval—a minute, say—and then to scale up this number proportionally with the total duration of the pain and suffering to determine the total award.[22] Even this rudimentary effort at quantification is not permitted in many states, perhaps because assuming that the pain and loss experienced is additive over each time interval may be a misleading economic approximation. Moreover, it begs the fundamental issue of what each unit of pain and suffering is worth.

The net outcome is that pain and suffering is generally recognized by the courts as a legitimate component of compensation but one for which we have no accepted procedure of measurement. Even more fundamentally, we do not have precise guidelines as to what should be measured if it were possible to do so. The standard procedure is to leave the issue to the jury, in the apparent hope that jurors can fill the intellectual void left by the courts and legal scholars.

The outcome has been that pain and suffering amounts are often the largest part of the damages award. A boy whose foot was wedged in an escalator at New York's Kennedy Airport received $50,000 for medical expenses and $1.2 million for pain and suffering.[23] A Minnesota jury awarded an eighteen-year-old man who suffered the loss of his right eye from a stone he ran over while using a Toro lawnmower $2.5 million, over half of which was for embarrassment, emotional distress, pain, disability, and disfigurement.[24] Awards such as these have given way to new developments regarding the possibility of obtaining awards for the fear of injury. After the 1989 crash of United Airlines Flight 232 in Iowa, survivors inspired by recent judicial trends contemplated filing "fear of death" lawsuits.[25] Even more dramatically, passengers whose plane did not crash have received such compensation.[26] More recently, the courts have permitted passengers on a tramway who witnessed a fatal accident to sue for the emotional trauma of witnessing the death of a woman whom they did not even know.[27]

The substantial uncertainties created by nonmonetary damages are reflected in the inability of juries to make reliable judgments. In an Illinois case of a worker killed in an oil refinery explosion (*Alex Bart v. Union Oil Co. of California*), a jury awarded the decedent's family $700,000 for pain and suffering, even though there was no evidence that the victim was conscious and able to experience any pain at the time of his death. As an additional bonus, the jury awarded the family $2.2 million for loss of love, affection, and kindness—$131,000 for each year of his expected remaining life. Upon appeal, the court found that there was no basis for the pain and suffering award and that the award for love, affection, and kindness was excessive. The wild swings in the financial stakes in this case are a result of the lack of meaningful criteria for guiding jury decisions.

In the absence of clear legal guidelines, jurors might make the pain and suffering award a minor addendum or perhaps the most important component of the award. The U.S. Department of Justice Tort Policy Working Group concluded that these awards were so subjective and unpredictable and that their magnitude was so substantial that a cap was required.[28]

These and other cries of alarm with respect to pain and suffering should not be taken at face value. Defendants in products liability cases would undoubtedly support any measure to reduce their economic burden. Pain and suffering has not been the sole target of reform proposals, nor the most prominent. Are companies simply seeking general relief or are pain and suffering awards a problem of substantial consequence?

To obtain an empirical perspective on pain and suffering I rely on the ISO data used to assess litigation patterns in Chapter 3.[29] Although jury behavior may have changed in the past decade, there has been no fundamental change in the basic principles for setting damages.

The average bodily injury loss experienced in this 1977 claims sample is $13,723, and the average bodily injury payment is $9,995. This latter figure includes claims for which no compensation was received. These dollar amounts are converted to 1990 prices by doubling them.[30]

Although the ISO data set includes a variety of questions on the nature of the injury and the disposition of the claim, the pain and suffering amount is not explicitly reported. For claims receiving a positive bodily injury payment, it is possible to calculate the pain and suffering value indirectly by netting out the compensation for economic loss.[31] Overall, 37.5 percent of the cases with positive awards had no pain and suffering compensation. This imputation is not an exact measure of the pain and suffering level, but it should provide an instructive index of the level of such compensation and its variation across injury groups.[32]

Table 5.4 summarizes the principal statistics on claims that received some positive payment for bodily injury (columns 1–3) and claims that also included a positive pain and suffering amount (columns 4 and 5). The prevalence of pain and suffering is particularly great for cancer and burn victims; over four-fifths of these accident victims received pain and suffering compensation. The mean value of pain and suffering, which includes claims for which there was a positive award but not necessarily a pain and suffering component, ranges from a low of $442 for dermatitis to high values of $67,628 for brain damage and $72,834 for paraplegia and quadriplegia.

There is considerably less variation in the share of the award paid for pain and suffering, which ranges from 30 percent to 57 percent of all awards in which bodily injury payment has been received. The

Table 5.4. Overall distributions of pain and suffering awards in 1977 ISO claims sample

Type of injury	Claims with positive bodily injury payments			Claims with positive pain and suffering payments	
	Fraction of claims compensated for pain and suffering	Mean pain and suffering awards ($)	Fraction of payment for pain and suffering	Mean pain and suffering awards ($)	Fraction of payment for pain and suffering
Amputation	.74	31,749	.51	42,801	.68
Asphyxiation	.68	10,349	.47	15,109	.68
Brain damage	.59	67,628	.38	114,324	.64
Bruise	.73	2,546	.49	3,502	.68
Burn	.82	22,841	.57	27,773	.69
Cancer	.86	25,642	.54	29,915	.63
Concussion	.76	9,022	.50	11,908	.66
Dermatitis	.66	422	.41	639	.63
Dislocation	.63	11,327	.42	18,124	.67
Disease—other	.79	8,440	.48	10,623	.61
Electrical shock	.61	3,439	.41	5,661	.68
Fracture	.51	6,187	.30	12,054	.58
Laceration	.75	3,397	.51	4,513	.68
Para/quadriplegia	.52	72,834	.26	140,065	.50
Poisoning	.72	510	.46	709	.64
Respiratory	.54	18,263	.41	33,918	.76
Sprain/strain	.76	10,418	.50	13,670	.65
Other	.53	4,505	.35	8,456	.65

Note: The sample size of claims with positive bodily injury payments is 8,116.

low end of the range indicates that there is no injury category for which pain and suffering does not constitute almost one-third or more of all compensation received. Indeed, for six of the eighteen categories listed, pain and suffering accounts for half or more of all compensation. The injury groups for which pain and suffering is responsible for a dominant share of the compensation include: amputations, burns, cancer, concussions, lacerations, and sprains/strains.

Even these rather impressive statistics may understate the importance of pain and suffering, however. When we exclude those cases where pain and suffering amounts are zero, awards for pain and suffering increase by about 50 percent in most cases. The mean values of pain and suffering now exceed $100,000 in two categories, para/quadriplegia and brain damage. In current dollars these amounts average above $200,000. The recommendation by the U.S. Department of Justice that noneconomic damages be capped at $100,000 would clearly be a binding constraint on average for these injuries, even if products liability awards had not increased with inflation over the past decade.[33]

The levels of compensation for brain damage and para/quadriplegia are extreme outliers. In fourteen of the eighteen injury categories in which there is positive pain and suffering compensation, the pain and suffering compensation is below $30,000.

These statistics show that pain and suffering amounts are fairly large in absolute terms and vary in a systematic fashion across injury categories. Jurors do not simply add a uniform pain and suffering amount to all claims. Pain and suffering amounts are neither completely random nor uniform. Major differences across accident categories can be observed. And yet a clearer and more consistent pattern can be seen in the final column in Table 5.4. For claims in which there is a positive pain and suffering award, the average share of pain and suffering compensation is consistently about two-thirds.

These results are noteworthy for two reasons. First, the contribution of pain and suffering is remarkably high. Noneconomic damages are not a minor afterthought but are the driving force of compensation levels when pain and suffering amounts are positive. Second, there is a tight clustering of the pain and suffering share, which ranges from 63 percent to 69 percent for fourteen of the eighteen injury groups.

This outcome is consistent with a rule of thumb that says compensation levels triple when pain and suffering is of consequence. There is no economic or legal justification for simply scaling up awards. Although more detailed statistical analysis indicates that pain and suffering awards involve more than a scale adjustment of the financial loss, a very strong component of awards is related to financial loss. In particular, a 100 percent increase in the financial loss will generate a 66 percent increase in the pain and suffering compensation amount.[34]

A desire to reduce the costs imposed by pain and suffering awards has led to proposed restrictions on these payments. In the extreme case one could advocate eliminating them altogether. Two less sweeping alternatives are to establish fixed schedules for pain and suffering awards and to impose dollar caps on them. The most prominent proposal of this type is the proposal by the U.S. Department of Justice to cap pain and suffering awards at $100,000.

Table 5.5 summarizes the effects of caps ranging from $50,000 to $150,000. In current dollars, these cap amounts are roughly $100,000 to $300,000. In each case, the table reports the fraction of all cases with bodily injury payments affected by the cap as well as the fraction of claims with positive pain and suffering for which the cap will be binding. To the extent that measured pain and suffering is depressed for cases settled out of court, these statistics understate the effect of caps.

If the problem with pain and suffering awards is that they are entirely capricious and completely random, one would expect caps to affect the most extreme claims in all injury types. The effect of caps is, however, much more selective. The three injury groups that will be most affected are para/quadriplegia, brain damage, and cancer. Over one-fourth of those claims receiving bodily injury payments will be constrained by a $50,000 cap. In the extreme case of para/quadriplegia, 40 percent of claims would be constrained by a $50,000 cap, and 77 percent of all claims receiving positive pain and suffering amounts would be affected.

In contrast, for the great majority of injury categories, pain and suffering is not substantial in absolute terms and a cap would be irrelevant. In nine of the eighteen injury groups, fewer than 5 percent of all claims would be affected by such a cap. Four additional injury groups have fewer than 10 percent of all claims affected by a cap.

As the level of the cap is raised, the fraction of cases affected by the cap declines by more than a proportional amount. Once the cap

Table 5.5. The fraction of claims that would be affected by a cap on pain and suffering payments in 1977 ISO claims sample

Type of injury	Claims with positive bodily injury payments			Claims with positive pain and suffering payments		
	$50,000	$100,000	$150,000	$50,000	$100,000	$150,000
Amputation	.169	.080	.061	.228	.108	.082
Asphyxiation	.068	.055	0	.100	.080	0
Brain damage	.338	.239	.141	.571	.405	.238
Bruise	.012	.003	0	.017	.004	0
Burn	.073	.052	.023	.088	.064	.028
Cancer	.286	0	0	.333	0	0
Concussion	.061	.030	.015	.080	.040	.020
Dermatitis	0	0	0	0	0	0
Dislocation	.094	.031	0	.150	.050	0
Disease—other	.027	.014	.014	.034	.017	.017
Electrical shock	.036	0	0	.059	0	0
Fracture	.029	.010	.005	.057	.019	.011
Laceration	.018	.006	.001	.024	.008	.001
Para/quadriplegia	.400	.240	.080	.769	.462	.154
Poisoning	.002	.001	0	.003	.001	0
Respiratory	.135	.019	.019	.250	.036	.036
Sprain/strain	.025	.011	.008	.033	.015	.011
Other	.021	.009	.005	.039	.017	.010

reaches $150,000, there are no cases above the cap in seven of the eighteen groups. Nevertheless, the caps will exclude substantial numbers of claims in particular injury groups. Even for a $150,000 cap ($300,000 in current dollars), 14 percent of all successful brain damage claims and 8 percent of all para/quadriplegia claims will be affected. For the claims receiving positive pain and suffering payments, the affected group is almost double this amount.

A products liability cap consequently will have very targeted impacts. Victims suffering brain damage, para/quadriplegia, and cancer will be most affected, while some classes of accidents, such as dermatitis and poisonings, will be largely unconstrained. To argue that caps will improve the products liability system is to argue that the very severe injuries involve the most excessive awards. There is no evidence that this is the case.

Capping awards would promote the objective of reducing liability costs, but caps would not provide for more consistent compensation. Claims for severe injuries with very large pain and suffering components would be most affected, but these cases are not necessarily most out of line. Since pain and suffering levels have an elasticity of less than 1.0 with the size of the claim, for any given injury type, it may be the small awards that are most unwarranted. Capping awards might increase the degree of inequity in the manner in which pain and suffering awards are set, because victims with major injuries would be limited in making their claims while those with minor injuries would be unaffected.

There is no compelling evidence that pain and suffering awards have escalated by more than, for example, the medical component of damages. What is clear is that these awards are not consistent—there is considerable inequity in the determination of pain and suffering damages. These inequities arise largely because of an absence of clear-cut criteria for setting pain and suffering levels. A more sensible approach to pain and suffering compensation is needed.

Has Voodoo Economics Come to the Courts?

Most estimates of the value of life and injury, made to assess appropriate deterrence levels, are based on studies of labor market decisions. Extensive data on wages and job characteristics yield statistical estimates of the quality-adjusted (that is, hedonic) wage rate. The key quality component of interest is the risk level faced by the worker.[35]

In a competitive market, the extra wage premium that workers receive for risk will reflect their attitudes toward bearing risk. The observed risk-dollar tradeoff can then be used to calculate the implicit value of life or injury. The average blue-collar worker receives an extra $300–600 in wage compensation each year for bearing an average fatality risk of one chance in 10,000, leading to an implicit value per statistical death of $3–6 million.

Since the observed risk-dollar tradeoffs reflect the preferences of the particular sets of workers being analyzed, one would expect to find differences across studies. The value of life is not a natural constant, like *e* or π, but a measure of one's willingness to bear risk. This willingness will vary across individuals just as will other individual tastes. Table 5.6 summarizes the results of a number of studies of the valuation of risk.[36] Although these estimates are reported for the mean level of risk in the sample, in general the value of life varies across the sample. In particular, workers who have selected themselves into high-risk jobs with an annual death risk on the order of 1/1,000 have estimated values of life of $1 million or less, whereas workers in very low risk jobs may have placed implicit values of life on the order of $10 million or more.[37] The variation in the estimates in Table 5.6 consequently reflects in part the different mix of workers as well as the different risks faced by the workers in the different samples analyzed. The $6.4 million estimate of the value of life has been obtained using the most recently available and most reliable death rate statistics.[38] The study yielding the $3.6 million estimate is

Table 5.6. Labor market studies of the value of life and health

Risk category studied	Value (in 1989 dollars)	Reference
Value of life	$3.6–4.8 million	Viscusi (1979)
Value of life	$9.0–13.4 million	Viscusi (1981)
Value of life	a. $6.4 million b. $6.4 million c. $2.4 million d. $2.8 million	Moore and Viscusi (1990), various samples
Value of nonfatal injury	$28,000–41,000	Viscusi (1979)
Value of nonfatal injury	$39,000–44,000	Viscusi (1981)
Value of nonfatal injury	$12,000–16,000	Viscusi and O'Connor (1984)
Value of nonfatal injury	$41,000–50,000	Viscusi and Moore (1987)

the most comprehensive in terms of the other job characteristics included in the analysis. It is currently the most widely used by government agencies such as OSHA and the Office of Management and Budget.

If used as deterrence values of life in wrongful death cases, these value-of-life estimates, even at the low end of the range, would all but ensure million-dollar damage awards. The extent of the potential impact can be assessed by comparing the present value of the earnings of the workers with the estimated dollar values of life. In the case of the $6.4 million estimates, the average workers in the sample had annual earnings of $17,826 (1980 dollars) and a remaining potential period of work until age 65 of 28 years. If their earnings were to grow at a rate equal to the rate of interest, then the present value of earnings lost would be just under $500,000. This estimate is an order of magnitude smaller than this sample's implicit value of life. Moreover, the average payment actually received in fatality cases is even less—only $132,811 for the 1977 ISO data.[39] Even after doubling this amount to put it in current dollars, it remains an order of magnitude below estimated values of life.

At first glance, this disparity may seem to be a contradiction. How can individuals value their lives from the standpoint of deterrence by so much more than their total lifetime resources? The explanation is that the deterrence values of life reflect individual attitudes toward small risks. Individuals may be willing to pay $600 to produce a reduction in their lifetime risk of 1/10,000, but this does not mean that we can extrapolate from this rate of tradeoff to assess how much individuals would be willing to pay for more substantial risk reductions. The amount that they would pay to purchase a 1/10 reduction in death risks generally will be far below $600,000.

The fact that the deterrence values pertain to individual valuations of small changes in risk does not in any way undermine their usefulness from the standpoint of tort liability. Indeed, from a deterrence standpoint this is exactly the valuation that we want. Product risks generally are not so high that all users of the product are killed. Fatalities and other serious injuries tend to be rare events. To value small risk reductions, we want a measure of how product users would have valued these risk reductions. The deterrence values of life give us this amount.

The valuation of nonfatal injuries yields much more modest estimates. Estimates range from $12,000 to $50,000 per injury, as shown in the table. Approximately half of this compensation is for the financial loss associated with the injury. More specifically, one can utilize these findings to derive an estimate of the value of the pain and suffering and noneconomic damage components of the injury, which ranges from $19,000 to $30,000.[40] Thus, approximately half of the injury valuation is for noneconomic loss, and the remainder is for the economic loss associated with the accident.

It is useful to put these estimates in perspective by considering the nature of the injuries involved. The average injury reflected in this table has a duration of seventeen days, which means that the value of the noneconomic damages is roughly $1,000 to $2,000 per day of work lost. Job injuries clearly involve more costs than time off the job, as these estimates indicate.

An important variation in the deterrence values is their relationship to individual income. Economic damages as now calculated are proportional to one's income. A similar relationship appears to pertain to the deterrence valuation figures. In particular, statistical estimates indicate that the valuation of health risk reduction increases on a one-to-one basis with one's income level.[41]

The deterrence valuation figures in Table 5.6 pertain to individual attitudes toward all consequences of the risk, not simply the noneconomic damages. Thus, the deterrence value of life reflects the value that the individual attaches to the risk of experiencing the injury, losing one's income, and losing one's ability to enjoy life. These deterrence values would never be used as an additional component of economic damages but instead would be used in lieu of the economic damage components.

The level of insurance compensation that is required and the overall desirability of pain and suffering compensation may, however, vary with the nature of the injury. For the typical job injury, the optimal level of insurance that workers would select with perfect markets would provide for 85 percent replacement of earnings rather than 100 percent.[42] For modest health effects, such as those resulting from exposure to household chemical products—for example chloramine gas poisoning from toilet bowl cleaner—consumers' deterrence values of prevention are on the order of $500–900 per incident.

Moreover, there is no evidence that the minor injuries reduce the welfare benefits one can derive from additional expenditures. Consumers would choose to insure these risks fully, for they treat them as equivalent to monetary losses. The pain and suffering valuations and the deterrence valuations of the minor injuries are identical. This result contrasts with the findings for more severe injuries, where generally it is not desirable to insure pain and suffering losses at all, and the deterrence values will greatly exceed the insurance values of the injury.

How, if at all, should these estimates be used by the courts? The focus of the controversy over deterrence values for injuries and death should not be over the validity of economics but over the objectives of the tort liability system. Agencies throughout the federal government have adopted the deterrence value approach to valuing the benefits of risk regulation, and the Office of Management and Budget has indicated that this approach should be used to assess all major new federal risk regulations.[43] The main question is whether the judicial system will choose to move to this new liability regime, in which the function of the damages award will be to establish incentives for safety, and not simply to compensate for the economic losses imposed.

Applying the Value of Life: The Ford Pinto Case

The potential applicability of deterrence values of life is illustrated by the Ford Pinto case of the 1970s. This inexpensive compact car dominated the American small car market in the 1970s, but it posed an added and unforeseen cost on consumers. The gas tank was located only six inches in front of the rear bumper, where it posed a potential risk of explosion upon rear impact. Moreover, Ford had made a conscious decision not to undertake an $11 per car improvement that would have prevented 180 burn deaths per year. As a result, Ford was the target of a number of lawsuits and attacks from prominent consumer advocates, including Ralph Nader.

Since Ford's design decision was based on explicit calculations of the benefits and costs associated with the improved design, it can be used to explore how the estimates failed to identify the risks and benefits of the safety improvements.[44] The design change would have eliminated 180 burn deaths, 180 serious burn injuries, and 2,100 burned vehicles, and Ford calculated how much each outcome would cost it in damages, on the basis of typical products liability awards in the 1970s. Fatalities were to be compensated by $200,000, burns by $67,000, and the economic loss incurred by the explosion to the cars themselves by $700 (see Table 5.7). The principal fallacy of Ford's

Table 5.7. Benefit calculations for increased safety in Pinto gas tank design

Outcome of faulty design	Ford's unit value	Ford's total value	Unit deterrence value	Total deterrence value
180 burn deaths	$200,000	$36 million	$5 million	$900 million
180 serious burn injuries	$ 67,000	$12.1 million	$2.5 million	$450 million
2,100 burned vehicles	$700	$1.5 million	$700	$1.5 million
Total		$49.6 million		$1,352 million

calculations is that these values, which were generated by the courts, were woefully inadequate.

A more appropriate set of values for valuing injuries in any design defect test is the deterrence values of life, which for illustrative purposes we will set equal to $5 million.[45] Valuing serious burn injuries is more difficult, because we do not have explicit data on these deterrence values. However, we do know that consumer valuations of chronic bronchitis are roughly one-third that of fatalities, or $1.5 million.[46] Since burn injuries are much more painful and serious than chronic bronchitis, a value of $2.5 million has been assessed in this instance. Finally, the property damage estimate by Ford, if it is in fact correct, was an appropriate estimate of the deterrence value of preventing burned vehicles. The total deterrence values show that the overall benefit of introducing the gas tank modification was $1.35 billion, which is 27 times greater than Ford's benefit estimate of $49.6 million.

Calculations of Ford's costs for the design change appear in Table 5.8 and are quite straightforward. With a unit cost of $11 per car of

Table 5.8. Cost calculations for increased safety in Pinto gas tank design

Number of units	Unit cost	Total cost[a]
11 million cars	$11	$121 million
1.5 million light trucks	$11	$ 16.5 million
Total		$137.5 million

a. Excluded is the minor cost component of the lost consumer's surplus of customers who do not buy Pintos because of the $11 price increase.

introducing the modification, the total cost for the entire fleet of affected cars and trucks would have been $137.5 million.

Ford's calculations using the incentives provided by the tort liability system indicated that making the gas tank improvement would not be worthwhile. Costs ($137.5 million) exceed benefits ($49.6 million) by a factor of almost 3 to 1. In contrast, proper calculation of the benefits of making the improvement ($1,352 million) showed them to be ten times greater than the cost.

The problem with Ford's decision was not that it undertook an explicit calculation of the tradeoffs. Nor was the difficulty that for $11 per car one should always undertake a safety improvement, since that is not always the case. Rather, the main problem was that in doing the calculation Ford drastically undervalued the lives that would be saved and the severe injuries that would be prevented. Ford's problem was not faulty mathematics. The company was simply responding to the incentives generated by the tort liability system.

Although Ford's experience is likely to be a sobering one for other companies contemplating explicit calculations of the merits of design changes, these kinds of tradeoffs should be encouraged. Moreover, if we truly wish the tort liability system to provide effective safety incentives, we must incorporate the deterrence values into the design defect test. Recognition of the deterrence values when setting damages will also provide companies with the correct incentives to promote product safety, but at the cost of providing too much compensation to the victim.

At the very minimum, the deterrence values should be used in assessing liability. Moreover, in extreme cases of inadequate safety decisions that traditionally would merit punitive damages, the deterrence values provide a sound basis for setting such awards, bringing both discipline and rationality to the punitive damages area. The degree to which the courts will adopt deterrence values more generally should depend on the relative importance of additional safety incentives to particular products and on whether creating these incentives warrants an award in excess of the optimal insurance amount.

Proposals for Setting Damages

There seems to be little dissatisfaction with the manner in which economic damages are calculated by the courts. Inflation, particularly with respect to medical prices, accounts for most of the increase in products liability awards over the past two decades. Since compensation for rising prices simply retains the purchasing value of the award, indexing for inflation is consistent with efforts to make victims "whole" financially.

The one component that has attracted the attention of products liability reformers is that of pain and suffering damages. The court system has no well-established methodology for setting pain and suffering and other noneconomic damages, and not surprisingly there have been claims that juries have often been inconsistent in establishing such damages. Examination of actual patterns of awards indicates that noneconomic damage compensation is quite substantial, and it varies in systematic fashion with the character of the injury.

Overall, depending on the injury category, pain and suffering and noneconomic damages constitute 30 percent to 50 percent of the total award. This level is not too dissimilar from the normal contingency fee share of one-third. Although legal reform debates may focus on the appropriate levels of pain and suffering compensation and treat such compensation at face value, this noneconomic damage component may simply be the mechanism by which juries compensate accident victims for their legal fees. If limits are imposed on pain and suffering, then juries may provide this compensation in other ways by, for example, increasing the amount of economic damages awarded.

One way to avoid this outcome is to include explicit compensation for reasonable attorney's fees as part of the award. Thus, pain and suffering awards would be governed by an advisory schedule, economic damages procedures would be unchanged, and attorney's fees would be addressed through a separate awards component based on a standardized fee schedule.[47]

Although a wide variety of pain and suffering caps have been proposed, by far the more fundamental reform task is to establish a firm conceptual basis for pain and suffering awards. One such basis is the deterrence value of compensation.

A second conceptual approach would be the insurance value. In general, the insurance value is below the deterrence value, particularly for major injuries. Except for minor injuries, pain and suffering damages are not outcomes that individuals would choose to insure, so the optimal insurance amount for pain and suffering will typically be zero.

The competing objectives of deterrence and compensation in tort liability consequently results in pain and suffering damages that will typically range from zero to the deterrence values associated with the injury. If there were greater emphasis on the deterrence function, juries could be provided with schedules of such deterrence values and descriptions of the health outcomes, and they could then assess where along this schedule the injury suffered by the plaintiff would fall. This scheduling process would assist juries in making these judgments and would also decrease some of the uncertainty now associated with tort liability awards. It would provide structure without imposing arbitrary limits that do not allow variations with injury severity.

This guideline approach appears preferable to a damages cap.[48] Caps will affect very few products liability claims and will have little overall financial impact. Some of the most highly publicized awards will, of course, be influenced by a cap, but the lion's share of the pain and suffering damages is generated by smaller claims, not by the few large claims at the extreme.

Moreover, noneconomic damage caps create a new class of inequities across injury groups. It is the minor injuries that tend to be overcompensated the most. The truly major injuries with substantial losses tend to be relatively undercompensated. Damages caps would leave the minor injuries unaffected and place a disproportionate burden on victims of injuries in only a few categories, such as brain damage and paraplegia.

There is no compelling rationale for caps other than the imposition of discipline. Rather than impose binding constraints on pain and suffering compensation, which does not even appear to be a driving force behind the liability crisis, it would be preferable to use suggested damages schedules that can be applied in a nonbinding manner.

Widespread adoption of deterrence values for pain, suffering, and the loss of life could, however, impose enormous costs. Moreover, even if one were indifferent to the price tag and simply wanted to create the correct incentives for safety, then utilization of the deterrence values of injury across the board is excessive except when firms completely ignore safety. Nevertheless, the courts could utilize the economic deterrence values in a very limited group of situations, as when it is important to establish effective deterrence incentives to promote appropriate recognition of product safety.

Deterrence values of life and health consequently can serve as the conceptual basis for setting punitive damages awards, thus providing greater certainty to a damages area where jury discretion is enormous. In addition, these values can be of general use in assessing whether firms undertook safety precautions sufficient to pass a risk-utility test. Finally, these estimates may be of use in other, very selected damages contexts where the courts' main interest is in establishing deterrence incentives rather than simply providing insurance to accident victims. These award levels would not be punitive in the sense of punishing firms, but they would be designed to redress imbalances when firms are ignoring the safety objectives at stake.

6

Regulation of Product Safety

Society has several institutional mechanisms for controlling product risks and compensating victims for income losses. Economic forces foster each of these objectives, deterrence and insurance, and social insurance programs, such as workers' compensation, also provide compensation and influence safety levels through merit rating. Two additional institutional mechanisms, which are the primary focus of this chapter, are tort liability and regulation, each of which has assumed a more active role in the last two decades.

Somewhat surprisingly, policymakers and economic analysts generally view each institution as the only societal response to risk. In the field of legal scholarship, this narrow approach has been termed the "tortcentric" perspective by Richard Stewart (1987a,b). A piecemeal approach may be necessary in some cases as an analytic convenience, but it neglects potentially important interactions.

The various institutions influence the management of risks in important ways. Without coordinating these systems, society will rarely invest optimally to achieve the goals of creating efficient incentives and providing appropriate compensation to injured parties. The solution to the problem lies in finding an appropriate allocation of institutional responsibilities.

Over the past two decades there has been an enormous expansion in government regulation relating to products. Many new agencies emerged in the 1970s, including the U.S. Consumer Product Safety Commission (CPSC), the Occupational Safety and Health Administration (OSHA), the Food and Drug Administration (FDA), the National Highway Traffic Safety Administration (NHTSA), the Federal Aviation Administration (FAA), and the U.S. Environmental Protection Agency (EPA). The controls imposed often were quite stringent, as the regulatory agencies generally were carrying out strong legislative mandates. With more product risks coming under regulatory control, the question arises how one should coordinate the various social institutions at work. Somewhat surprisingly, reliance on products liability has increased at the same time regulation has become more extensive, and there has been little concern with assigning responsibilities to the different institutions.

Regulations are better suited to addressing many product risk concerns. As the scope of regulation increases, the optimal mix of risk-reduction institutions will require decreased use of the tort system. There are good reasons for retaining the tort system, but its role should diminish as that of regulation expands. The new practical and analytical question is how to restructure products liability to better complement the activities of other social risk management efforts.

The Adequacy of Incentives

Deterrence is efficient when the marginal cost of the incremental reduction in risk equals the benefit of the reduction to society. The efficient level of risk is typically nonzero, because the risk-dollar tradeoff values are finite and additional risk reductions tend to become increasingly expensive. In perfect markets, risk-reduction incentives are adequate and efficient. As the risks associated with any product become known, the market price adjusts to reflect the price of persuading individuals to engage the risk.

However, as Chapter 5 indicated, current levels of products liability damages will never provide efficient deterrence levels when it is life and limb rather than property damage at stake. Products liability may nevertheless augment existing incentives and provide the additional financial inducement needed to alter firms' behavior in the desired manner.

Regulations are distinctive because they arise from a variety of sources, not a single set of accident claims. Agencies promulgate regulations on the basis of scientific evidence or widespread accident patterns. This process is subject to the same political forces that drive other types of government action. Individual parties exposed to risk can sometimes initiate action as well, as in the case of OSHA inspections prompted by worker complaints or fatalities. Similarly, when a significant number of product-related accidents suggests a defect, NHTSA or the CPSC can initiate product recalls.[1] In extreme cases, government may ban certain products or activities altogether. Moreover, some statutes empower individuals and organizations to bring citizen suits to force firms to comply with regulatory standards.[2]

The regulatory process often involves substantial delays. An agency must identify a problem area, prepare a regulatory analysis, receive approval from the Office of Management and Budget (OMB), and provide for extensive comment before issuing an authoritative regulation.[3] The regulatory process shapes fairly permanent rules that provide clear guidance in creating risk-reduction incentives. The difficult part is designing *efficient* incentives.

Since regulators are not limited by damage amount provisions and other constraints, there is substantial leeway for establishing efficient safety incentives. Indeed, the typical regulatory mandates push the agencies to go beyond the efficient level of precautions in setting the risk level. The usual legislative provisions call for stringent health and safety standards limited only by very weak balancing considerations. OSHA, for example, is prohibited from setting regulations on the basis of benefit-cost analysis, although there is an effort to avoid regulations that will cause major economic dislocations. The CPSC has greater leeway, but in practice it continues to adopt a risk-based orientation.

When regulations establish an effective safety floor, this safety level should meet a reasonable economic standard of adequacy. The record in Table 6.1 of the costs per life saved of twenty-seven major government regulations indicates that inadequate stringency is not generally a problem. If we take as our measure of the appropriate cutoff a value of life of $5 million, then thirteen of the regulations listed cost more than this cutoff. Moreover, the less expensive regulations in terms of cost per life saved are generally not low because the regulation was lenient. Rather, they are usually discrete actions that can be taken to promote safety, such as installing passive restraints in automobiles, and their stringency cannot be enhanced. The principal exception is the FAA, which has long based its safety efforts on the same inadequate basis as the courts, the present value of lost earnings.

Table 6.1. The cost of regulations per life saved

Regulation	Year	Agency	Thousands of dollars (1984) per life saved
Steering column protection	1967	NHTSA	100
Unvented space heaters	1980	CPSC	100
Cabin fire protection	1985	FAA	200
Passive restraints/belts	1984	NHTSA	300
Fuel system integrity	1975	NHTSA	300
Trihalomethanes	1979	EPA	300
Alcohol and drug control	1985	FRA	500
Servicing wheel rims	1984	OSHA	500
Seat cushion flammability	1984	FAA	600
Floor emergency lighting	1984	FAA	700
Children's sleepwear flammability	1973	CPSC	1,300
Side doors	1970	NHTSA	1,300
Hazard communication	1983	OSHA	1,800
Benzene/fugitive emissions	1984	EPA	2,800
Radionuclides/uranium mines	1984	OSHA	6,900
Asbestos	1972	OSHA	25,600
Arsenic/glass plant	1986	EPA	19,200
Ethylene oxide	1984	OSHA	7,400
Arsenic/copper smelter	1986	EPA	26,500
Uranium mill tailings/inactive	1983	EPA	27,600
Acrylonitrile	1978	OSHA	37,600
Uranium mill tailings/active	1983	EPA	53,000
Coke ovens	1976	OSHA	61,800
Asbestos	1986	OSHA	89,300
Arsenic	1978	OSHA	92,500
Asbestos	1986	EPA	104,200
DES (cattlefeed)	1979	FDA	132,000

Source: Morrall (1986), p. 30.

Not surprisingly, all three FAA policies listed save lives at a cost per life of under $1 million, which in this case is a signal of a complacent regulatory agency rather than a highly efficient one.

Similarly, the cost per life estimates swamp the level of products liability awards for fatalities. Suppose that every fatality from product accidents were compensated at a rate of $200,000. Even if all fatalities were compensated at this level, rather than just those plaintiffs making successful claims, the resulting safety incentives would be less than those specified in all but three regulations in this table. The safety incentives of products liability are dwarfed by those achievable through regulation.

This contrast is greatest in instances of apparent regulatory excess, such as the ten regulations that impose a cost per life saved above $25 million. Although there may be a greater need for regulatory moderation in some instances and greater regulatory control in others, as an institutional mechanism regulatory agencies are ideally suited to establishing effective product safety incentives. Yet regulations have their shortcomings. First, regulations are not fully comprehensive. Not all product risks are addressed by regulation. OSHA has issued hundreds of standards but does not specify all workplace safety conditions. The CPSC has done little by way of issuing regulatory standards and has focused primarily on recalls and voluntary standards. For many large areas of product risk, products liability will be the main institutional mechanism augmenting whatever market incentives may exist.

The second deficiency of regulations is that of inadequate enforcement. The regulations assessed in Table 6.1 are regulatory *guidelines*. Agencies do not always take the steps needed to ensure compliance. OSHA enforcement efforts, for example, are notoriously weak, generating very low financial incentives for compliance.

Table 6.2 summarizes many of the studies assessing the performance of regulatory agencies. Enforcement problems vary by agency. Proper enforcement is a function of information, monitoring costs, and sanctions for violations. In some instances, agencies enforce standards strictly; for example, FDA must approve new pharmaceuticals before they can be sold.[4] FDA regulations receive full compliance, as do requirements that cars have seatbelts[5] and that medicine bottles have safety caps.[6] Similarly, EPA water pollution regulations have reasonably high rates of compliance[7] because they require firms to submit monthly reports regarding their discharges, and EPA inspects these firms roughly once a year. Thus, if information and monitoring costs are relatively low, compliance rates tend to be quite high.

In contrast, weak enforcement sanctions and infrequent monitoring hamper regulatory performance. OSHA regulations reduce worker injuries only modestly because the agency undertakes only rare inspections and because their sanctions for noncompliance are usually inconsequential.[8] The odds of seeing an OSHA inspector at a firm in any given year is comparable to the chance of seeing Halley's Comet. Other classes of regulations that lack strong enforcement provisions include those governing the dumping of toxic wastes, where the injuring party often cannot be identified. In these and other in-

Table 6.2. Summary of effects of regulation

Class of regulations (Reference)	General conclusion
Product safety	
1. CPSC—General (Viscusi, 1984a,c, 1985b)	Few standards and no significant beneficial effects on safety.
2. CPSC—Mattresses (Linneman, 1980)	No significant beneficial effect on safety.
3. CPSC—Safety caps (Viscusi, 1984c, 1985b)	No significant beneficial effect on safety because of offsetting behavioral response.
4. NHTSA—Seatbelts (Peltzman, 1975)	No significant beneficial effect on safety because of offsetting behavioral response.
5. NHTSA—Seatbelts (Crandall and Graham, 1984)	Offsetting response to seatbelts exists but does not negate their beneficial effects.
6. FDA—Pharmaceuticals (Grabowski and Vernon, 1983)	Excessively stringent drug screening leads to lag in obtaining health-enhancing drugs.
7. FDA—Prescription drugs (Peltzman, 1987)	No significant health benefits of prescription requirements.
8. FDA—Food additives (Lave, 1981)	Need to set priorities and promulgate more balanced regulations.
Worker safety	
9. OSHA (Viscusi, 1986a,c)	Weak enforcement. No significant effects until 1980s, when small effects are observed.
Environmental risks	
10. EPA—Air (Crandall, 1983)	Improvements are needed in enforcement; a market-based pollution tax should be implemented.
11. EPA—Water (Magat and Viscusi, 1991)	Frequent enforcement and substantial effect on pollution by pulp and paper mills.
12. NRC—Nuclear (Wood, 1984)	Need to reorganize entire agency and streamline licensing process.
Hazard warnings	
13. Worker and consumer (Viscusi and Magat, 1987)	"Educational" efforts that provide no new information are unsuccessful, but warnings that convey new knowledge can be effective.

stances in which enforcement is not effective, regulations will not promote product safety adequately.

Society has substantial discretion in setting health and safety standards. For risk regulations to realize their potential, however, regulatory design and enforcement must improve. Agencies can resolve these problems more easily than the problems associated with both tort liability and social insurance can be resolved. In addition, once an agency promulgates regulations, social costs need not be incurred again. Compared with insurance or tort liability, regulation is a larger investment in a more permanent solution.

Perhaps the major shortcoming of regulatory solutions is that they have emphasized the role of technological solutions as opposed to behaviorial ones. In this vein, for example, OSHA has promulgated meticulous standards for the design of ladders and the shape of toilet seats. The CPSC has mandated narrowly specified requirements for the design of bicycles, which many observers believe were primarily intended to keep inexpensive Taiwanese bicycles off the U.S. market. In the extreme case, technology-oriented regulation may be counter-productive rather than simply ineffective.

A dramatic case in point is that of safety caps. Many children have been poisoned by ingesting various household products, and there has long been an effort to reduce the number of injuries. In the 1960s widespread educational efforts urged parents to limit their children's access to drugs, such as aspirin. These efforts were re-placed in 1972 by mandatory protective bottlecap requirements for aspirin, which were subsequently extended to other products, such as prescription drugs and furniture polish. Unfortunately, the regula-tions were not successful. One difficulty is that safety caps were rou-tinely designated as being "child-proof" rather than "child-resistant," even by CPSC officials.[9] As a result, they may have lulled parents into a false sense of security, making them believe that the products were safer than they actually were and decreasing their efforts to keep children away from harmful products. I have termed this effect "lull-ing effect" of regulations.[10] Even if parents' sense of security is war-ranted, problems arise from the decrease in parental caution that may result. For much the same reason as one would choose to drive more safely on an icy street than on dry pavement, one would need to exercise greater care with products that have a safety cap as com-pared with those that do not. Parents quite rationally will become more lax about products with safety caps.

Finally, safety caps will not have their intended effect if they are not used. If adults find these caps too difficult to open, they may leave the caps off.

Statistical analysis of the effect of safety caps indicates quite disap-pointing results. In no case in which safety caps were introduced has there been a statistically significant downward shift in poisoning rates.

Moreover, once caps were introduced for aspirin, poisonings from analgesic products such as Tylenol increased. The apparent decreased responsibility with respect to storage of medicines led to an additional 3,500 poisonings per year that would not have taken place if parents had exercised the same care as they did before the introduction of safety caps.[11] Conclusions such as these are reached by looking at the actual patterns of usage of aspirin and related products. Table 6.3 summarizes the pertinent statistics. The percentage of aspirin sold with safety caps was relatively invariant from 1972, the year the caps were introduced, to 1978. The share of poisonings from products with safety cap bottles rose from 40 percent of all poisonings in 1972 to 73 percent of all poisonings in 1978. These poisonings occurred in part because the bottles were left open. Almost half of all poisonings are attributable to bottles being left open, a problem that safety caps cannot solve. Moreover, the share of poisonings from open bottles rose after the advent of safety caps.

What these findings indicate is not that regulations are bad or that adoption of safety caps was necessarily a misguided policy. They do suggest, however, that technological "improvements" alone may not solve the problem of product safety. Sound regulations and a sensible products liability structure must adequately recognize the actions and behavior of consumers as well as the safety aspects of the product design. The chief method of bringing consumer habits into the picture is the hazard warning, which is the subject of the following chapter.

Regulatory Violations and Products Liability Litigation

Although government regulations and products liability law have as an objective the control of product safety risks, neither the general regulatory agencies nor the special mission agencies make any specific allowance for the effects of the tort liability system on safety incentives. To the extent that products liability lawsuits do influence the regulatory environment, they may stimulate excessive governmental action. For example, the wave of asbestos litigation was followed by greater OSHA regulation of asbestos, with an average cost per life saved of $89 million. EPA subsequently issued asbestos regulations with a cost of $104 million per life saved. Rather than substituting for regulation, products liability lawsuits may generate additional regulation.

Table 6.3. Poisoning incidents since the introduction of safety caps

	1971	1972	1973	1974	1975	1976	1977	1978
Aspirin								
Sold with safety caps (%)	—	53	56	59	56	56	55	52
Poisonings from safety-capped bottles (%)	—	40	52	60	59	67	71	73
Share of poisonings due to open bottles (%)	—	41	43	44	48	46	44	49
Aspirin and analgesics								
Poisonings from safety-capped bottles (%)	—	34	44	53	54	63	67	66
Share of poisonings due to open bottles (%)	—	43	43	44	47	44	39	47
Total poisonings	168,930	167,270	153,670	126,520	137,010	112,860	112,840	111,420

Source: This table is drawn from Viscusi (1985), table 8. It is based on unpublished Poison Control Center computer printouts and pharmaceutical industry data on aspirin sales.

Compliance with government regulation likewise does not ensure that the product will not be the subject of products liability suits. Regulatory compliance is admissible as a defense but is not conclusive. The problems arising from inadequate recognition of the effects of regulation was a major theme of a National Academy of Sciences (1990) panel that addressed products liability costs and their contribution to a decline in U.S. contraceptive innovation. The panel observed that "although manufacturers introduce evidence of compliance with FDA regulations in a products liability lawsuit, this evidence has no special status in most states. FDA approval, for example, does not entitle the manufacturer to a presumption that it acted with care."[12] Similarly, the National Traffic and Motor Vehicle Safety Act explicitly states that compliance "does not exempt any person from liability under common law." Regulatory compliance is not entirely irrelevant, as companies may introduce evidence of compliance to show that the product has a favorable risk-utility balance and as a consequence should not be considered defective.

Although regulatory compliance at best provides a weak defense, regulatory violations have much greater impact in demonstrating manufacturer negligence. Some courts have concluded that such violations constitute evidence of negligence per se. One such instance involved an oral contraceptive manufacturer's failure to include the package insert mandated by the FDA, which would have advised patients of proper use and overall product risks. Moreover, it is generally accepted that courts cannot set safety standards lower than those of a legislative body, which all but ensures that products liability and regulatory enforcement sanctions will both be applicable to firms that violate regulations. In cases of noncompliance, products liability costs augment the inadequate incentives for compliance created by the regulatory enforcement mechanism. In this class of instances, the institutional mechanisms complement one another.

The extent of the overlap is suggested by the ISO data on closed products liability claims presented in Table 6.4. Overall, regulatory violations are cited by claimants in 19 percent of products liability claims and 28 percent of job-related claims. The expanded scope of government regulations over the past decade no doubt has increased the institutional overlap, which was already substantial a decade ago when these data were collected. Just under half of the violations in products liability claims are for OSHA and CPSC standards, the

Table 6.4. The effects of regulatory violations on products liability litigation off and on the job

Litigation category	No violations alleged	Violations alleged	Originating agency of alleged violation		
			CPSC	OSHA	Other
Claims unrelated to employment					
Claims	.81	.19	.06	.02	.11
Successful claims	.76	.81	.80	.83	.82
Claims dropped	.20	.13	.13	.13	.13
Claims settled out of court	.77	.83	.81	.85	.84
Court cases won by claimant	.41	.33	.29	.19	.36
Bodily injury loss	$6,253	$14,772	$6,582	$7,948	$20,051
Bodily injury payment	$5,640	$16,091	$11,311	$12,570	$19,100
Claims for on-the-job injuries					
Claims	.72	.28	.04	.08	.16
Successful claims	.60	.72	.66	.71	.74
Claims dropped	.28	.15	.23	.15	.13
Claims settled out of court	.65	.75	.74	.77	.75
Court cases won by claimant	.25	.40	0.00	.40	.43
Bodily injury loss	$50,084	$56,855	$77,386	$26,461	$67,994
Bodily injury payment	$21,002	$38,062	$20,559	$32,262	$45,190

OSHA standards being more prominent in job-related claims for obvious reasons.

Regulatory violations enhance the chance of a successful claim, as one might expect given the legal framework. For off-the-job injuries, claims alleging regulatory violations have a 5 percent success differential. The greater effect for job-related claims may be due in part to the greater marginal improvement that is possible for a claims group with a lower rate of success. The success rate for job-related product claims is below that for off-the-job injury because third-party suits are often inappropriate and may be used simply as a means of evading the requirement that workers' compensation be the exclusive remedy against one's employer.

The influence of regulatory violations on the disposition of claims is also apparent.[13] Claimants will be more reluctant to drop a claim if their probability of success in court is enhanced by a regulatory violation. For product injuries, the drop probability is 7 percent lower if some regulatory violation has been alleged. For on-the-job injuries, the probability of dropping is 13 percent lower when there are regulatory violations. In each case, the type of violation alleged has the expected effects; the weak influence of OSHA violations for off-the-job injuries and of CPSC violations for job-related injuries follows from the emphasis of these policies.

Regulatory violations also influence out-of-court settlements. In particular, they have a relatively greater effect on the willingness of firms to settle than they have on claimant reservation prices.[14] Out-of-court settlements are 6 percent greater for on-the-job injuries when there are regulatory violations.

The effect of regulatory violations on the probability that a claimant will win a court case is less precisely understood since few claims reach a court verdict. Claimants alleging regulatory violations win more on-the-job claims and fewer product claims, but these patterns are influenced in a complex manner by the mix of claims going to trial.

Overall, regulatory violations enhance the prospect of a claim's success and appear to affect the firm's expected losses more than the claimant's expected gains. Regulatory violations reduce the probability that a claim will be dropped, increase the likelihood of an out-of-court settlement, and increase the size of such settlements.

Restructuring the Institutional Interactions

To promote more efficient levels of risk and insurance, I propose the following modification of the tort liability structure. Firms should be exempted from potential liability in design defect cases if they can demonstrate either compliance with a specific government regulation or the use of a hazard warnings program that is sufficiently effective that it leads to informed market decisions. More generally, the risk-utility test applied to assess product design defects should be amended to exempt all products for which manufacturers can demonstrate that the risk level is efficient. (Chapter 7 will explore the use of warnings in greater detail.)

If these market incentives for safety are not adequate, risk regulation programs that in effect provide a minimum safety constraint are well-suited to the task, for they are targeted explicitly at firms' safety decisions. Most government regulations are designed to promote a level of safety that is more stringent than the economically efficient risk level, which means that regulatory compliance is often an indication of adequate safety levels.

One might also envision the possibility of restricting the regulatory compliance test to situations in which the regulation is shown to promote efficient risk levels. Doing so, however, would effectively eliminate the compliance defense since juries still must undertake a full risk-utility task. Because the legislative mandates of risk regulation are quite stringent and regulations reflect society's judgments regarding the appropriate level of product safety, the courts should take advantage of these judgments. Broadly based design defect exemptions for pharmaceutical products would be one consequence of adopting such a regulatory compliance defense.

Regulatory constraints do not provide any incentives once compliance has been achieved. In terms of institutional overlap, this on-off character of regulatory incentives is one advantage over injury taxes and pollution taxes. There is no combined effect of regulatory incentives and products liability incentives once compliance at an efficient safety level is reached. For firms out of compliance with the regulation, which is often the case, one can view products liability awards against noncomplying firms as an additional compliance incentive. Under the current legal framework, if a firm complies with an adequate standard, it will face the prospect of additional tort liability. These potential costs will create inefficient incentives for safety, leading firms to produce safety above the level of the regulatory standard.

One cannot rely on tort liability in lieu of regulation because products liability incentives are ill-suited to the task. Not all injured parties file claims, and court awards are far below what is required to promote efficient safety incentives.

The impetus for this proposal is not a desire to reduce the products liability burden but a desire to establish a coordinated strategy that recognizes the actions of the multiple institutions at work. The presence of multiple institutions affecting safety, not just one, defines the nature of firms' economic environment and should begin to be recognized by economists and legal scholars.

Table 6.5 summarizes the general assessments of institutional performance that emerge from Chapters 4, 5, and 6. Not all of the measures listed in the first column are mutually exclusive concerns, so one should be cautious of the method used to combine the ratings. Moreover, the importance of each category varies in different contexts. The table does provide, however, a convenient checklist of fac-

Table 6.5. A summary assessment of the ability of institutions to control risk

Measure of performance	Market forces	Tort liability	Social insurance	Government regulation
Timing, vis-à-vis accident	*Ex ante*, also *Ex post*	*Ex post*	*Ex post*	*Ex ante* and *Ex post*
Scope of risk coverage	All perceived risks traded in markets	Injuries and illnesses for which it is possible to establish harm, link to injurer, and show liability	General social insurance and coverage of specific classes of risk	Risks covered by broad-based regulations or recall power
Information requirements	Risk perceptions, market value, and risk-reduction	Causality, damages, and level of care	Base wage and nature of injury	Risks and costs of risk-reduction
Adequacy of risk-reduction incentives	Adequate, if perceived	Inadequate	Inadequate	Great potential if not too stringent or poorly enforced
Institutional overlap	Institutional reference point	Potential overlap in compensation and incentives	Potential overlap, more for compensation than incentives	Fine-tuning mechanism
Adequacy of compensation	Ideal if perfect insurance	Inadequate	Reasonably adequate floor	No compensation

tors that are important in assessing institutional performance. Overall, the more we rely on regulation and both private and social insurance efforts the more likely we will be able to decrease the scope of products liability litigation.

The superiority of regulation in creating deterrence and social and private insurance in providing compensation does not mean that tort liability cannot play a constructive role in managing risks. Rather, it implies that the tort system should be subsidiary to the other institutions. Tort liability can create significant risk-reduction incentives and compensate some of those who are injured. In addition, the tort system provides a useful forum for identifying potential targets for regulation and for addressing idiosyncratic risks not covered by broadly based regulations. However, tort reformers should recognize the subsidiary role that tort liability must play in the future and focus on achieving the traditional goals of the tort system through increased use of government regulation and social insurance.

Such a policy shift will enhance the power of regulatory policies as well by increasing the benefits to firms from regulatory compliance. The existence of such a compliance defense will not, however, completely eliminate the need for tort liability. The performance of regulatory agencies has often been disappointing, and there is a continuing need for more vigorous and effective risk regulation. Moreover, even with stronger regulatory policies, tort liability will still be necessary. For manufacturing defects, products liability will remain the dominant mechanism of redress.

7

Hazard Warnings

Over the past two decades the idea that inadequate hazard warnings are a type of design defect has greatly expanded the scope of products liability. If a potentially risky product does not include an adequate warning, the firm can be found liable for an accident even in the absence of a manufacturing defect or defective physical attribute. This is not an innocuous change. It is not comparable to including, for example, machine guards as a potentially defective product component. The major issue is no longer the physical properties of the product but rather how the product will interact with the product user. In particular, does the product include sufficient information for the user to be informed of the risk of its use and the necessary precautions?

Resolving this issue is not a matter for engineering studies, as it would be in the case of other alleged defects. Rather, one must turn to different classes of evidence regarding how individuals process information and make their subsequent decisions. This new requirement has been accompanied by a decrease in the reliability of the evidence used to assess liability, since warnings cases are seldom based on objective, scientific criteria for assessing a product defect. The net effect is to augment the already considerable degree of uncertainty that firms face with respect to their prospective liability.

The increased attention to hazard warnings is not an idiosyncratic property of tort liability. There has been an emerging "right-to-know" movement at several governmental levels and in society at large.

There have, of course, been many long-standing warnings programs. Chief among these are the FDA's risk labeling efforts for pharmaceutical products and EPA's pesticide labeling efforts. Beginning in the 1960s, the government's emphasis on hazard warnings increased. Congress mandated hazard warnings for cigarettes in 1965 and subsequently modified them in 1969 and 1984.[1] Similarly, Congress imposed hazard warnings on products containing saccharin in 1977.[2]

The 1980s witnessed a proliferation of warnings efforts throughout the federal government. The Occupational Safety and Health Administration initiated mandatory hazard communication provisions for all manufacturing workers exposed to hazardous chemicals. The Environmental Protection Agency initiated similar right-to-know efforts for homeowners' exposure to radon and citizens' exposures to hazardous wastes. Even some individual states introduced warnings measures. The most extensive of these has been California's Proposition 65, which requires that California residents be informed of all carcinogenic exposures from food products, their jobs, or the general environment.[3]

The increased reliance on warnings emerged in part from the greater recognition of the limits of technology-oriented regulations. Accidents generally are the result of the interaction of the behavior of the user and the technological characteristics of the product within the context in which the product was being used. Although some studies of job-related accidents attribute the overwhelming majority of such accidents to the failure of workers to take appropriate precautions,[4] precise assignments of responsibility are infeasible. What is clear is that fostering efficient risk management requires that we address all contributors to product risks, not simply the physical attributes of the product alone.

Another impetus for warnings programs is the difference in risk information possessed by the producer as compared with the consumer. The producer is responsible for the product design and has a larger base of direct research as well as accident reports to draw upon in forming assessments. Companies should not, however, be expected to provide warnings with respect to information that we cannot reasonably expect them to have. Asbestos companies should not, for example, be found strictly liable for having failed to warn about risks that at the time were unknown and unavoidable.[5]

The rationale for providing this information to product users is to foster improved decisions. Unfortunately, the popular designation of such efforts as "right-to-know" policies is to some extent a misnomer. The main concern is not with individual rights in circumstances in which no actions will be affected. Rather, the justification for risk communication requirements is that it will be more efficient for people to know about the risk since they will be better able to choose their risk exposures and their risk precautions after this information has been provided.

Since the ultimate objective is to promote improved decisions, the limitations that individuals have in processing information and in making decisions involving risks must be taken into account in the design of hazard warnings. It is for this reason that assessments of the adequacy of a warning is more complex than simply noting whether a particular risk has been mentioned. Ensuring that a warning is adequate is so difficult because cognitive factors pertaining to the processing of risk information are so complex. If individuals could be assumed to understand all information, in all forms, warnings could simply refer individuals to an appropriate bibliography of scientific articles.

The Objectives of Hazard Warnings

The overall objectives of hazard warnings should be to convey the risk level, appropriate precautions, and an indication of the particular risks that will be reduced by these precautions. The ultimate intent is to influence the individual's decisions, which are made in two different contexts. The first set of choices might be labeled threshold product decisions: will the consumer purchase the product or choose to use it in a particular circumstance? The second class of decisions concerns precautionary behavior: what efforts to reduce risk will the individual make when using the product?

Consider first the threshold product choice decision, a discrete decision an individual makes to purchase or use a product. The intent of warnings for cigarettes, for example, is to apprise consumers of the potential risks of smoking so that they can make an informed choice. If our objective were to eliminate smoking altogether, then it would be more appropriate to ban the product. Society has banned some products, including heroin and crack cocaine. In addition, it restricts the use of products in particular instances; some drugs may not be sold without a prescription, and there are age requirements for the purchase of alcoholic beverages. In a democratic society, our objective should be to allow individuals to make informed choices except in cases of extreme danger, when bans are warranted.

Most studies of hazard warnings equate a reduction in use of a product as a sign of efficacy.[6] Observers note with approval drops in consumption of a product after a warning has been given, such as the decline in cigarette smoking and in the purchase of diet soft drinks containing saccharin following the issue of congressionally mandated warnings concerning these products. Reduced use indicates a negative shift in attitudes toward a product, but it does not tell us whether the warning has been adequate or whether it has been unduly alarmist. If declines in product use are a signal of success, then a product ban would have produced the greatest gains. Presumably, society has more limited objectives in issuing a warning, and these should be recognized.

Certain cognitive factors govern how individuals perceive risk. In particular, individuals tend to overestimate risks that are called to their attention[7] and to overestimate the risk of low-probability events.[8] Since product risks tend to be small, informing individuals about these risks may make people believe that the risks are larger than they actually are. The dangers of overly alarmist warnings are illustrated by the language adopted for food cancer warnings under California's Proposition 65, an initiative intended to promote broad consumer awareness of cancer risks. Although the exact implementation of the warning continues to evolve, the wording of the warning mandated by the regulation is the following:

WARNING: This product contains a chemical known to the state of California to cause cancer.[9]

Products to be covered by this warning include all consumer products that pose a lifetime risk of cancer of one chance in 100,000, or a risk from annual consumption of the product of one in 7,000,000. This probability is smaller than the chance of being struck by lightning, which is too small a risk for most people to think about precisely.

The wording of the warning does not, however, convey a minimal risk. Rather, a survey of individual assessments of the impact of this warning as compared with others indicates that it conveys a very powerful message. Fifty-six percent of all individuals believe the saccharin warning ("Use of this product may be hazardous to your health. This product contains a chemical that has been determined to cause cancer in laboratory animals.") indicates a product with less risk than the risk identified by Proposition 65 warning.[10] Yet, the California warning addresses risks that are estimated to be as much as 400 times smaller than the estimated lifetime risk of cancer from saccharin—1/2,500.[11] Only a minority of consumers believe that the California Proposition 65 warning alerts them to a greater risk than the various cigarette warnings that have been used; 48 percent regard the Proposition 65 warning as comparable in severity to the 1969 cigarette warning ("WARNING: The Surgeon General has determined that cigarette smoking is dangerous to your health."), and 69 percent view the Proposition 65 warning as being comparable to the 1965 cigarette warning ("CAUTION: Cigarette smoking may be hazardous to your health.").

Similarly, consumers view the risk of getting cancer from eating breakfast cereal bearing a Proposition 65 warning as comparable to that of getting cancer from smoking 0.58 packs of cigarettes. Perhaps most dramatically, consumers estimate that twelve of every 100 consumers of the product bearing such a warning would die of cancer—an estimate that dwarfs the actual risk that may be posed by these products by a factor of 1,000 or more.[12]

This stunning example of overestimation of small risks identified in warnings highlights the potential hazards of issuing a warning. Because individual risk perceptions are so sensitive to the particular wording of warnings and the very presence of a risk warning, warnings must be carefully designed to avoid the competing dangers of underwarning and of unduly alarming consumers. Misguided policies will jeopardize the credibility of other, more legitimate warnings.

Individuals' proclivity to overestimate low-probability events also suggests that warnings regarding visible or publicized risks associated with products are not likely to be needed since risk perceptions for these risks should be adequate. In contrast, however, there are many classes of risks for which product users may have no knowledge whatsoever. This class of hidden risks includes those posed by pesticides, food additives, many pharmaceutical products, and long-term carcinogenic risks. Given that there are risks about which consumers are ignorant, there is a strong demand for providing risk information, but as the Proposition 65 example illustrates, doing so may give consumers an impression of the risks that is equally as wrong as their initial impression of no risk. The problem of striking an appropriate balance is reflected in the common sales maxim that "safety doesn't sell." Calling consumers' attention to the safety properties of a product may in and of itself boost the consumers' risk perception in an adverse manner. The best practical solution to the problem of competing risks of labeling is pre-testing the warning—its language and its presentation of information—for its ability to accomplish the intended objective.[13]

Warnings intended to promote precautionary behavior raise a somewhat different class of issues. In this case the objective is not simply to apprise individuals of the risks they face but also to indicate how they can reduce these risks through their actions. Consumers generally know how to handle obvious product risks, such as those posed by sharp knives. The emphasis of warnings should be on precautions about which the producer has some superior knowledge.

It will seldom be the case that the yardstick for judging precautionary labeling will be the extent to which all individuals take a particular kind of precaution. Precautions are often onerous. Individuals could, for example, rationally choose not to use particular kinds of protective equipment if they felt it was too burdensome to do so. When we wish to require precautionary behavior, as opposed to only suggesting it, labeling is not an adequate measure. The more appropriate solution is regulation. Society, for example, requires that motorcyclists wear helmets because it has a stake in controlling the costs of accident-related damages, costs that are rarely borne by the victim alone. Unfortunately, when behavior is decentralized and cannot be monitored, strongly worded precautions may be the only mechanism available to promote risk-averting activities. We can monitor motorcycle helmet use much more easily than we can determine whether consumers dilute pesticides to the proper concentration.

The nature in which hazard warnings influence precautions is illustrated by the effects of different labels for a drain opener (summarized in Table 7.1)—a frequent target of hazard warnings litigation. Three different warnings were considered by a group of consumers assessing three hypothetical products with professionally drawn labels. The first label is patterned after a composite of those used on Drano and Red Devil Lye. A second product with a redesigned label not similar to any now used was also examined. This test label incorporated a clear labeling format, but it carried much less extensive

Table 7.1. Effect of warnings on precautions taken with drain openers

Precaution	Percent of sample taking precaution			Maximum incremental effect (%)
	Drano/ Red Devil Lye label	Test label	No warning	
Wear rubber gloves	82	73	63	19
Store in childproof location				
Households with children under five	90	83	70	20
Households with no children under five	63	61	48	15

Source: Viscusi and Magat (1987), tables 4.3 and 4.6, and calculations by the author.

information than the composite label did. Finally, a third group of consumers considered the Drano/Red Devil Lye label but with the warning information deleted from it. The two major precautions for the products examined in the survey were that consumers should wear rubber gloves to avoid hand burns and that they should store the product in a child-proof location to decrease the risk of child poisoning.

Several results are noteworthy. First, even in the absence of any warning information, many consumers will take precautions such as these. Even when using products without any warning information, the majority of all respondents would wear rubber gloves, and the majority of all individuals with children would store the product in a child-proof location. Individuals may be generally aware of the types of risks that arise with respect to a class of products, perhaps in part due to past warnings efforts. The second result of interest is that in none of the cases did the warning result in universal precaution taking. The maximum incremental effect of labels was to boost the fraction of individuals with children under five who would store the product in a child-proof location: this fraction rose from 70 percent when no warning was given to 90 percent when the Drano/Red Devil Lye warning was provided.

Compliance is not universal for a variety of reasons. First, not all individuals will read, process, and take actions in response to hazard warnings. Second, and perhaps more fundamentally, it will not always be rational for them to do so. The consumers participating in this study indicated that they would be willing to pay an extra 17 cents per bottle to avoid having to wear rubber gloves while using the product. Individuals who found wearing gloves more costly than the expected injury costs imposed by a hand burn might rationally choose to forgo the recommended precaution.

The final noteworthy feature of the results in Table 7.1 is that the degree to which people take precautions will be influenced by the particular risks that they face. Households with children are more likely than adult households to store drain opener in a child-proof location. The hazard warning label also has a greater impact on households with children, even though these households are already more likely to store the product in a safe place than adult households are. This evidence suggests that individuals can use warning label information to make sensible risk-balancing decisions.

Assessing the Quality of Warnings

There are two classes of critieria for assessing whether warnings fulfill the objective of providing appropriate information with respect to risks and precautions. Each will be governed by the fact that not only warning but also the ability of the recipient to make use of the warnings must be taken into account.

Principle 1: Warnings should be judged from the perspective of a hazard communication system. To judge a warning on the basis of a particular risk posed by a single product is to take a myopic view of the problem, which must be approached at two separate levels. First, for all the risks posed by the product and the different ways in which the risk is communicated, is it desirable to incorporate a warning for the hazard involved in a particular case? Second, for the entire class of risks faced by the individual, would adopting a particular warning strategy lead to a sensible overall warnings policy?

When claiming a warnings defect, plaintiffs frequently take full advantage of the wisdom conferred by hindsight. The plaintiff was injured because of a particular risk posed by the product, and if only there had been a bold hazard warning with respect to that risk the injury could have been averted. The problem with this argument is that if a warning had included information about not only that risk but about all other comparable risks posed by the product, then it might have been ineffective. The problem is one of information over-load. Detailed examination of the information that individuals retain from hazard warnings indicates that even with very detailed and well-designed warning labels, individuals can seldom recall more than six pieces of information from a label.[14] Much of what is retained regards aspects of the product other than precautions and risk levels—for example, how to use the product. With the addition of more information, individuals eventually reach a saturation point.

There is a fundamental tradeoff in terms of the information that is retained by consumer. Pesticide warnings that include much greater amounts of risk information may be more easily recalled, but there is also a tendency for consumers to forget or not to process at all the information with regard to appropriate product use. Since the formulation of commercially sold pesticides is such that the major risks of pesticide products are due to misuse (using an inappropriate concentration of pesticides) rather than to inadequate precautions during proper use, excessive risk information may actually increase the overall risk posed by the product.

With excessive amounts of information pertaining to product risks, consumers tend to be cognizant of the risks that are present but to have a more muddled sense of the *particular* precautions that should be undertaken to reduce the risks. In short, not only is there a tradeoff in terms of the kinds of information that individuals retain, but there is also a chance that the message will be distorted if excessive information is provided.

This result should serve as a precautionary warning for the courts, which through their decentralized treatment of case-specific risks generate incentives for a proliferation of warnings. In some cases it may not be desirable to include warnings with respect to particular risks if doing so would detract from awareness of the more fundamental risks posed by the product. One should assess not only the impact of the case-specific warning but also the efficacy of the entire hazard communication system that would result if warnings for all risks were governed by similar principles.

In recent years, for example, a number of lawsuits have been brought against manufacturers of lift trucks that have tipped over, usually when they were being driven very fast and the driver made a sharp turn. Although plaintiffs' experts have testified in such cases that there was a need for a very prominent hazard warning on the lift truck concerning this risk, simplistic assessments such as these ignore the demands that are placed on the hazard communication system. Lift trucks pose the entire range of hazards associated with motor vehicles, as well as the additional risks arising from carrying cargo. There are also other risks associated with the specific features of this vehicle. The training manual for this product identifies approximately three dozen potential sources of fatal injuries. Plastering warning signs for each of these hazards on the lift truck may mute some of the manufacturer's potential liability, but it will not improve the quality of the hazard communication system.

The multiplicity of risks does not mean that we should take no action at all when we wish to communicate more than a handful of pieces of information. Rather, in such situations we should explore other informational mechanisms. In the case of lift trucks, the main mechanism will be the training program given to operators and the training manual accompanying the lift truck. Other information that can be provided in this context includes training films.

Similar concerns arise in other contexts as well. When evaluating pharmaceutical warnings, for example, the labeling on the product is only one concern. Information disseminated in medical journals, through detail men, in professional seminars, and in the general media also should be considered. Courts should shift their focus from warnings and labeling to broader assessments of the entire hazard communication system. Instead, emphasis is placed on the product. One such case involved an industrial toilet bowl cleaner company, which was found liable for a worker's skin burns.[15] The product warning indicated the risks of chemical burns from skin contact and the need to rinse immediately if skin contact occurred. Moreover, the overall hazard communication system for this worker included a warning from her supervisor to wear rubber gloves, a warning that was ignored. Since the worker's set of risk information would not have been augmented by a warning label, a proper application of risk communication principles would not have indicated that the warning was defective. Nevertheless, the court ruled that the warning was inadequate because it did not include the need to wear rubber gloves.

The warnings test should not ask whether the on-product labeling was adequate. Rather, it should ask whether the entire hazard communication system adopted by the company was sufficient given the character of the entire class of product risks, the limitations on human information processing abilities, the availability of other mechanisms to convey information to product users, and the willingness of product users to take the particular precaution. Hazard warning judgments should be made from the context of the entire risk communication system, not simply the on-product labels.

Principle 2: The key criterion for judging a warning is the extent to which it provides new information in a convincing manner. In other words, the adequacy of a warning depends on how much information consumers *already possess.* The primary determinant of the impact of warnings regarding workplace hazards, for example, is not the risk level conveyed by the warning but the informational content of the warning message.[16] Warnings that are forms of persuasion or that are intended as reminders will generally have less impact than those that provide new knowledge. A widely publicized series of accidents—the explosion of tires on which there were no warnings concerning the maximum safe inflationary pressure—illustrate the legitimate need for information.[17] Manufacturers are much better situated than consumers to ascertain limits of this kind, and they should be expected to bridge the "information gap."

Similarly, there may be an information gap even in situations for which some risks are apparent. People who play softball or baseball are generally aware that they may be hit with a ball, but it is likely that few know that the risk of brain damage from being hit in the head with a softball thrown at normal speed is greater than the risks from being hit by a baseball.[18]

If the hazards are widely known or readily apparent, warnings have no new information to convey. Manufacturers of forklifts are not required to warn of the hazards of operation on uneven surfaces because the danger of operating on rough terrain are apparent to the driver.[19] Similarly, bullet manufacturers do not have a duty to warn about the risk of gun accidents because the risks posed by bullets are open and obvious.[20] Airplane manufacturers also needn't warn pilots to lock their seats into position before takeoff because "the pilot, just as the automobile driver, would, through the exercise of common sense, innately appreciate the difficulty in reaching and stably operating the controls and foot pedals from a seat which had not been secured into position."[21]

A similar principle has arisen in a series of highly publicized cases involving the link between excessive alcohol use and birth defects. Would a pregnant woman who drinks half a fifth of Jim Beam whiskey a day alter her behavior because of a warning on the bottle concerning potential birth defects? A federal jury concluded that Jim

Beam was not negligent in failing to warn pregnant women about the risks of excessive drinking.[22]

Although the courts have sometimes recognized the role of existing information, in other instances products have been found to be defective because of inadequate warnings even though the new informational content of these warnings appears to have been minimal. Somewhat surprisingly, tire manufacturers have been found liable for failing to warn purchasers that a blowout could result if a vehicle is carrying an excessive amount of weight.[23] Similarly, a federal appeals court ruled that Uniroyal was liable for the fatality of a professional truck driver because it had failed to provide a warning of the risks of underinflated tires.[24] Plaintiffs have also begun suing liquor manufacturers, alleging inadequate warnings about risks of alcoholism. In each of these cases, the new knowledge that would have been provided by warnings appears to be insubstantial.

Seemingly misguided warnings verdicts have affected other industries as well. Football helmet manufacturers have been particularly hard hit. A California court awarded a high school football player $11 million because the helmet manufacturer, Riddell Inc., did not include a warning label pertaining to the risks of ramming opposing players.[25] In Indiana a jury awarded $485,000 to a woman—apparently credited with little product knowledge—for injuries following the collapse of her improperly opened chaise lounge. The firm was held responsible for not including instructions explicitly indicating that an improperly opened chair could collapse.[26]

The net effect of such cases is that whenever there is a remote possibility that some class of consumers may not be fully informed, or could successfully argue *ex post* that they were caught by surprise even when they were not, the firm will have an incentive to introduce a product warning. There is no penalty for overwarning, only for underwarning. The courts consequently create incentives for a proliferation of warnings that will ultimately inundate consumers with risk messages. The net effect will be excessive warnings that dilute the impact of warnings that could reduce risk if they were followed.

Assessing whether there is an informational gap depends on who the target of the information is. Although the product user is usually the key group, often some other intervening economic agent is the principal recipient of the information. Physicians, for example, serve as the "learned intermediary" between pharmaceutical companies and their patients. The producer's task is to inform the physician, who is better trained to process the risk information and convey the risks to the patient for this particular situation. The learned intermediary doctrine shields pharmaceutical companies from liability for failure to warn provided that the physician is adequately informed.[27]

The knowledge of intervening economic agents arises in other contexts as well. The expertise of parties other than the product supplier was recognized in a court decision regarding silica sand; the original supplier of the sand was not found to be liable for failure to warn workers of the risks of silicosis because the manager of the company where the sand was being used was a "sophisticated user" and was best able to warn the workers.[28] Similarly, carbide tool manufacturers are sophisticated users of cobalt and can be relied upon to warn their employees of the potential risk of bronchitis from cobalt dust.[29]

These two principles are the criteria that should guide an assessment of whether a warning does or will do what it is intended to do—inform a product user of a risk and of behavior that will reduce that risk. In examining a particular warning, a regulatory agency, a court, or a manufacturer should use these criteria to evaluate the evidence before it. Hazard warnings are not only relatively new to the courts, but they are also comparatively new to academic research. In any developing field, there is a danger that "junk science" will be mistaken for solid evidence. So-called warnings experts may provide misleading information to juries, for example, and regulatory agencies may mandate changes in wording that make no improvements in or that actually impair a warnings program.

Warnings assessments should be based on scientific principles rather than on conjecture of self-proclaimed expertise. Four types of scientific evidence are best suited in this regard. First, the actual impact that the warnings have had on risk perceptions, precautions, and safety outcomes should be studied. Interview studies can address narrowly defined issues such as those pertaining to risk perceptions and precautions, and in many situations market data are available to assess the effect of warnings on the quantity of the product consumed. For example, warnings about Reye's Syndrome that were disseminated in the media, through doctors, and through on-product warning labels produced a substantial drop in aspirin use among young children.[30] Similarly, there was a modest drop in the sale of soft drinks containing saccharin after the advent of on-product warnings about the sweetener and the publicity that attended the warnings program.[31] The decline in cigarette use also is attributable to the surge of adverse publicity regarding cigarette hazards, including the succession of warning labels that have been placed on cigarette packs.[32]

It is important to note, however, that in all these instances, the particular contribution of the warnings to changes in sales or behavior cannot be isolated. Other information about risk that might have been received in addition to the warning may have been responsible for the changes. To utilize market data successfully, one needs to take into account changes in the environment other than the warning label by undertaking a carefully controlled study. Though difficult to collect, extensive data may make it possible to draw such refined distinctions, as we will see below in the case of the market impacts of tetracycline warnings.

A second source of evidence that can be used to assess the efficacy of warnings is experimental studies. The results on warnings reported in Table 7.1 were of that form. The reliability of experimental results depends on the degree to which one re-creates the context in which consumers are exposed to information and make decisions.

A third procedure for evaluating impact of warning labels is to apply the principles that have been developed in the scientific literature. This procedure is generally the simplest to undertake since no new research is required, but it is important to rely upon scientifically established principles for label design as opposed to conjecture.

Finally, established labeling guidelines may be used as a reference point for assessing whether the particular warning chosen is appropriate. A number of institutions have established procedures for warnings. The American National Standards Institute, for example, has issued guidelines for choosing the appropriate word for mechanical hazards, such as "danger," "warning," and "caution." Similarly, the detailed warnings programs for pharmaceuticals and pesticides provide reference points regarding past warnings practices for these classes of products.

Use of these reference points is instructive insofar as it indicates the extent to which a particular warning has adhered to the appropriate labeling vocabulary for the type of risk, but it is often not definitive. Moreover, little of this work has been based on formal scientific studies of labeling efficacy. The efforts have generally been the outgrowth of an attempt to promote uniformity. The principles underlying such guidelines may not be sound, and the domain in which they can be applied may be limited. Nevertheless, reference points may establish some guidance with respect to how different types of warning language are used.

Warnings and the Risk-Utility Test

The risk-utility test described in Chapter 4 has several implications with respect to warnings. First, if hazard warnings are effective in fully communicating the risk, then any additional examination of whether a product design is defective is redundant since the market has already performed such a risk-utility test. The second implication is that one should apply the same kind of risk-utility balancing in assessing warnings as one would in analyzing other aspects of product design.

Consider first the automatic character of the risk-utility test. If the warning message is received and processed reliably, individuals making consumption decisions will incorporate the value of the risk reduction to them. This value in turn will be transmitted to the producer, thus establishing incentives for the producer to take the efficient level of care.

The date in Table 7.2 indicate the way in which this mechanism operates in a warning situation. Two different groups of workers in

Table 7.2. Workers' risk-utility tradeoffs

	Chloroacetophenone	Asbestos
Initial risk assessment (0–1 probability scale)	0.10	0.09
Risk assessment after warning (0–1 probability scale)	0.18	0.26
Additional wage premium for risk required ($1982)	1,919	2,996
Implicit value of an injury (value per statistical injury)	23,988	17,624
Workers refusing to stay on job at any wage (fraction)	0.02	0.11
Workers intending to quit if no wage increase (fraction)	0.23	0.65
Workers who would take the job again if no wage increase (fraction)	0.58	0.11

Source: Based on calculations by the author and data in Viscusi and O'Connor (1984).

the chemical industry received warnings for chemical products and were asked how working with a chemical bearing such a warning would alter their attitude toward their jobs. The first chemical is chloroacetophenone, which is an industrial chemical that is an irritant. Although this chemical will make you cry, it will not have serious or irreversible health impacts. In contrast, the second chemical for which a professionally drawn label was given to the workers was asbestos, a rather well-known carcinogen.

In each case workers were asked what their initial assessment of the risk of their job was, which is given in the first row of the table. In particular, what was the probability of a standard job accident that is equivalent to the risk of working with the chemical for which the warning was given. Before receiving the warning workers set the risk at 0.10 for the chloroacetophenone sample and 0.09 for the asbestos group. A risk of 0.10 indicates that the riskiness of the job is comparable to an annual chance of one in ten of experiencing an on-the-job injury. After being shown the warning label for a chemical that would replace the chemicals with which the individual currently worked, the risk assessments increased to a level of 0.18 for chloroacetophenone and 0.26 for asbestos.

Labeling will generate market incentives for safety if workers demand additional wage premiums to remain on the job after being apprised of the risks. These premiums averaged $1,919 for chloroacetophenone and $2,996 for asbestos. Viewed in terms of the amount that workers required for each additional expected injury on the job, these figures translate into an implicit value for each expected injury of approximately $20,000.[33] This order of magnitude for the implicit value of an on-the-job injury is comparable to the amount that workers now receive for risks. As a result, risk labeling will generate the same kind of risk reduction incentives in the labor market as are now generated through the wage mechanism. A risk-utility test is superfluous in situations where these market processes are effective.

Additional financial incentives for safety will be generated through turnover costs. In the case of asbestos, 11 percent of all workers indicated that they would not work with asbestos for any wage, and 65 percent of workers indicated that they would quit if their wage were not increased.[34]

The risk-utility test is based on a balancing of the benefits and costs of risk. Sound warnings efforts promote this balancing for precautionary decisions. Table 7.3 summarizes information relevant to con-

Table 7.3. A private risk-utility analysis of precautions for use of a drain opener

Costs	
Disutility per bottle of wearing rubber gloves	$0.17
Number of bottles of drain opener per year	1.78
Annual value of costs of wearing rubber gloves	$0.30
Benefits	
Annual risk of hand burn from drain opener if no precaution is taken	0.000061
Effect of hand burn	Temporary discomfort
Benefit-cost comparison	
Minimal dollar value of hand burns for expected benefits to exceed costs of precaution [value × (.000061) > $.30]	$5,200.00

sumers' decisions to wear rubber gloves when using a product with the Drano/Red Devil Lye composite label that was considered in Table 7.1. The main cost of warnings typically will not be the cost of placing a label on the container but rather the cost to the individual of the recommended precautions. In this case, the disutility of wearing gloves is valued at seventeen cents per bottle, or thirty cents per year for the average product usage. Individuals who wear rubber gloves will reduce their risk of hand burns that are severe enough to require medical treatment by an average of 0.000061. Whether or not it is desirable to undertake this precaution depends in large part on how valuable the injury reduction is. Above some threshold benefit level precautions are desirable, and below this cutoff they are not. The calculations in Table 7.3 indicate that if the value of the hand burns prevented by using rubber gloves exceeds $5,200, then it is economically desirable for individuals to take precautions. If the loss imposed by the hand burn is less than this amount, then it would be rational to forgo the precaution.

Overall, 18 percent of the sample receiving the Drano/Red Devil Lye warning chose to forgo this precaution. This behavior is not necessarily irrational, given the threshold benefit level before precautions are desirable. Once the information has been given, received, and processed, there is often leeway for individuals to choose in a rational manner not to take the recommended precautions. Their personal risk-utility test with respect to the precautions may indicate that it is not worth their while to exercise the recommended degree of care. This element of choice and the freedom to ignore warning instructions is sometimes a rationale for instituting warnings efforts as opposed to mandatory stipulations.

Regulatory Compliance

The primary recommendation of Chapter 6 was that evidence regarding a product's compliance with specific regulatory requirements should be exculpatory. This proposal is particularly pertinent in the case of hazard warnings that are approved by government agencies. For compliance with warnings standards, or other standards, to be a valid defense, however, the company must have provided to the regulatory agency on a continuing basis any available information relevant to setting the regulatory standard. In addition, the regulation must deal explicitly with the hazard warning and its content. This latter requirement hinges primarily on the degree to which there is a specific regulatory requirement as well as the extent to which this requirement is based on an established and effective warnings vocabulary.

Three different regulatory contexts involving warnings arise, and the extent to which regulatory compliance should be exculpatory will vary among them. In the first situation the agency drafts the specific warning language, which is based on an effective warnings vocabulary. Compliance with those warnings requirements should be exculpatory. The chief examples of such warnings are the pharmaceutical warnings mandated by the Food and Drug Administration. The congressionally mandated warnings for cigarettes and saccharin may be in this category as well.

In some cases, most prominently in litigation over cigarette use, compliance with the warnings requirements has been ruled exculpatory, at least from the standpoint of warnings defects. Simultaneously there are, however, limits to the extent warnings may serve as a defense. In a case involving toxic shock syndrome and tampon use, the courts have ruled that compliance with federal warnings requirements preempts claims based on inadequate warnings but not claims based on defective product design or construction.[35] Unless one can also demonstrate that the warnings are fully informative, this limitation is correct from a warnings policy standpoint.

Since this situation in which warnings are effective will be the principal reference point for assessing other warning contexts, consider the character of the warnings requirements and their performance in detail. Since our principal case study will be warnings for tetracycline, let us consider the components of one brand of this drug—Sumycin—in detail. The primary audience for this warning is the physician who will write the prescription. This warning is included in an annual compilation of warnings known as the *Physician's Desk Reference*, and it is also distributed with the product itself. As a result, there is access to the warnings.

The audience for the warnings is not the consumer but a learned intermediary, the physician, who will act as the patient's agent. The content of the warning can therefore be much more complex and scientifically detailed than would a warning directed to consumers.

Nevertheless, for any recipient group it is essential to provide the information in a clear and organized manner. For pharmaceuticals the FDA has adopted a standardized warnings vocabulary. In particular, each section of the warning addresses a different class of issues. The first segment of the warning information provides a general description of the product. The second section deals with the clinical pharmacology, part of which raises issues that would be familiar to physicians—all of whom take pharmacology courses in medical school. The third component of the warnings message consists of indications of usage, thus summarizing the particular situations in which the medicine will be effective.

The first of several paragraphs in the warnings section highlighted the potential risks of tooth staining:

WARNINGS

THE USE OF DRUGS OF THE TETRACYCLINE CLASS DURING TOOTH DEVELOP-MENT (LAST HALF OF PREGNANCY, INFANCY, AND EARLY CHILDHOOD TO AGE OF EIGHT YEARS) MAY CAUSE PERMANENT DISCOLORATION OF THE TEETH (YELLOW-GRAY-BROWN). This reaction is more common during long-term use of the drugs but has been observed following repeated short-term courses. Enamel hypoplasia has also been reported. TETRACYCLINE DRUGS, THEREFORE, SHOULD NOT BE USED IN THIS AGE GROUP UNLESS OTHER DRUGS ARE NOT LIKELY TO BE EFFECTIVE OR ARE CONTRAINDI-CATED.[36]

The degree to which adding the tooth staining warning to the label affected tetracycline usage will be explored below.

The contraindications section addresses situations in which the drug should not be administered because of particular risks. The next section is devoted to various kinds of warnings with respect to the drug that arise both generally as well as in particular contexts, such as usage during pregnancy. Risks that may arise but on a less general basis are addressed in the precautions section of the warning, which is followed by a section on adverse reactions. After being given all of this information regarding the product risk, the physician then obtains information regarding dosage and administration as well as the manner in which the product is supplied.

Processing of this information is facilitated not only by the prior training of the physician but also by the standardization of labeling information. Although some sections may not appear, the ordering of the different component sections of the label and their content is always identical. Thus, descriptive information always precedes discussion of clinical pharmacology. Moreover, the risk warnings will always appear in the appropriate section and will not, for example, be subsumed into a clinical pharmacology section. A standardized format allows the user of the information to develop expertise in processing the labeling information in a systematic manner.

A second noteworthy feature is that the degree of prominence given to various kinds of information has also been standardized. The manner in which warnings are developed for pharmaceutical products ensures such comparability. The pharmaceutical company applies for the approval of a product, and the specific wording of the warning is drafted by a group of physicians and pharmacologists within the Food and Drug Administration. A national group of this kind helps to establish a degree of uniformity and a common vocabulary across warnings.

In contrast, if one were to adopt a warnings strategy with the objective of minimizing one's risk of liability, the solution would be to box and put in large bold lettering all warnings pertaining to products, however ineffective this approach might be as a method of communication. The company taking such apparently ambitious measures could then argue that it had done all that it could to convey the warning. Such overwarning may reduce liability costs, but it will not lead to a sensible warnings policy. If we box and otherwise highlight warnings related to minor health impacts, then there will be no option left in our warnings vocabulary to convey more serious classes of risks. What do we do for an encore? We will dilute the effectiveness of the messages that merit greater concern.

The degree to which warnings can have an impact is illustrated in Figure 7.1. Hazard warnings indicating the tooth staining risk to young children taking tetracycline began in April 1963. Although the consequences of tooth discoloration are only cosmetic, awards in these cases have often been substantial—sometimes in the range of $65,000–$75,000.[37] The age ranges shown in Figure 7.1 are for the affected group, children up to age eight, and what might be viewed as a control population group not affected by the risk, consumers age nine and above. The usage of tetracycline declined for young children beginning in 1963 from approximately 400 mentions (which consist primarily of prescriptions and renewals of prescriptions) per 1,000 population to under 100 mentions per 1,000 population by 1975. Physicians continued to prescribe the drug for age groups not susceptible to tooth staining, at a modest but steady pace until other competitive drugs began to decrease its market share in the 1970s.

This type of market evidence provides a nice comparison of what the trajectory of tetracycline usage for young children would have been in the absence of the warning. The clearcut implication is that the hazard warning was effective in this particular market context.

Usage of tetracycline in the age group susceptible to tooth staining did not completely disappear since physicians must make risk-utility tests on behalf of their patients. If a particular drug is more effective in reducing serious risks to one's well-being, then it may be worthwhile to accept a risk of cosmetic damage. For example, tetracycline is more effective than other drugs in combatting Lyme disease and Rocky Mountain spotted fever. In this situation, by comparing the market segment affected by the warning with the market segment that would not be directly affected by the warning, one can establish evidence of the warnings impact that, in effect, takes into account changes in disease patterns and drug availability that might have otherwise accounted for the shift in tetracycline usage.

A second class of warnings regulations consists of those with less clearcut implications for a firm's potential liability. Often, warnings are approved without a firmly established vocabulary, perhaps the best example of which is the EPA's labeling requirements for pesticides. Although pesticide labels must be formally approved in advance of marketing by EPA, the structure and content of these labels varies considerably even for products within the same product class. There is no well-established warnings vocabulary as there is for phar-

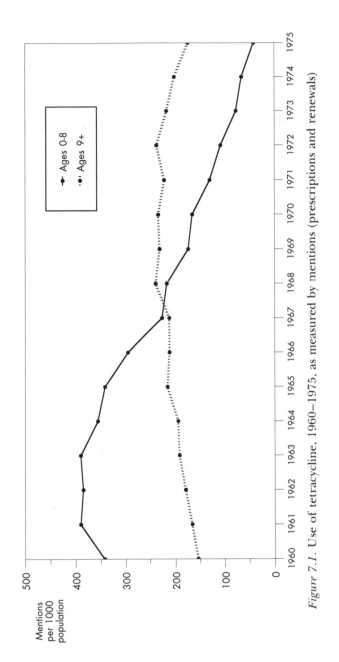

Figure 7.1. Use of tetracycline, 1960–1975, as measured by mentions (prescriptions and renewals)

maceuticals. The structure, content, and the format of the warning differ considerably across products in part because the warning is often drafted to accommodate the broader marketing function of the labeling material.

The variations in the efficacy of pesticide warnings are borne out in a study of different EPA-approved warnings for bleach, which is officially classified as a pesticide by EPA because of its biocidal properties.[38] The placement and content of the warnings message varies considerably for different nationally marketed brands. The effectiveness of these warnings differs in large part because the EPA is not explicitly concerned with establishing a common and effective approach to warnings, as the FDA is. Although regulatory compliance with guidelines such as those administered by EPA may be exculpatory, the guidelines are not sufficiently detailed to ensure that this will always be the case.[39] Compliance with federal labeling requirements, such as EPA-approved labeling, currently does not generally exempt companies from tort suits, and this view is consistent with my warnings proposal.[40]

The third situation in which warnings requirements can arise is with respect to regulatory provisions that impose warnings but do not indicate their specific form and content. OSHA's large-scale hazard communication effort for job-related chemical hazards is of this type. Manufacturing firms are required to warn their workers about hazardous chemical exposures, but there are no regulatory stipulations whatsoever regarding the form, content, structure, or other aspects of the warning. There is not even any explicit regulatory guideline that one can use to assess whether the warning is in compliance with the regulatory standard. Even in situations in which the company has been subjected to a government inspection and found to be in compliance, one cannot be confident that the warnings system is sound. This type of regulatory violation may not have even been addressed by the inspector. In addition, even if the inspector did assess the warnings, the absence of a precise standard to be used for judging warnings limits any inference about the desirability of the warning.

The regulatory compliance defense for warnings at the present time consequently should be limited to a very few special situations in which there are explicit, standardized guidelines describing what kind of hazard warning is appropriate.

Toward a National Warnings Policy

For the regulatory compliance defense to be of consequence for any more than a small segment of liability cases, Alan Schwartz and I have proposed a national warnings policy to establish a uniform national vocabulary for warnings.[41] The general approach would be to establish standards for situations in which particular words, means of emphasis, indications of risk severity, and formats would be used. This approach would extend across all contexts and would not be limited to a particular product group. Its effect would be a substantial broadening of efforts at standardization that have been undertaken by governmental groups such as the Food and Drug Administration and private organizations such as the American National Standards Institute.

There are several rationales for adopting this approach. The first dividend would be to establish objective criteria to serve as a reference point for assessing warnings. Rather than relying on an uncertain battle of experts with regard to the efficacy of a particular warning, one could simply assess whether a warning was in compliance with the guidelines of the national warnings policy. In particular, did the firm adopt the appropriate language and structure given the risk of the product?

A second advantage is the greater ease with which individuals will be able to process information once we move to a common language and warnings format. As the number of warnings proliferates, there is a need for standardization of the language and the manner in which the information is presented. In the absence of such structure, it will be more difficult for individuals to process the information given to them. Moreover, even if warnings are processed, their content may be misconstrued because of the absence of a well-established and common vocabulary. Thus, a systematic means of communication will more reliably convey pertinent information. One of the purposes of warnings is to enable consumers to make across-product comparisons so that they can allocate both their product purchases and activity choices to better manage the risks in their lives. Establishing a commonality in the language of warnings is essential for promoting more informed consumer choice.

Standardization alone is not the objective. In particular, in designing the national warnings vocabulary, we should take advantage of the capabilities scientific studies offer in developing sound and effective warnings formats.

The best method of achieving a well-designed warnings system is not to let the warnings systems emerge from a series of decentralized court cases. This can only lead firms to try to limit their liability by adopting an overly conservative approach. In the long run this overwarning will mute warnings' impact. A preferable option would be to expect firms to meet clear and well-established criteria. The major beneficiaries will be the product users themselves, who are now confronting an avalanche of warnings, health claims, and other risk-related information. Risk information is now widely disseminated but not effectively communicated.

A major theme that has emerged during the products liability crisis is the attitude that responsibility for accidents does not lie with the accident victim. Liability cases have turned into a search for the "deep pocket" rather than an examination of whether or not the producer met his obligations. The main message of hazard warnings is that safety is a joint responsibility, not simply a responsibility of producers. Proper use of hazard warnings will increase the accountability of product users, but before we can demand this accountability, the warnings systems themselves must be held to a higher standard.

8

Environmental and Mass Toxic Torts

Mass toxic tort cases differ from textbook models of products liability litigation in terms of the nature of the problems they pose. Consider the simplest case of a manufacturing defect. Suppose that the brakes on a car may be manufactured imperfectly and, as a result, function with some rate of failure. The resulting injuries will be isolated events that depend on the stringency of the quality control process and that will lead to a modest level of litigation. This scenario is what the courts generally have in mind when they envision the manufacturer (and the product purchasers) as the insurer of the accident victim's losses.

Now consider a design defect that extends across an entire product line. If the brakes for an entire model of a car are defective, then the manufacturer becomes liable for the brake-related accidents for all cars in that model group. Because of their potentially widespread impact, design defects impose greater cost burdens on the firm.

A third class of products liability cases is the mass toxic tort, which is frequently the result of environmental risks. Suppose that the brake linings of the car in the example are made of asbestos and that the exposure of manufacturing workers and mechanics to the asbestos leads to cancer; suppose also that there is a twenty-year lag before the link between exposure and cancer will be apparent. This is not a case of a series of isolated manufacturing defects leading to liability, nor of a single model year imposing risks. Rather, twenty years of products will generate a much greater degree of liability that will begin to be manifested only once there is a considerable backlog of cases that have not yet emerged.

Because of this lag in the time of the risk exposure and the time when liability is imposed, the tort liability system cannot create effective risk reduction incentives for producers. The system would work only if this potential liability were fully anticipated and taken into account by the managers of the firm at the time when the risk was generated. Standards of liability change over time, however, and firms may not be able to recognize the deferred impacts of remote prospects of litigation, so tort liability will fare particularly badly as a safety incentive mechanism.

The tort liability system will also serve as a poor insurance system. Even in the case of design defects, the scale of the problem limits the insurance role of products liability. When the injury a product causes is a disease whose onset may be delayed for decades, the system is burdened by the added problem that consumers today will be paying for the insurance benefits of consumers many years earlier. This lag breaks the link between the product price and the insurance provided to such an extent that the insurance market will not be viable. Consumers of less risky products produced now will have no interest in providing high levels of insurance benefits to previous consumers of highly risky versions of the products.

Finally, the scale of losses incurred by product-related diseases may be so great that there may be little that can be done without threatening the financial viability of the firm and their insurers.

Overall, mass toxic torts undermine the essential functions of the products liability system. Tort liability will be unable to provide either effective insurance or effective deterrence. Mass toxic torts are not simply scaled-up versions of manufacturing defect cases. Rather, they pose a new class of products liability issues. As the statistics presented in Chapter 2 indicated, mass torts make up a dominant share of all products liability litigation in the federal courts. The key issue for liability reform issue is what role, if any, products liability should play when a product causes injury on a very large scale.

The focus of this chapter will be on cases involving asbestos, Agent Orange, and the Dalkon Shield. This emphasis is not random. As Figure 8.1 indicates, the overwhelming proportion of mass tort litigation involves these three lines of litigation. The estimated 340,000 asbestos claimants alone account for roughly half of it. The 210,000 claimants for the Dalkon Shield and the 125,000 claimants for Agent

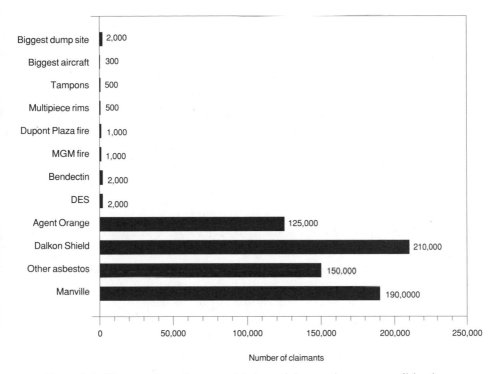

Figure 8.1. The number of personal injury claimants in mass tort litigation
Source: Rheingold (1990), p. 150

Orange also dwarf the numbers of other instances of mass tort litigation. The numbers illustrated in Figure 8.1 do not reflect the ultimate scope of mass tort litigation. In all likelihood, new cases will arise with increasing frequency as the science of establishing causal linkages improves. These mass tort cases will demand sounder legal remedies than have been offered to date.

The Market Paradigm and Why It Fails

Product-related diseases would be largely eliminated if people could make fully informed, voluntary market choices. Unfortunately, this is not how markets work. Informational inadequacies and externalities make the free market particularly ineffective in reducing disease and environmental risks.

The standard economic model rests primarily on the assumption that individuals perceive and understand the risks they face. The risk of disease, however, is cloaked in informational inadequacies for all parties concerned. Workers and consumers are likely to be particularly unaware of the risks associated with current and future exposures to chemicals and other health hazards, as compared with visible safety risks. Risk assessments are very complex; one cannot expect the general public to understand the ongoing debates in the scientific community over the relationship between exposure and health risks.[1] Health may be affected by factors one would not expect to be relevant. For instance, different demographic groups have different susceptibilities to some risks. There also may be complex synergies with behavior patterns, such as diet, unrelated to a particular product risk. The long time lags involved and the difficulty of inferring the correct causal links make it hard for individuals to learn by experience about certain risks.

Environmental risks represent the extreme case of market failure, for no market transaction is involved. No incentive to avoid risk can be generated by a market for products that impose the risk on individuals who do not purchase the products. The extent of this breakdown in risk incentives is, however, no different from the failure of market mechanisms when individuals are completely ignorant of the hazards they face in the market.

The failure of the market to eliminate product-related diseases is felt in today's market on a massive scale. Consider the case of diseases arising from occupational exposures. Although it is difficult to ascertain direct cause-and-effect links, the overall scale of the occupational disease problem is staggering. Over 190,000 occupational illnesses are documented each year by the Bureau of Labor Statistics.[2] These figures probably understate the problem, however, since other Department of Labor statistics indicate that there are two million people severely or partially disabled by occupational disease, of whom 700,000 suffer long-term total disability.[3] Some estimates indicate that 85,000 workers are victims of asbestos-related diseases alone.

Several factors make it difficult to estimate precisely the level of liability that will ultimately arise from product-related diseases. In part, it is impossible to know the exact number of disease victims because some illnesses have long latency periods (that is, symptoms do not appear until many years after exposure to the hazard). Even when victims can be identified, it may be difficult or impossible to ascertain the cause or causes of disease. Few illnesses are "signature" diseases, ailments that can be traced to a single cause.[4] Although well-defined scientific relationships exist in some instances, most diseases may be caused by exposure to any one of several substances or by participation in any one of several activities. Lung cancer, for example, may be attributed to inhalation of cigarette smoke, asbestos, air pollution, or numerous other potential carcinogens.

Whatever the precise scope of the problem, product-related diseases will have important effects on the growth of products liability litigation. During the past decade, for example, workers have filed numerous suits against manufacturers of hazardous products used in the workplace in order to circumvent the restrictions of workers' compensation systems and thus obtain additional compensation for job-related disease.

Rapid growth in the number of products liability suits may threaten the viability of entire industries. For instance, the estimated value of valid claims against the asbestos industry exceeded the combined financial resources of all asbestos producers and insurers.[5]

Products Liability—an Inadequate Remedy

To prevail under a strict liability theory, a victim must establish that the product was defective, that the defect proximately caused the injury, and that the defendant was the manufacturer of the defective product.[6] A plaintiff charging that the injury incurred by the product is a particular disease encounters uniquely difficult problems with each of these three elements.

Under strict liability doctrine, a defective product is one that is unreasonably dangerous.[7] Consumer products are typically found to be unreasonably dangerous because of a manufacturing flaw or an unsafe product design that does not pass a risk-utility test. However, a product also may be unreasonably dangerous if the manufacturer fails to give warnings or directions to users of the product as to its safe use.[8] Failure to warn has been the basis for holding manufacturers liable in most cases in which a product was alleged to have caused a disease.[9] The victim must establish that the manufacturer knew or should have known about the hazards at the time of the failure to warn[10]—a difficult task given that the link between many products and diseases has been established only recently. As a defense, the manufacturer can present evidence that the victim was aware of the risk and incurred it voluntarily.[11]

The second requirement, that a plaintiff must show that the manufacturer's product was the proximate cause of his disease,[12] can be extremely difficult to fulfill. Uncertainties in the relationship between exposure levels and health effects, problems of multiple causes, and long latency periods between exposure and manifestation all significantly reduce the probability of establishing proximate cause. Most observers believe, for example, that actor Steve McQueen's mesothelioma was due to his exposure to asbestos as a World War II shipyard worker, but the asbestos in his auto racing suit may have been the causal link.

Finally, the plaintiff must show that the defendant manufactured the hazardous product that led to his injury.[13] This burden is easily met in some situations, but very difficult to meet in others. Consider, for example, a worker who has been exposed to asbestos while working for several different employers, each of which used several different asbestos suppliers.[14]

Other problems can also prevent recovery. The relevant statute of limitations may expire before many disease victims know that they are ill or that their disease is related to exposures to particular products.[15] Even when the victim wins a jury award, recovery may still be thwarted by a judgment-proof defendant. A firm faced with multiple, unanticipated tort claims may not have adequate resources to compensate all the victims and may have to reorganize under bankruptcy law.[16] Alternatively, mass tort claims against an insured manufacturer may exceed the resources of its insurance company.[17] Finally, workers exposed to risk in the manufacture of hazardous products cannot bring products liability suits against their employers because workers' compensation is their exclusive remedy.[18]

Products liability is not only difficult to apply, it also leads to inequities. Suits by individuals with comparable product-related diseases may have quite inconsistent outcomes because a plaintiff's success in a products liability suit often hinges on such unpredictable factors as the length of the latency period or the availability of evidence showing whose products caused the illness.

Products liability also may be an inefficient mechanism for compensating disease victims. The high transactions costs inherent in the tort liability system are illustrated by recent studies of asbestos litigation. One study indicated that asbestos litigation costs an average of $95,000 per closed claim for defendants and about $25,000 for plaintiffs.[19] Overall, 41 percent of the compensation award is devoted to plaintiffs' legal fees, and defendants devote an amount equal to 58 percent of the award to litigation expenses. As a result, $2.71 in compensation has been paid for every $1 received by plaintiffs. Similar results are borne out in a sample of 513 asbestos claims resolved from 1980 to 1982. Of the average expenditure per case of $101,000, $37,000 was for defendant expenses, $25,000 was for plaintiff expenses, and $39,000 was for the net compensation.[20] In this sample, plaintiffs' net compensation is 39 cents per dollar expenditure, or a total expenditure of $2.56 is required to transfer $1 in compensation.

Agent Orange and the Economic Stakes of Mass Toxic Torts

One of the most unusual cases of products liability litigation stemmed from the use of the defoliant Agent Orange during the Vietnam War. Although originally hailed as a model herbicide, Agent Orange is contaminated by dioxin, which has been called "the most toxic molecule ever synthesized by man."[21] Exposures to the herbicide, which possibly contributed to thousands of cases of cancer, birth defects, and other ailments, may be considered an example of an occupational hazard, but it is an unusual example because the employer in this situation was the United States government.

Furthermore, exposure to Agent Orange did not occur within the context of a standard market. Wage rates for soldiers are not set competitively—if that were the case, there would have been no draft during the Vietnam War. Moreover, in a competitive labor market wages are adjusted so that workers would transfer voluntarily to positions within the army rather than being assigned to them, with no option of changing jobs or quitting. For these reasons, chemical product risks encountered during military service more closely resemble environmental risks than occupational risks. And these risks, which pertained to an entire product line and which did not become evident for years, had reached mass proportions long after decisions on the use of Agent Orange had already been made.

The scale of the ensuing litigation was immense: 600 different actions were brought for over 15,000 named individuals.[22] The estimated number of claims that will eventually be filed is 125,000. News of the chemical's toxicity and suits claiming damages from exposure to Agent Orange were highly publicized. Here we are interested in tracking the economic effects of these news stories, which illustrate how products liability suits influence firms' well-being.

Table 8.1 summarizes the impact the major legal events had on six

Table 8.1. The effect of Agent Orange suits on the value of individual firms

Firms	Change in value ($ millions)	
	Same day	Ten-day period
A. Yannacone files class action suit, January 8, 1979.		
Diamond Shamrock	35.03	−32.04
Dow Chemical	−60.74	−50.69
Hercules Inc.	−6.24	−30.82
Monsanto Co.	−20.68	9.76
North American Phillips Corp.	−1.09	1.57
Uniroyal Inc.	−1.93	3.80
Total change	−55.65	−98.42
B. Judge Pratt rules federal common law applies, November 20, 1979.		
Diamond Shamrock	9.51	40.02
Dow Chemical	43.78	−178.83
Hercules Inc.	−2.12	17.45
Monsanto Co.	−14.52	−118.63
North American Phillips Corp.	−9.09	−18.71
Uniroyal Inc.	0.86	−8.74
Total change	28.42	−267.44
C. Agent Orange suit for $310 million reported in Wall Street Journal, May 30, 1980.		
Diamond Shamrock	−32.49	−80.33
Dow Chemical	38.44	−220.68
Hercules Inc.	−0.94	27.28
Monsanto Co.	−9.33	193.41
North American Phillips Corp.	−5.12	30.57
Uniroyal Inc.	0.07	12.12
Total change	−9.78	−37.63
D. Agent Orange suit reported in Wall Street Journal, July 10, 1980.		
Diamond Shamrock	−18.11	−136.42
Dow Chemical	−80.98	−97.23
Hercules Inc.	−13.47	−64.49
Monsanto Co.	33.49	−5.39
North American Phillips Corp.	−5.62	−15.81
Uniroyal Inc.	0.56	21.07
Total change	−151.11	−298.27

Table 8.1. *(continued)*

Firms	Change in value ($ millions)	
	Same day	Ten-day period
E. Judge Weinstein announces decision, May 7, 1985.		
Diamond Shamrock	− 11.63	20.86
Dow Chemical	83.35	300.69
Hercules Inc.	23.75	128.76
Monsanto Co.	66.27	204.26
North American Phillips Corp.	− 16.567	28.61
Uniroyal Inc.	N.A.	N.A.
Total change	145.17	683.18

Source: Viscusi and Hersch (1990).

of the largest producers of Agent Orange, measured by the estimated change in the value of the firm on the date of the event and by the estimated change during a ten-day period surrounding the event. A longer time frame is useful because there may be some anticipation of the event and because there may be some lag before the market can fully process the implications of an event. These estimates pertain to overall shifts in stock prices, irrespective of their cause, so it may be that information pertaining to aspects of the firm other than Agent Orange may have influenced stockholders.

The first major event in the Agent Orange litigation, the filing of the class action suit against the producers of Agent Orange by Victor Yannacone,[23] had a modest effect on the major producers of Agent Orange. The total change in the value of the firms was $56 million on the day of the suit and $98 million for a ten-day period surrounding this event. As one might expect, Dow Chemical Company, the largest producer of Agent Orange, experienced the greatest drop in value.

The major issue in the initial suit was whether the government or the companies would be held liable for the illnesses. Under the Feres doctrine (from the 1980 decision in *Feres v. United States*), the government is immune from liability for torts that are committed against soldiers in situations "where injuries arise out of or in the course of activity incident to service." Moreover, the Stencel doctrine precludes third-party claims that are derived from service-related claims that would be barred by the Feres doctrine. Judge Pratt ruled on November 20, 1979, that federal common law did, however, apply to this case and that the key issues would be those of liability and causation. Although this ruling had a negligible effect on the date of the decision, over the ten-day period surrounding it the producing firms dropped in value by $267 million, with Dow Chemical Company experiencing a loss of $179 million. From the standpoint of the stock market, the stakes had clearly increased.

During the subsequent year, the press also began to devote more attention to the litigation. An article in the *Wall Street Journal* on May 30, 1980, reported Agent Orange suits claiming a total of $310 million. Although the overall market effects of this information appear to have been modest because of the rise in the value of Monsanto stock, possibly due to other economic influences, once again Dow Chemical Company experienced a negative effect from the information, with a loss of $221 million over the ten-day period surrounding the news article. A subsequent report in the *Wall Street Journal* on July 10, 1980, led to a single-day loss of $151 million, with Dow Chemical Company contributing $81 million of this amount. In addition, there was a ten day loss of almost $298 million, where Dow Chemical Company experienced a loss of $97 million.

The Agent Orange litigation was resolved by Judge Weinstein, who did not want to encourage groundless mass tort litigation, especially when, as he saw it, the link between the exposure and the injury was very weak. Judge Weinstein fashioned a settlement among the parties for $180 million, which is a small fraction of the potential jury award. For the 15,000 plaintiffs in this particular case, this award averages $12,000—a modest sum indeed compared with the awards levels summarized in Chapter 5.

Although this was the largest total products liability award granted, the small scale of the award relative to the potential losses was generally regarded as a victory for the defense. The market also perceived that this was the case. On the date of award there was a $145 million increase in the value of the firms, with Dow Chemical Company experiencing an increase of $83 million. Perhaps even more noteworthy, over the ten-day period surrounding the ruling, the value of the companies jumped by a total of $683 million, almost half of which was for Dow Chemical Company. The stock market reaction to the various stages of the litigation indicates that both favorable and unfavorable news is transmitted to investors. The extent of the final, positive impact was somewhat smaller than the negative effects of the first four events, so on balance there were net costs.

The Agent Orange litigation is noteworthy from another standpoint as well. Because of the difficult causality problems, Judge Weinstein opted for a fairly minimal settlement. There was no justification for imposing the usual level of liability. Even with a larger award, the tort liability system would not have functioned as an effective deterrence mechanism.

Compensation Funds

Because the damages that must be paid in mass toxic torts cases may exceed a defendant's resources, the result of some cases has been financial reorganization for the producing firms, and compensation funds have been set up to meet the costs of the claims. The performance of these funds thus far has been disappointing, with the chief problems being inadequate resources, uncertainty of future payments, and continued litigation costs.

Consider first the case of the leading asbestos producer, now known as the Manville Corporation. Manville established a $2.6 billion trust fund in 1988 to compensate asbestos victims.[24] Eighty percent of the company's total worth and insurance payments received by the firm's insurers went toward the fund's resources. In addition, Manville set up a $300 million fund to cover property damage claims. Initial settlements with claimants on this fund varied widely, but the average settlement was in the range of $40,000.

As experience with the fund progressed, problems emerged. Less than one year after the fund's establishment, the claims exceeded the cash resources. Although the share of the initial Manville fund earmarked for personal injuries was set at $2.5 billion, all of these resources were not liquid.[25] Only $670 million was actually on hand, most of which represented payments to Manville by insurance companies. As a result, the fund encountered cash flow problems after paying off about 15,000 pre-bankruptcy claims an average amount of $40,000. Within a year after the fund was established, the trust began encountering difficulties in paying off the new claims, which were being filed at the rate of 11,000 to 12,000 per month.

In 1990 the company, to meet the shortfall, offered claimants settlements that consisted of up to 40 percent of the value of the claim in cash and the rest in nonmarketable long-term notes payable in

1991 or later.[26] With an average settlement of $41,907 that was over 50 percent higher than the original estimate of $25,000, the long-term viability of the fund came into question.

The result is that the prospective claims anticipated in 1990 greatly exceeded future resources. Although the trust's remaining resources (not all liquid) in 1990 were at most $1.5 billion, it faced claims and administrative costs likely to equal $7.5 billion.[27] This disparity and the absence of available resources to pay current claims led the court to observe: "The trust cannot pay one widow in Brooklyn today and a widow living elsewhere, whose husband died of the same disease, 20 years from now . . . A national uniform plan is required."[28] By mid-1990, with the fund's resources all but depleted, Judge Jack B. Weinstein—the key player in the Agent Orange litigation—pressured Manville into adding $520 million to the fund over a seven-year period.[29] Ensuring the fund's long-term ability to pay the estimated 130,000 remaining asbestos claims will continue to be a matter of concern.

Moreover, in addition to uncertainty regarding eventual payment, doubts have been raised about the effectiveness of the fund in providing compensation. Even after Manville established the asbestos trust fund to reduce the litigation burden, litigation costs remained substantial. Plaintiffs' lawyers, for example, have received more than one-fourth of the compensation paid.[30] An administrative compensation mechanism provides no assurance that legal fees will be eliminated, but the level of litigation expenses has been reduced.

A. H. Robins has established a similar type of fund to deal with claims against it contraceptive device, the Dalkon Shield. As in the case of asbestos litigation, the company established the fund as part of its bankruptcy reorganization.[31] The 195,000 claimants (as of 1989) will each receive payments based on the extent of the injury. Most claimants (80,000 by 1989) had accepted modest payments of $725. More severely injured claimants will receive settlements based on proof of injury and medical evidence; these settlements ranged from $25,000 to $250,000 before the bankruptcy filing. The level of compensation is consequently not great in most instances.

The terms of the payments are actually well below those of typical tort awards.[32] Women who incurred minor and unsubstantiated injuries can receive $725. Women who can prove that they used the device and as a result suffered injuries such as spontaneous abortions and sterility after its removal can receive $850 to $5,500—a low price indeed for such serious consequences. A third option, involving payments after complete review of medical records and proof of Dalkon Shield's causality (and not some other intrauterine device), can lead to higher awards. The proposed payments can be appealed in a civil suit or binding arbitration in a process not much different from the requirements of current tort litigation.

In 1989 the fund had resources of $2.5–2.7 billion to pay prospective claimants.[33] As in the case of the asbestos fund, the adequacy of these resources is uncertain. One consulting firm estimated that the amount A. H. Robins would ultimately need to compensate the Dalkon Shield victims was $7.2 billion, which greatly exceeded the company's estimate of $1.2 billion and Aetna's estimate of $2.3 billion.[34] Providing for an uncertain amount of future damages is a highly problematic exercise for toxic torts cases in which risk relationships are not well understood.

The administrative costs associated with the Dalkon Shield fund have also been quite high. The lawyers for women collecting from the fund are believed to be receiving about $700 million in legal fees.[35] Moreover, the bill to A. H. Robins for its bankruptcy reorganization and defense included $70 million in legal fees and $4.8 million in consulting from investment bankers.[36] Overall, administrative compensation funds of this sort do not seem to be the ideal solution on any dimension.

Strategies for Mass Toxic Torts

The current tort liability system cannot successfully address the problems posed by mass toxic torts. The large scale of the litigation creates substantial transaction costs as well as enormous congestion in the courts.

The main problem is that these cases involve indeterminate causation. It is difficult to make a link between the behavior of the firm, or for that matter individuals' exposure, and the subsequent disease. In the absence of such a link, it becomes difficult to assign liability. Because of these problems, the option of retaining the current products liability approach to mass toxic torts is simply not viable.

A second option would be to reform the manner in which mass tort cases are treated. One reform would be to abandon the current "preponderance" standard and assign liability on a proportional basis according to the contribution of the particular product exposure to the disease risk—in effect, to move to a rule of proportional liability.[37] Although this approach is attractive in instances in which relative contribution to causality can be ascertained, the fine-tuning this approach requires may be infeasible when complex scientific information and dimly understood scientific relationships are involved. If, however, the proportional liability approach were coupled with the utilization of scientific panels to resolve underlying technical issues that are beyond the capabilities of any jury, then courts might be able to assign liability in a reasonable fashion.[38] Even so, if the risks were not well understood at the time of the original risk exposure, as in the case of asbestos, then a proportional liability rule would still not have the desired incentive effect.

If our sole objective were to compensate victims, then an alternative to the tort liability system would be to set up an administrative compensation system. This option has been considered by Congress in the case of asbestos exposures.[39] Under proposed legislation that was not adopted by Congress, an administrative scheme would have been set up in which workers would be granted an irrebuttable presumption that asbestosis or mesothelioma were caused by exposure to asbestos. The program would also presume that lung cancer was caused by asbestos exposure, but this presumption would become irrebuttable only if there were evidence showing that asbestos had caused changes in the lung or pleura.

Although administrative compensation schemes would eliminate many of the transaction costs associated with asbestos litigation, the price tag would be enormous. Cost estimates for compensating all fatalities resulting from asbestos exposure run from $16 billion to $30 billion.[40] It is impossible, however, to determine which cases of lung cancer in asbestos workers were caused by asbestos and which were caused by other factors. As a result, all lung cancers in asbestos workers could be compensable under the program, raising the present value of the total cost of compensation to between $54 billion and $108 billion.[41] In contrast, estimates of the present value of the cost of asbestos products liability suits based on similar assumptions range from $8 billion to $91 billion.[42]

Not only would this scheme lead to enormous financial burdens because of the difficult causality problems involved, but it would also create no effective incentives for asbestos risk reduction. When causality cannot be ascertained, the usual compensation system approach is to define broad industry groups, such as the chemical industry,

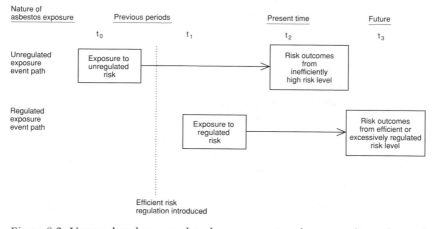

Figure 8.2. Unregulated vs. regulated exposures to asbestos: a chronology of outcomes

and tax these firms according to their output. This is the procedure adopted for the black lung fund and Superfund. There will be no deterrent effect in these cases.

The difficulty of relying on compensation policies for deterrence is illustrated by Figure 8.2. (The same kind of approach may be applied to other toxic torts as well.) Before regulation, workers are exposed to asbestos at time t_0. The effects of exposure are not felt until the present time, t_2. Anything we do in period t_2 in terms of social insurance, tort liability, or government regulation will do nothing to alter the exposure levels in t_0. As a result, the tort system will have an effect only on compensation, not deterrence. Suppose, on the other hand, that government regulation beginning at period t_1 has led to an efficient level of deterrence. Exposures in this period will result in outcomes in period t_3 that will be efficient even in the absence of tort liability incentives.

The cost per life saved through regulation provides a good index of how this deterrence function has been taken over by regulatory agencies. OSHA asbestos regulations in 1972 imposed regulations that cost $7.4 million per life saved, but by 1986 the cost had escalated to $89.3 million. This amount is exceeded by the $104.2 million per life saved of EPA asbestos regulation, as noted in Chapter 6. The end result of the regulatory battle against asbestos is that EPA has banned virtually all products containing asbestos by 1996.[43] Compliance with these regulations will ensure more than adequate risk deterrence, and there is no need to superimpose an additional products liability penalty. Doing so provides overdeterrence.

From the standpoint of deterrence, products liability no longer has a role to play in the regulated exposure event path in Figure 8.2. Past asbestos cases involve previously made decisions that cannot be altered by products liability awards. Future and current asbestos exposures are already addressed by regulatory systems. Augmenting these mechanisms with additional incentives from products liability would provide excessive deterrence.

Regulatory mechanisms are also more effective than products liability in situations involving highly complex scientific information and society-wide judgments regarding product risk.

The only remaining potential objective of products liability would be to provide compensation to the victims of asbestos and other mass toxic torts. The most equitable use of tort liability in this instance is not clear-cut. Under current policies, similarly situated disease victims often receive widely different levels of compensation. One person may win a multimillion-dollar judgment in a products liability suit, while the claim of an equally deserving victim may be dismissed by a court or rejected by a workers' compensation board because of difficulties in proving causation. Similarly dramatic inequities arise between victims of occupational injuries and victims of occupational illnesses. A fundamental equity issue is whether victims of product-related diseases deserve to receive more generous compensation than victims of diseases not related to products.

When compensation fails to provide deterrence, presumably victims of product-related disease should be treated the same as victims of diseases of unknown origin or victims of diseases caused by contact with hazardous waste sites. Society has the same impulse to provide a minimum level of income support and medical care to a disease victim whether the cause of that person's affliction is occupational, environmental, or unidentifiable. The appropriate level of compensation should not hinge on how the victim contracted the disease or whether the illness is job-related or product-related. In general, the compensation decision should depend instead on the effects of the disease on the victim's well-being and the consequent need for income support.

Similarly situated disease victims should be eligible for similar levels of public compensation, regardless of the cause of their illnesses. Existing private and social insurance efforts, such as the Social Security disability compensation system, can better serve as the principal mechanism for income support.

Social Security disability insurance is a particularly attractive remedy because it provides income support for workers with long-term disabilities whether the cause is occupational or not. The program thus treats victims of similar diseases similarly. It also has the crucial advantage of being funded through a broad-based payroll tax rather than through a tax targeted at particular firms. In one sense, this type of funding is unfair, because firms not responsible for causing the disease will be treated the same as those that were responsible. On the other hand, this perceived inequity arises only in cases where responsible firms can be identified. It is generally impossible to make a precise causal connection between a particular disease and one's job or product usage. Compensating victims of past diseases through the Social Security system will provide fair levels of income support without penalizing firms for conditions that can no longer be changed.

Failure to establish sound liability criteria for long-term risks may not only perpetuate the problems posed by previously marketed products but may also discourage the introduction of safer substitutes. Ideally, products liability should lead firms to internalize safety costs. In practice, matters are more complicated, particularly when long-term risks are involved. Monsanto chose not to market a fiber (calcium sodium phosphate) it had developed as an asbestos substitute because the scientific uncertainties regarding the low-level cancer risks possibly posed by the product created a potential for tremendous future liability exposure.[44] In this instance the prospective liability burden exceeded many observers' assessments of the likely injury costs, but the difficulty of proving the fiber's safety led Monsanto to abandon the product.

There is a clear-cut need for establishing more definitive guidelines that firms can meet so that they will not be putting at risk the entire value of the firm when they consider marketing products with long-term risks. The inability of the courts to address these issues successfully creates an enormous range of uncertainty for the firm, which ultimately may be hit with a liability bill far in excess of the injury costs specifically attributable to its product. The regulatory compliance defense proposed in Chapter 6 is particularly essential for products associated with long-term health hazards.

The solution to mass toxic torts and related problems of environmental disease is to eliminate the involvement of the products liability system. Deterrence for previous actions is irrelevant, and deterrence for current and future risks is best provided through effective government regulation of risk exposure levels. Regulation that directly addresses these issues can succeed in providing the risk incentives that a remote chance of ultimately incurring a products liability burden will not succeed in generating.

The compensation problems are more problematic, since ideally one would like to provide equitable compensation to disease victims. Distinguishing who should receive compensation and who should not is not feasible when causal relationships are not well understood. Promotion of broadly based social insurance compensation for all disease victims, irrespective of cause, would meet society's objective of providing insurance to individuals in need. If these levels are inadequate, the task for policy is to raise these levels to an appropriate amount for all illness victims, not simply to award substantial prizes to the few who succeed in the litigation lottery.

9

Workers' Compensation

Recent assessments of the expansion in products liability have high-lighted the increased use of tort remedies for individual accidents and diseases, such as those attributable to asbestos. Before the advent of workers' compensation, workers pursued legal remedies for individual accidents in much the same manner.[1] Early in this century states replaced tort liability remedies with administrative compensation systems, but in recent years tort liability suits have re-emerged as a prominent source of compensation for job injuries.[2]

The significance of the different means of addressing on-the-job injuries is suggested by a review of the economic rationale for adoption of workers' compensation systems. Because of the substantial litigation costs and the uncertainty of receiving adequate compensation, reliance on liability for *ex post* compensation of work-related injuries was not an ideal approach, so states established workers' compensation systems as the exclusive remedy.

Workers' compensation provides for more certain and rapid financial support, thus promoting society's objective of insuring workers against medical expenses and drops in earnings. Moreover, linking workers' compensation premiums to firms' safety records maintains incentives for avoiding risk that would have been provided by tort awards.

The advent of workers' compensation marked a shift in the basis for determining whether compensation would be paid. Under tort remedies, fault is the key issue. Is the employer responsible for the accident through, for example, negligence in the provision of safety equipment? Under workers' compensation, the focal point is not on fault but on causation. Was the accident or illness one that "arose out of and in the course of employment?" Thus, there must be evidence that the adverse outcome was indeed job-related. The worker's contribution to the accident is not an issue.[3]

The rationale for establishing a no-fault compensation mechanism is not entirely inconsistent with injury prevention. Employers exert substantial control over and are responsible for monitoring workplace conditions. A financing scheme for compensation that varies with the risk levels maintained by particular firms will generate financial inducements among those firms to provide safe capital equipment and to ensure safe work practices. Tort liability remedies can establish such incentives, but litigation is a cumbersome process that imposes substantial costs on both sides. Workers' compensation offers an administrative compensation remedy that imposes lower transaction costs on claimants and avoids the confrontational aspects of a products liability case, which might damage relations between employer and employee.

The job-relatedness test imposed by workers' compensation is not innocuous. Particularly in cases of occupational disease,[4] it has led to many claims being denied. Overall, the requirements that must be met under workers' compensation are much more stringent than under general social insurance programs for which the existence of an adverse health effect and economic loss is a sufficient basis for compensation.

Workers' compensation is the most prominent *ex post* remedy for job-related injuries, but it is not the exclusive remedy. Products liability continues to play an important role. Workers cannot generally sue their employer, but they can file third-party suits. A worker driving a lift truck that tips over and disables him can, for example, sue the lift truck manufacturer. Similarly, the workers' compensation insurance company that pays off the claim for the injured driver could file a subrogation action to obtain compensation from the firm that manufactured the defective lift truck.

The total share of job-related claims is a minority of all products liability claims—about 13 percent—but their dollar losses are several times larger. Because of the lower probability of showing that a third party should be liable, the cases that lead to third-party suits involve larger stakes than the typical products liability suit. Job-related cases with small losses are unattractive targets for litigation because of the high litigation costs involved.

Moreover, from the worker's standpoint, the net gain from even a successful third-party suit may not be great unless the stakes are substantial. Collateral source rules prevent the courts from lowering a tort award because the injured worker has received workers' compensation benefits. The worker, however, cannot generally obtain a double recovery since the employer or the insurer who paid the claim is typically subrogated to the worker's tort claim, up to the amount of the workers' compensation benefit.[5] There are a few exceptions, however, as some jurisdictions (Georgia, Ohio, and West Virginia) do not have subrogation rights. The injured party's financial incentive to file a products liability claim will be diminished by the extent of the workers' compensation benefits that have already been received. As a result, the cases for which litigation is worthwhile will tend to be only those with larger losses.

The workers' compensation experience is of interest to products liability reformers for two reasons. First and most important, it represents a major social experiment in the way in which liability claims are handled. This administrative compensation structure moved a substantial segment of tort liability claims out of the courts. How well does an administrative compensation mechanism work, and what lessons can be learned from it in terms of redesigning the way in which other products liability cases are handled? Is there evidence that the safety incentives created by this system are of consequence? Second, workers' compensation now interacts with products liability to an increasing extent. In this chapter I will explore the character of the suits and how their performance differs from other products liability actions.

Lessons from the Workers' Compensation Experience

Lesson 1: Incentives matter. Workers' compensation is not simply a social insurance mechanism for which employers make tax contributions independent of the risks posed at the workplace. The link between premiums and benefits paid is not just a nicety or a matter of fairness.[6] Ties of this sort will provide safety incentives. The premium-risk linkage is not always perfect. Large firms will self-insure or be charged rates that are strongly related to their past experience, but smaller firms will pay rates based largely upon their industry's riskiness, thus muting any specific link to the particular hazards of the firm.

Whether workers' compensation does, in fact, establish meaningful and constructive safety incentives has long been a matter of debate. The 1987 *Economic Report of the President* (p. 197) declared that the program's impact was counterproductive: "A growing body of research has found that workers' compensation benefits have unfavorable effects on safety. Higher benefits appear to increase both the frequency of work injuries and the number of compensation claims filed." This rather surprising conclusion was based on studies of nonfatal injuries. More generous workers' compensation benefits increase the incentive of workers to file claims for job-related injuries and, in some cases, for injuries that did not occur on the job at all, such as problems of lower back pain. Moreover, more generous benefits increase the amount of time workers will remain out of work after an injury.

The adverse effect of insurance on the behavior of the insured, known as moral hazard, is exemplified by the claims filed against the Chicago Transit Authority.[7] Over a five-year period, 200 of the CTA's employees accounted for 1,200 injury claims. This concentration of claims is hardly consistent with accidents being a rare event. One worker filed claims for fourteen injuries in less than a single year for "accidents" such as falling off the front bumper of her bus while adjusting the rear-view mirror. Another driver claimed benefits for *eighteen* different injuries, including such dubious claims as falling onto the floor of the bus while she was driving it.

Since assessments of workers' compensation's effects on nonfatal accidents are clouded by the influence of frivolous claims, a more instructive test of the safety incentive is to examine the effect of workers' compensation on the number of fatalities. In that case, workers' compensation provides a dramatic safety incentive. If the safety incentives of workers' compensation were removed, fatality rates in the United States economy would increase by almost 30 percent.[8] Over 1,200 more workers would die from job injuries every year in the absence of the safety incentives provided by workers' compensation.[9]

This number of lives saved dwarfs the estimate of the impacts of federal risk regulations. For example, the highest estimates of the effect of OSHA regulations indicate that at most this agency has reduced injuries by 2–4 percent—a small fraction of the impact that workers' compensation has had.[10] That there should be such a disparity is not surprising. Workers' compensation premiums are over 1,000 times as large as the total penalties levied by OSHA in any year.[11]

Proponents of administrative compensation schemes for products liability should not be too cavalier in treating costs to firms as simply a general revenue tax. The link between liability costs and the risks posed by a firm's product will create safety incentives in much the same manner as does the workers' compensation system. Superfund and toxic tort compensation schemes that levy taxes on firms irrespective of their particular contribution to an injury will fail to generate these safety incentives.

Lesson 2: Workers' compensation benefits are valued by those who receive them; this value lowers the net costs to the firm. The link between benefits and costs implies that workers will accept a lower wage to work on a hazardous job for which they will be covered by workers' compensation. Similarly, the provision of products liability for potentially hazardous products will increase consumers' willingness to pay for the goods, since in effect they are purchasing both a product and an insurance policy. This notion was at least partially understood by some of the early proponents of strict liability, who viewed strict liability as a means of spreading the costs of insurance among the product purchasers. What should be emphasized is that by adopting an administrative compensation scheme we are not simply shifting the cost and taxing the product user. Rather, we are providing product users with a valued product attribute, namely insurance, for which they may be willing to pay a substantial sum.

In the case of workers' compensation, one can explicitly estimate the wage offset that has occurred as a result of the presence of workers' compensation benefits. Not only are workers willing to give up wages in return for higher workers' compensation benefits, but the extent of this wage reduction exceeds the total premiums paid by firms. As a result, the workers' compensation system more than pays for itself through this wage offset.[12] Workers accept an offset that exceeds the expected benefits that they will reap because they value the insurance function of workers' compensation. For much the same reason, risk-averse consumers who purchase life insurance, home insurance, or automobile insurance are willing to pay more for this insurance than the expected amount that they will receive from this coverage. Because insurance provides income support when it is needed, individuals are by no means irrational in placing such a high value on insurance.

Although it is unlikely that firms fully understand this wage offset mechanism, which economists have documented only recently, firms are not necessarily irrational in opposing recent benefit increases. Workers' compensation more than pays for itself overall, but the recent benefits increases have not paid for themselves. The earlier benefit inadequacies have been eliminated, and we have reached the point where the value that workers place on additional increases in benefits no longer exceed their cost.[13] Insurance is beneficial, but going beyond it to a situation of overinsurance is not.

Lesson 3: Administrative compensation systems can be fairly efficient. Roughly eighty cents of every workers' compensation premium dollar reaches individuals as benefits. Very little of the premium is absorbed by overhead and similar expenditures. Dismayed by the high fraction of tort liability awards devoted to legal fees and other expenses, products liability reformers have viewed administrative compensation as an attractive alternative because of the lower administrative costs.

The cost savings from shifting products liability to a workers' compensation–type system will, however, be less than one might expect. Although only one-fifth of the premium dollar goes toward administrative expenses, the worker often pays additional fees to a lawyer (often on a contingency fee basis) to represent the claim before a workers' compensation board or similar administrative body. In addition, the relative efficiency of workers' compensation in transferring social insurance dollars to injured parties stems largely from the program's focus on acute injuries. As it has begun to deal increasingly with diseases, for which causality is much more difficult to ascertain, the same kinds of problems that have led critics of products liability to urge adoption of an administrative compensation system for product-related diseases have also hindered the workers' compensation system. Litigation costs are high, and few cases of occupational disease are covered by the program. Indeed, the system has remained relatively efficient administratively largely because the lion's share of the diseases caused by on-the-job exposures have been excluded from coverage. In contrast, the majority of all products liability cases in federal courts now involve asbestos and similar diseases for which the litigation costs are likely to be particularly high. Such cases will pose severe problems for a workers' compensation–style approach as well. Indeed, the compensation funds for asbestos and the Dalkon Shield have performed much more poorly than has workers' compensation overall.

Lesson 4: Health risks and associated diseases pose major difficulties for compensation, irrespective of the liability mechanism. As indicated in Chapter 8, compensation of all job-related cancers of asbestos workers would cost over ten times as much as the cost of compensating only those cases of cancer specifically attributable to asbestos exposures—if they could be identified. Even in a program with as broad a sweep as workers' compensation, health risks pose major problems because of the diverse sources of causality, which may not be limited to the job environment.

Lesson 5: One should be cautious in generalizing from the workers' compensation experience. Both product and job markets are based on exchanges between a firm and an individual exposed to the risk. There also may be price or wage adjustments to account for the insurance being provided by administrative compensation funds. There is, however, one critical difference between the situations. Firms exert a substantial degree of control over the actions of workers. They assign workers to jobs, control the work environment, specify the job tasks, assign the co-workers whose actions are likely to affect the worker, and generally monitor worker actions as well as all other activities relating to safety. Firms also can monitor whether most "job" injuries occurred on the job.

The producers of products do not have control over product users. They do not supervise the product in use, and they do not even know how the product will be used. They are unaware of the specific attributes of the individual who will be using the product or whether it will be used in conjunction with some other product. In many instances, it is not even known whether an individual was using a particular product at the time of an accident. An enterprising homeowner who slipped on a ladder while doing some weekend painting may complain that the ladder collapsed under him, but no one will know whether the ladder did in fact collapse or even whether the injury was incurred while the ladder was in use.

Because of these difficult monitoring problems, ultimately any administrative compensation scheme for product-related injuries of a comparable scale to workers' compensation would not be the kind of traditional liability system in which there is an effort to establish a financial link between the benefits paid and the firms producing the particular products. Instead, it would more closely resemble a social insurance effort because of the difficulty of ascertaining causality.

Job-Related Products Liability Claims and Workers' Compensation

Workers' compensation is relevant to assessments of tort liability not only because of the lessons it provides but also because of interactions between the two systems. We will investigate these interactions by considering the job-related component of the ISO survey of products liability claims discussed in Chapter 3. Analysis of the 1,447 closed claims for job-related injuries will illuminate a variety of concerns, including the following: What factors lead to cases being dropped or lead to successful attempts to receive compensation? How do aspects of the injury, such as the size of the loss, affect this outcome? Do subrogation actions by insurers follow the same litigation pattern as do workers' third-party lawsuits? Many of the patterns of influence, which are explored in Appendix B, are similar to those for products liability cases overall. Cases involving large losses, for example, are less likely to be dropped because of their high expected payoff.

The dollar magnitudes involved in job-related claims are impressive. The average bodily injury loss is $51,800 and the average bodily injury payment, including cases with zero award, is $25,645 (each of these figures is in 1977 dollars, roughly half the current value). Losses are measured by the reports by the insurance companies of the combined total medical expenses, wage losses, and other financial losses associated with the claim.

Figure 9.1 provides an overview of the disposition of these claims. Almost one-fourth of the claims are dropped without ever going to court or receiving an out-of-court settlement. Of the claims that are not dropped, the great majority (89 percent) are settled out of court. The small portion of litigated claims consists largely of cases in which the plaintiff loses (69 percent), as most of the successful claims are resolved at the settlement stage. The pattern of job-related claims disposition differs from that of all products liability claims. The drop rate for job-related claims is 6 percent higher than for other products claims, and the settlement rate is 10 percent lower. Whereas 4 percent of other products claims are litigated, 8 percent of job-related claims go to a court verdict. This high litigation rate may be due to the substantially greater stakes involved in job-related claims, as compared with other products claims. Claims involving injuries not incurred on the job have an average loss value of $7,821 and an average payment value of $7,570, each of which is considerably below the comparable values for claims involving on-the-job injuries. The

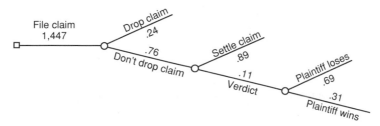

Figure 9.1. The disposition of job-related products liability claims

greater stakes of job-related claims decrease the claimant's propensity to drop a case by boosting the expected payoff from litigation.[14]

The tendency for job-related claims to be dropped or taken to court more often than other products claims is not unexpected, given the factors that affect the loss levels in the claims that are filed. The general presumption in the law is that for job-related claims workers' compensation is the exclusive remedy for seeking redress from one's employer. Third-party products liability suits will consequently exclude a group of potential defendants (employers). The prospects of plaintiff success will consequently be lower and the litigation costs will be higher than for products liability claims in general. Victims of job injuries will be less likely to pursue job-related claims than comparable product claims because the inability to sue one's employer reduces the likelihood that the claim will be successful. The substantial costs involved in subrogation actions also will tend to limit these suits to the larger claims, and workers will be reluctant to press products liability claims unless they can receive more than their workers' compensation benefits. Nevertheless, some of the claims that are filed may not be completely warranted, for employee negligence is an issue in one-quarter of the claims.

The injury mix of claims also reflects the need for greater incentives to file a products liability suit for a job-related injury. The fraction of claims involving fatal injuries is 11 percent, which is almost four times the average fatality rate for all products liability cases. Job-related products liability claims tend to involve injuries that are more severe than the typical product injury.

Many of the claims are not initiated by injured workers. Almost one-fourth of all job-related products liability claims are the result of subrogation actions in which employers or insurers are seeking reimbursement for their payment of worker losses.[15] The defendant of a subrogation action, usually an insurer, may in turn seek protection by initiating what we will designate an "indemnification action." A single injury, then, may spur a number of suits—the worker may sue the employer (the initial claim), the employer may sue the insurer (the subrogation action), and the insurer may sue yet another party, such as the manufacturer of equipment used at the time of the injury (the indemnification action)—each party seeking compensation for losses of one type or another. Almost one-fourth of plaintiffs' actions included in the survey are subrogation actions and almost an equal number of the insurance companies responding to the survey have initiated indemnification or subrogation actions of their own. Similarly, in 24 percent of the cases there are cross complaints involved. Thus, roughly half of all job-related claims are attempts to recover benefits paid to workers. They do not represent claims by workers to obtain reimbursement for their injuries. The extent of overlapping and multiple lawsuits for job-related products liability claims is quite substantial.

The extent of the overlapping among the key legal characterizations of the claims is summarized in Table 9.1. Each row of the table gives the sample group for which the conditional value was obtained—such as cases involving a subrogation action—and the columns list the fraction of cases in that group that satisfy particular characteristics. For example, for 69 percent of the claims involving a subrogation action, there is an indemnification action as well; in 44 percent of cases in which there is a workers' compensation lien against the insurer who responded to the survey, there is an indemnification action too; and in 35 percent of cases for which the state has adopted the sole remedy rule (whereby the employee most likely would seek compensation from workers' compensation or his employer for that type of claim), there is also an indemnification action.

All the variables overlap, but there are no perfect correlations. Some of the most prominent linkages are the following. For about half of all claims in which the defendant is seeking indemnification, contribution, or subrogation from some other party, the defendant is also a target of other subrogated claims by an employer or other insurer. The reverse linkage is even stronger; 69 percent of the cases in which the defendant is the target of subrogation claims by an employer or insurer also involve an indemnification suit by the defendant against some other party. In some but not all cases, these suits involve the same pair of parties. The frequency of cross complaints

Table 9.1. Overlapping of the workers' compensation doctrine variables

	Mean value of variable for group[a]				
Conditional group	Subrogation actions	Nonzero value of workers' compensation lien	Indemnification action	Cross complaints	Sole remedy rule
Full sample	0.23	0.57	0.33	0.24	0.46
Subrogation actions	1.00	0.87	0.69	0.15	0.48
Nonzero value of workers' compensation lien	0.35	1.00	0.44	0.26	0.50
Indemnification action	0.47	0.77	1.00	0.34	0.48
Cross complaints	0.14	0.63	0.47	1.00	0.56
Sole remedy rule	0.24	0.62	0.35	0.29	1.00

a. Mean values correspond to the fraction of the values of the variable that equal 1.

reaches a high value of 34 percent in the case of claims involving indemnification actions. The presence of a subrogation action by the workers' compensation carrier or employer greatly increases the likelihood that there is a reported value of the workers' compensation lien against the insured since the workers' compensation lien variable represents the magnitude of the subrogation action when this dollar value is known. The relative invariance of the data in the last column of Table 9.1 indicates that the applicability of a sole remedy rule has little effect on the presence of other various interactions between workers' compensation and tort liability. The primary interactions appear to be among cross complaints, indemnification actions, subrogation actions, and the scaled variant of subrogation actions, which is workers' compensation liens.

These institutional overlaps are of substantial consequence for legal policy reform. Some observers have recommended the abolition of subrogation actions for job-related injuries.[16] Policy proposals such as this would not be minor tinkerings with arcane legal doctrines but instead would engender a fundamental transformation in the functioning of the tort liability and workers' compensation system. Given the substantial deterrence effect of workers' compensation overall, one would be hard-pressed to justify the abolition of subrogation and indemnification actions in the absence of any empirical support indicating that the loss in controlling risks will be minor.

It is clear that any discussion of tort liability reform for job-related accidents must take into account the role of workers' compensation. Moreover, since job-related claims are an important component of the total products liability burden, in terms both of the number of claims and of their magnitude, any comprehensive program for tort liability reform must examine the workers' compensation–products liability linkage. In addition, the performance of workers' compensation highlights several key lessons for tort liability more generally. Safety incentives matter, and the expected benefits provided to the injured are valued by those exposed to the risk and will lead to at least a partial financial offset. Although compensation structures modeled on workers' compensation will not solve the problems posed by toxic torts, the lessons learned from workers' compensation may better inform participants in the tort liability reform debate about the economic ramifications of liability systems.

10

Will Products Liability
Reform Matter?

The desirability of products liability reform proposals hinges on whether they will in fact be effective. In particular, will the kinds of products liability reforms advocated here result in a real improvement, or are the judicial outcomes of products liability cases unlikely to be altered except by drastic changes, such as a return to a negligence regime? One way to obtain some perspective on this question is to compare the outcomes in jurisdictions whose liability laws differ on the same points that are being proposed for reform. The escalation of the products liability burden over the past three decades can be traced to the evolution of liability standards over time, but the precise timing of these changes in different jurisdictions is not identical, so it is difficult to identify the causal influences. Another natural experiment has been the adoption of different liability statutes across states. By analyzing the impact of these state differences, one can obtain a sense of the potentially major influence of the structure of liability law.

The focal point for the assessment in this chapter will be the effect of state differences in liability law on the performance of insurance markets from 1980 to 1984. By necessity, this analysis predates the insurance crisis of 1985–1986 and recent reform measures.[1] The data analyzed are the insurance files of the Insurance Services Office for bodily injury coverage in the products liability insurance line. The files were then aggregated on the basis of interstate differences in the products liability statutes.

I have divided states into a succession of binary groupings according to the particular products liability statutory provisions in effect in each state. I show that there are systematic differences between each pair of groups. First, though, several caveats are in order. The sets do overlap to some extent. Hence, the analysis does not distinguish the magnitude of the effect of each class of influences.[2] Moreover, these statutory provisions may reflect in part the general character of the products liability regime across states, including a diverse set of legislative and legal factors that extend far beyond the details of the particular statutory provisions.

The states were grouped according to whether there is in each state a statute providing for

1. definitions of key products liability concepts,
2. a state-of-the-art defense,
3. a statute of limitations for producer liability,
4. collateral source rules, or
5. damages rules.

Most of these statutes should improve the liability climate for the insurance industry. The principal exception is that of damages rules, some of which may increase the amount of damages paid. These five distinctions embody broad sets of statutory differences identified in the literature on state differences in liability law, and they provide a systematic basis for categorizing these differences in a way that avoids subjective judgments in classification.

Three aspects of these categorizations should be noted. First, there is some heterogeneity within the groups. For example, provisions on statutes of limitations vary among the states that have them. These provisions do not, however, always lend themselves to ordering and quantification, so it is not feasible to develop a quantitative metric to capture the statutory distinctions. Thus, each state will be in one of two groups, rather than assessed using a scaled variable. The statistical breakdowns will consequently reflect the average performance of the category. Second, the statutory provisions are for specific products liability statutes rather than torts statutes of various types. If there is a correlation between general torts statute provisions or other aspects of the states' legal environments with products liability statutes, then the analysis would reflect these differences as well. Third, the categorizations involve overlapping groups. For example, states with products liability definitions include as subsets almost all of the subsequent provisions. The intent of the analysis is not to assess the incremental effect of each liability provision, but rather to assess whether differences in legal regimes matter. Each of the statutory provisions consequently will serve as a proxy for differences in legal environments.

State products liability rate regulations were not a binding constraint during the time period under consideration, when there was substantial price competition, as noted in Chapter 2. It is the tort environment rather than the regulatory environment that will be the main source of variation.

The ISO data give the state in which the insurance policy was written. For the types of smaller product operations represented in the data set as well as the particular industry mix, it is likely that most product operations will be local rather than national. Plaintiffs are therefore likely to be injured in the state in which the policy was written and file their lawsuits there. In particular, as a total average annual premium level for bodily injury coverage of $317 million over the 1980–1984 period suggests, many of the largest firms self-insured rather than purchased insurance through ISO affiliates. Notable examples of firms that have self-insured or sought special coverage not included in the data are those firms in the pharmaceutical industry and the asbestos industry.

In addition, many of the firms in the sample have construction-related activities, which will tend to be local in character. The top ten product groups for products liability premiums in 1984 included many products with predominantly local operations: miscellaneous services, carpentry, general contracting, lumberyards, general contracting, and electrical wiring. The services and construction-related product groups make up the dominant portion of the products covered.

The state indicators also could be unreliable if firms used out-of-state offices to get coverage written in a state that had lower rates than the state where their products are used. There is, however, little incentive for firms to seek insurance by establishing an out-of-state office to purchase the insurance. Not only are state insurance regulations not a binding constraint during the period being considered, but the rate-setting process is on a product basis, not a state basis. The ISO establishes manual rates on the basis of five-digit product codes, and these rates are national in scope. The insurance underwriter can make a deviation in these rates because of state differences in liability regimes, but it will be unlikely to depart from these rates on the basis of the insured's corporate headquarters rather than, for example, the location of its principal place of business. The latter seems a more reliable index of the pertinent law. In particular, the law that will be applied to any tort is usually the substantive law of the jurisdiction in which the suit is brought, but this is not always the case.

One should also note the direction of the bias, if any, that results from assuming the law governing the policy is the law of the state in which the policy is written. To the extent that firms in the sample market their products nationally rather than within a particular state, there will be a muting of the patterns that are observed. Random measurement error of this type will imply that the actual linkages between products liability statutes and insurance performance are greater than those implied by the data in the subsequent tables.

This sample consists of the information base used by the Insurance Services Office in providing ratemaking guidance for products liability coverage. The sample is quite extensive—over two hundred thousand liability policy observations, where the unit of observation is a policy written for a product in a particular year. This sample provides a statistically reliable basis for assessing insurance trends, but it is less instructive in assessing the total liability burden than the overall statistics reported in Chapter 2.

Insurance Availability

An examination of each of the five measures follows, but first consider the extent of the differences statutory provisions can make. Table 10.1 shows how the provisions affected the availability of insurance during the early 1980s. The first column summarizes the percentage of premiums for policies that experienced an increase in exposure, or amount of coverage, from 1980 to 1984. Since policies involve different levels of total coverage, some weighting system was needed to establish the share of the market experiencing an increase in exposure. The weights used are the premiums for the policies; the values given here are the premiums of policies that experienced an increase in exposure levels divided by the total value of the premiums of all policies written in states with a particular liability regime. The percentages of the total premium levels in 1980 in states with and without various provisions are given in the second column to provide

Table 10.1. Differences in exposure levels and premium levels as a function of statutory provisions

	Percentage of 1980 premiums with increase in exposure, 1980–1984	Percentage of total premiums in 1980
Product liability definitions		
States with	68.7	44.8
States without	54.5	55.2
State-of-the-art defense		
States with	70.5	16.7
States without	54.3	83.3
Statute of limitations		
States with	76.6	28.6
States without	49.4	71.4
Collateral source rules		
States with	64.4	8.4
States without	56.0	91.6
Damages rules		
States with	69.3	38.1
States without	53.2	61.9

a sense of the difference in the prevalence of the various legal provisions, which is substantial.

The share of premiums that experienced exposure increases from 1980 to 1984 provides a measure of insurance availability. One would have expected substantial growth in insurance coverage over that period. Prices for the economy as a whole rose by 26 percent, and the GNP grew by 38 percent.[3] Failure of exposure levels to rise at all is consequently a measure of a substantial decline in expected coverage. As the data in Chapter 2 indicated, premiums also declined during this same period, which may be a sign of an insurance crisis, but the trend could also be a reflection of declining losses and lower prices of insurance. As a result, a better single summary statistic of insurance availability is the total exposure level.

Although the exposure level is typically measured in terms of dollars of coverage, in some instances it is not. The units may be physical rather than monetary. Thus, it is not always possible to aggregate units of exposure across product groups. To avoid this problem, Table 10.1 focuses on the percentage of premiums representing individual insureds that experienced an increase in the total exposure amount for the coverage written over the 1980–1984 period. The problem of noncomparable units of measurement consequently can be overcome. Given the substantial rise in both prices and GNP, the failure to exhibit an increase in exposure should be a signal of a substantial denial of coverage for that type of policy.

With respect to each kind of products liability statute, exposure levels were more likely to increase for a given type of policy in states with the statutory provision. The differences involved are of considerable magnitude. The smallest difference is for collateral source rules, where there is an 8.4 percent gap in the premium percentage exhibiting an increase in exposure. The greatest difference is a 27.2 percent gap for statute of limitation provisions. By most usual standards for empirical research, the observed differences offer stunning support of the hypothesis that differences in tort law affect the availability of insurance.[4]

The strength of these effects suggests that other forces may be at work as well. For example, fourteen states that have adopted one particular set of statutory provisions may have undertaken other measures as well. Such definitions serve in part as a proxy for whether the state has a statute that addresses products liability issues in a comprehensive manner. Even with this broader interpretation, however, the existence of differences across states suggests that state variations in legal structure can be of substantial import.

The failure of the insurance market to adjust completely for differences in statutory regimes illustrates its distinct character as well as a general failure of insurance pricing to adjust rapidly to the profound economic consequences of changes in the structure of tort law. Geographical differences in products liability law currently play little role in current ratemaking procedures.[5] These findings and those below suggest that such differences often have quite stark effects on insurance market performance.

Products Liability Definitions

Products liability definitions may be of several types—the most general define the character of the parties and some of the legal concepts. What attributes must one have to be classified as a "seller," a "manufacturer," or a "user or consumer"? Similarly, what constitutes a "product," or a "harm," a "state-of-the-art" design, a "reasonably foreseeable alteration," or "reasonably anticipated conduct"?

Twenty-five of the fifty states have statutes that include such defi-

Table 10.2. Differences in loss ratios as a function of state products liability definitions

	1980	1981	1982	1983	1984	1980–1984 average	Percentage change, 1980–1984
States with products liability definitions							
Loss ratio	0.76	0.67	0.87	0.97	0.77	0.81	0.74
Premiums ($ millions)	152.14	128.54	108.58	106.45	126.91	124.52	−16.59
States without products liability definitions							
Loss ratio	0.97	0.96	0.98	1.07	0.88	0.97	−9.75
Premiums ($ millions)	209.03	194.73	171.50	178.50	206.37	192.02	−1.27
Ratio of states with to states without							
Loss ratio	0.78	0.70	0.89	0.91	0.88	0.84	12.82
Premiums	0.73	0.66	0.63	0.60	0.62	0.65	−15.07

nitions.[6] The definitions usually are a part of a products liability statute. All states have statutory provisions relating to tort law more generally and all but one state (Wyoming) has a statute that relates to specific doctrines that may arise in products liability contexts, such as strict liability. The presence of products liability definitions thus serves in part as a proxy for whether a state has specific statutory provisions that articulate the character of the products liability law in that state rather than tort law more generally.

Moreover, definitions tend to be restrictive in nature. By defining principles such as "state of the art," the legislature inhibits the leeway of the courts in these areas. Although definitions are to some extent neutral, in practice they limit the scope of products liability. In the short run, these statutory provisions may temporarily increase ambiguity because courts must interpret them. In the long run, however, definitions reduce ambiguity, and it is this ambiguity that some observers believe has contributed to the liability crisis.

The data in Table 10.2 illustrate the connection between liability definitions and products liability insurance. The main insurance measure included is the loss ratio by year. In general, the loss ratio is defined as the ratio of losses paid to premiums in any given year. The inverse of the loss ratio, the premium charged per dollar loss, consequently serves as a measure of the effective price of insurance. If the loss ratio were 1.0, then insurance would be actuarially fair if we ignore the lag time before the losses are filed with the insurer. Given administrative costs and the need for a reasonable rate of return, loss ratios must be below 1.0 if an insurance company is to be viable in the long run, if again we ignore the effect of the time lag.[7]

The loss ratios in Table 10.2 represent a mixture of actual and estimated economic effects. The premium information in the denominator of the loss ratios pertains to actual premiums paid. The loss figures reflect losses incurred in the initial years of the policy, which have been extrapolated to assess their ultimate impact using the ISO's loss projection factors. The losses experienced were matched to the year the policy was written. Thus, a loss that is paid in 1987 on a policy written in 1980 is charged against the loss ratio in the original insurance year, 1980. Several factors may account for the delay between the time when policies are written and the date the losses are recorded. First, the loss may not occur in the year the policy is written. There may be a lag before the accidental event occurs (for example, when a part breaks) or before the ramifications of an adverse product effect become apparent (such as deferred health effects). Delays also arise because of the nature of the claim settlement process. There is typically some lag between the time of the accident and the filing of a claim, after which there may be a period of prolonged negotiation and perhaps litigation as well.

Because of these lags, the losses that appear in the loss ratio are generally incurred after the premiums are collected. Insurance firms can invest the premiums and earn a return before the losses must be paid, which means that the estimated loss ratios in Table 10.2 overstate the present value of the loss ratio. Moreover, the longer the tail of the distribution curve of claims initiated over time (that is, the more claims that are brought long after the policy was made), the more these estimated loss ratios will understate the profitability of insurance.

Furthermore, the observed losses to date do not fully capture the losses that ultimately will be experienced. To adjust for these lags, the losses in the numerators of the loss ratios in Table 10.2 consist of two components—the actual loss to date plus the additional amount that is expected to occur.[8]

For both loss ratios and premiums, Table 10.2 summarizes the pertinent trends from 1980 to 1984, the five-year average, and the five-year percentage change. Premium trends reflect the combined influence of the price of insurance and exposure levels, which were considered earlier. Although the number of states with and without statutory definitions for products liability are equal, the division of the premium income is not. States without such definitions write about half again as much insurance, a result that reflects the presence of some very large states, such as California and New York, in this group.

Wholly apart from the distinctions across states in terms of the presence of statutory provisions pertaining to products liability, several quite striking characteristics are evident in the table. One would expect a smoothly functioning insurance market to behave differently. Assuming that the number of claims paid does not change greatly from year to year, with a large sample of products liability policies in the companies' portfolios, these losses should be relatively uniform over time and the loss ratios should remain reasonably stable. But Table 10.2 provides a quite different picture of this segment of the insurance industry. First, the loss ratios are quite unstable, particularly for the states with products liability definitions, where they fluctuate from 0.76 to 0.97. For more narrowly refined categories, such as particular product groups, this pattern becomes even more volatile. Second, the source of the industry's complaints about a products liability crisis is apparent, as the profitability of insurance is much lower in states that have not adopted statutes with limiting definitions.

Perhaps the most surprising result from an economic perspective is the persistence of the different levels of loss ratios across the two state groups. States with statutory products liability definitions tend to exhibit consistently lower loss ratios than those without such definitions. Although some effect is expected, it should not persist over a long period of time. Assuming similar numbers of claims over time, competitively priced insurance policies should have the same expected loss ratios across both groups of states, because price competition will force insurance companies in states that have undertaken successful reform efforts to lower their rates. In the long run the terms of the policies should adjust so that the last policy offered in each state is equally profitable as the first.

If one views the loss ratio as the principal measure of the viability of an insurance market, then the implications of Table 10.2 are clear. States that have statutes that include products liability definitions have a consistently lower loss ratio than those that do not. Over the five-year period analyzed, the gap has been narrowing, as one would expect in a competitive market. The loss ratios for the states with products liability definitions were relatively invariant from 1980 to 1984, but there was a decline in the loss ratios for the states without definitions.

The comparisons that appear at the bottom of Table 10.2 are perhaps most telling. The loss ratio in states with products liability definitions relative to states without definitions were quite low in 1980 and 1981, but for the 1982–1984 period they were roughly 0.9. These ratios provide a more stable pattern than the figures in the first two panels of Table 10.2 because they control at least in part for factors that affect loss ratios in all states similarly, such as changes in insurance market competition or fluctuations in interest rates. Premium information is less relevant because it reflects other economic factors, such as the growth in the industries in the affected states. In the case of both state groups, premiums fell in the middle time period and rose by 1984, in parallel with general economic trends.

These data suggest that states with statutes including products liability definitions provide a consistently more profitable context for product risk insurance. It would be an oversimplification to conclude that it is the definitions themselves driving this result. Because such definitions tend to be an integral part of the statutory treatment of liability, a more reasonable interpretation is that the definitions variable serves as a proxy for statutory provisions that on balance foster a more profitable environment for the insurer.

State-of-the-Art Defenses

Less prevalent than the products liability definitions are statutory provisions that relate to the state-of-the-art defense.[9] Fourteen states have products liability statutes dealing with the state-of-the-art concept, twelve of which also had statutory products liability definitions.[10] Thus, states with state-of-the-art provisions are roughly a subset of states with products liability definitions.

A precise definition of the state-of-the-art concept has proved elusive. What constitutes a state-of-the-art design? Is it sufficient for a manufacturer to comply with standard industry practice at the time of the product's manufacture? Must it take advantage of other technologies that are available when it is feasible to do so, and if so, what yardstick should be used to assess feasibility? These generic issues

Table 10.3. Differences in loss ratios and number of claims as a function of state-of-the-art defenses

	1980	1981	1982	1983	1984	1980–1984 average	Percentage change, 1980–1984
States with state-of-the-art defenses							
Loss ratio	0.67	0.83	0.93	0.84	0.69	0.79	3.14
Number of claims (thousands)	2.89	2.88	2.85	2.73	2.51	2.77	−13.05
Premiums ($ millions)	58.96	49.50	43.90	45.07	54.58	50.38	−7.60
States without state-of-the-art defenses							
Loss ratio	0.93	0.85	0.94	1.07	0.86	0.93	−6.64
Number of claims (thousands)	17.35	18.34	16.33	17.51	16.02	17.11	−7.66
Premiums ($ millions)	302.21	273.76	236.19	239.88	278.79	266.17	−7.75
Ratio of states with to states without							
Loss ratio	0.72	0.98	0.99	0.79	0.80	0.85	11.11
Number of claims	0.17	0.16	0.17	0.16	0.16	0.16	−5.88
Premiums	0.20	0.18	0.19	0.19	0.20	0.19	0.00

arise in regulatory contexts as well, and they are very hard to resolve.[11]

Actual state-of-the-art statutory provisions reflect this uncertainty. In some states, such as Indiana and Kentucky, a firm is not responsible for incorporating technical advancement in the design of a product.[12] There is not a similar exemption for warnings, but a producer may be obliged to disseminate warning information to consumers subsequent to their purchase of the product even if the product risk became known only after the sale. A second form of state-of-the-art provision that appears in statutes in several states (including Tennessee and Washington) is that a rebuttable presumption is established that the product is not unreasonably dangerous if it is in compliance with government standards.[13]

To assess the impact of state-of-the-art provisions, consider the data in Table 10.3, which summarizes several of the key series of insurance data for states with and without products liability statutes that have provisions relating to the state-of-the-art defense. The rather infrequent adoption of such provisions is reflected in the low percentage (16 percent) of premiums paid in 1980–1984 in states having such provisions. Nevertheless, the distinctions across the states with and without such provisions is both dramatic and consistent with the earlier results for products liability definitions. Over the 1980–1984 period, the loss ratio averaged 0.79 for states with state-of-the-art provisions, as compared with a 0.93 average for states without them. The patterns appear to be quite volatile, however. Although the loss ratios for the two groupings are almost identical in 1981 and 1982, for 1980 and the 1983–1984 period there is a major gap. Over the entire 1980–1984 period, the loss ratio for states with state-of-the-art defenses displays a somewhat modest 3 percent increase, and the loss ratios for the other group of states are declining, resulting in some narrowing of the loss ratio gap.

This narrowing is expected, but what is striking is that there appears to be a large and persistent spread. The loss ratios in the state-of-the-art defense states are 0.26 lower in 1980 and 0.17 lower in 1984. As the bottom panel of the table indicates, the loss ratio in states with state-of-the-art provisions relative to states without such provisions is roughly 0.8 in 1983–1984. The major economic issue raised by this disparity is how such substantial differences could persist in the long run. One potential explanation for the discrepancy is that the current ratemaking procedures are not sufficiently refined to reflect differences in liability regimes.

The trend in the number of claims summarized in Table 10.3 is also instructive. State-of-the-art provisions presumably affect the plaintiff's prospects of success more than they influence the amount of damages. Thus, they are primarily relevant to determining whether a claim will be successful, and if these provisions diminish the prospects for success they will also dampen the incentive to file a claim. Over the 1980–1984 period, the total amount of premiums paid declined by almost 8 percent for both state groups. One would have expected a similar decline in claims levels in the two groups of states, but somewhat surprisingly the drop in the number of claims is 1.7 times as large in the states with state-of-the-art statutory provisions.

As in the case of the loss ratios, these data suggest two sets of conclusions. First, differences in state torts statutes have a strong effect on the performance of insurance markets in these jurisdictions. Second, the observed differences suggest the presence of a liability environment that is more favorable to insurance firms in states with liability statutes. To the extent that the exposure results indicate a decrease in denials of coverage, this relationship has normative significance as well.

Statutory provisions pertaining to state-of-the-art defenses are not as consequential as the state differences in Table 10.3 suggest. Most states that do not have such statutory defenses have adopted a common law state-of-the-art defense. What these and the other results suggest is that passing liability reform laws provides reassurance to firms and may reflect more general aspects of the litigation atmosphere in states that pass such measures.

Statutes of Limitation

Fifteen states have special statutes of limitation for products liability cases.[14] Eleven of these overlap with the group of states having products liability statutes with definitions provisions. The fifteen states in this group account for 27 percent of all products liability premiums.

Statutes of limitation are particularly pertinent with respect to older products, those that were developed with earlier technologies and that may develop defects over time.[15] The provisions vary across states. In some instances, there is a time limit for filing a claim after an injury occurs, as in the case of Alabama, where this limit is one year.[16] A second form of limitation focuses on the useful life of the product, as in Idaho.[17] States may also place a limit on the time after which the original purchaser of the product parted with possession or control of the product, as in the case of Connecticut, where this limit is ten years.[18] Similarly, there may be a time limit imposed after the original delivery to the consumer, such as that imposed in Indiana.[19] Although the character and nuances of the liability provisions vary considerably, the essential thrust of these provisions is similar. In each case the imposition of a time limit for potential liability should enhance the ability of the insurer to limit the potential losses associated with the policies that have been written.

The data in Table 10.4 do not provide the sharp contrasts we saw earlier. Perhaps the main reason for this difference is that some of the key long-tail insurance lines (those lines for which cases are brought long after the policy was drawn up) are not included in the

Table 10.4. Differences in loss ratios and losses per claim as a function of statutes of limitations

	1980	1981	1982	1983	1984	1980–1984 average	Percentage change, 1980–1984
States with statutes of limitations							
Loss ratio	0.93	0.87	0.99	1.02	0.85	0.93	−8.21
Loss/claim ($ thousands)	19.40	12.76	13.41	14.13	15.25	14.99	−21.39
Premiums ($ millions)	99.97	85.97	76.04	77.46	94.72	86.83	−5.25
States without statutes of limitations							
Loss ratio	0.86	0.84	0.92	1.04	0.83	0.90	−4.32
Loss/claim ($ thousands)	14.61	12.88	13.85	14.68	14.91	14.19	2.01
Premiums ($ millions)	261.20	237.30	204.04	207.49	238.55	229.72	−8.67
Ratio of states with to states without							
Loss ratio	1.12	1.04	1.08	0.98	1.02	1.03	−0.09
Loss/claim	1.32	0.99	0.97	0.96	1.02	1.06	−0.23
Premiums	0.38	0.36	0.37	0.37	0.40	0.38	+0.05

sample. Chief among the omitted products is asbestos, which is by far the product with the largest amount of claims for which statutes of limitation are relevant. The loss ratios are somewhat higher in the states with products liability statutes that include statutes of limitation provisions. The relative loss ratios in the bottom panel of the table illustrate this relationship perhaps most clearly. This minor difference may not represent an adverse influence but instead may be a consequence of the claims mix. The severity of the losses is greater in states with these provisions, at least in part because of differences in the product mix. For the 1980–1984 period, the loss ratio was 3 percent higher for states with statutes of limitations, but the loss per claim was 6 percent greater. Statutes of limitation may be effective in limiting the number of successful claims, but they are not so influential that they offset the influence of the difference in loss severity. The trend in the loss ratio is, however, favorable for states with statutes of limitation, which means that the provisions may be influential in terms of limiting any decrease in the viability of insurance.

Collateral Source Rules and Damage Rules

The size of the payoffs that insurance companies must make will decline if there are collateral source rules or other damages provisions that prevent plaintiffs from obtaining multiple recoveries for a particular injury. The character of these provisions is fairly similar, and I consider each of them in turn.[20] Collateral source rules are included in products liability statutes infrequently. Only seven states representing 8 percent of the premiums have such provisions.[21] Other damages provisions, which often are quite similar in character to collateral source rules, are more prevalent.[22] They are present in fifteen states that have 28 percent of the total insurance premiums.

Collateral source provisions tend to be fairly limited in terms of their scope. For example, the state of Alabama limits the plaintiff's recovery of medical and hospital expenses to only one source.[23] The rationale for this restriction is to avoid "double-dipping": "It is the intent of the legislature that plaintiffs be compensated fully for any medical or hospital expenses incurred as as result of injuries sustained from a breach of products liability laws, but that plaintiffs not receive compensation more than once for the same medical and hospital expenses."[24]

The damages provisions often are similar in character to the collateral source rules even though they are not designated as "collateral source rules." For example, in addition to its collateral source rules, Alabama's products liability statutes also provide that "evidence of medical expenses reimbursement mitigates damages."[25] In some states, the damages provisions in the statute arise in the context of joint torts, under which the liability of each party is tied to the percentage of the fault attributable to each of the parties. The ramifications of the often complex damages provisions frequently are not clear, as they may improve the legal environment of the plaintiff.[26] This cautionary warning will be borne out in the character of the supporting empirical results.

The insurance rate trends in Table 10.5 provide a detailed perspective on the character of the liability crisis that emerged in the mid-1980s and on the effects of collateral source provisions. A rise in loss ratios leading to loss ratios in some instances that are at or close to 1.0 will reduce the profitability of insurance. The drop in coverage is consistent with explanations that cite an availability crisis, but it should also be noted that even without quantity rationing a quantity

Table 10.5. Differences in losses per claim and loss ratios as a function of collateral source rules

	1980	1981	1982	1983	1984	1980–1984 average	Percentage change, 1980–1984
States with collateral source rules							
Loss/claim ($ thousands)	12.21	13.26	12.80	14.48	14.74	13.50	20.67
Loss ratio	0.70	0.91	0.78	0.82	0.72	0.79	2.60
Premiums ($ millions)	30.08	26.79	24.05	23.86	27.21	26.40	−9.52
States without collateral source rules							
Loss/claim ($ thousands)	16.08	12.81	13.80	14.53	15.03	14.45	−6.52
Loss ratio	0.90	0.84	0.95	1.05	0.85	0.92	−6.03
Premiums ($ millions)	331.09	296.48	256.03	261.09	306.06	290.15	−7.56
Ratio of states with to states without							
Loss/claim	0.76	1.04	0.93	1.00	0.98	0.93	0.29
Loss ratio	0.78	1.08	0.82	0.78	0.85	0.86	0.09
Premiums	0.09	0.09	0.09	0.09	0.09	0.09	0.00

decline would also be observed in response to higher prices. Explanations of the liability crisis that attribute the phenomenon to collusion among firms do not appear to be consistent with the data, particularly given the unfavorable implications of high and volatile loss ratios for insurance firms' profitability. Increased costs associated with changes in tort liability are certainly influential, but perhaps the most critical factor is that these higher costs have been coupled with long tails for the loss distribution curves. Thus, there will be a substantial time lag before losses under a policy occur and can be incorporated into the premium structure for subsequent years.

The loss ratio in states with collateral source rules is substantially below that in the other state group. Although the 1980 loss ratio difference of 0.20 had narrowed to 0.13 by 1984, the discrepancy was still substantial and difficult to reconcile with efficient insurance pricing. The statistics in the bottom panel of Table 10.5, which give the relative loss ratios in the two groups of states, indicate consistently lower loss ratios in the states with collateral source provisions, except in 1981. Over the 1980–1984 period, the loss per claim amount was

Table 10.6. Differences in loss ratios and losses per claim as a function of damages rules

	1980	1981	1982	1983	1984	1980–1984 average	Percentage change, 1980–1984
States with damages rules							
Loss ratio	0.86	0.70	0.90	0.97	0.86	0.86	− 0.59
Loss/claim ($ thousands)	21.85	12.26	14.56	14.89	16.12	15.94	− 26.22
Premiums ($ millions)	108.91	92.22	77.41	75.04	90.87	88.89	− 16.57
States without damages rules							
Loss ratio	0.89	0.90	0.96	1.06	0.83	0.93	− 7.32
Loss/claim ($ thousands)	14.10	13.04	13.44	14.41	14.61	13.92	3.63
Premiums ($ millions)	252.26	231.05	202.67	209.91	242.40	227.66	− 3.91
Ratio of states with to states without							
Loss ratio	0.97	0.78	0.94	0.92	1.04	0.92	+ 0.07
Loss/claim	1.55	0.94	1.08	1.03	1.10	1.15	− 0.29
Premiums	0.43	0.40	0.38	0.36	0.37	0.39	− 0.14

7 percent lower in states with collateral source rules, which is also consistent with the expected effect. Most of this difference stems from the loss per claim difference in 1982 and particularly in 1980.

It is especially remarkable that premium trends are identical in both sets of states, at least for the 1980 and 1984 reference years. The difference in the percentage of premiums experiencing an increase in the exposure level was also narrowest in the case of the collateral source rule (see Table 10.1).

There is also a substantial discrepancy in the loss ratio between the state groups with and without statutory provisions for damages. The loss ratios reported in Table 10.6 average 0.07 lower in the states with damages rules, indicating that once again the existence of specific statutory provisions relating to damages enhances the profitability of the insurance. Although the loss per claim amount is somewhat greater in states with damages rules, over the 1981–1984 period this difference is dramatically reduced, as illustrated by the 26 percent drop in the loss per claim amount in the states with damages rules. Indeed, the early high loss per claim amounts may have served in part as the impetus for adopting damages limits.[27]

Table 10.7. Effect on premiums of liability provisions

	Percentage effect on premiums[a]	
	Overall effect	Effect on premium change
Definitions relating to product liability	−4.5[b]	−3.6
State-of-the-art defense	−49.1	−4.9
Statute of limitations	−29.9	−3.3
Collateral source rule	−17.4	−1.0[b]
Damages provisions	47.8	+3.3

a. These results are based on regression analysis reported in Viscusi (1990).
b. These results were not statistically significant at the 5 percent level, one-tailed test.

Effects on Premiums

The final criteria for assessing the effect of liability law reforms are their effect on insurance premiums. Since a variety of factors affect premium levels, this discussion will be based on results derived from a more formal statistical analysis of premium determinants that takes these diverse influences into account.[28] The analysis above, which focused on loss ratios, incorporated such controls by examining the relationship between premiums and losses, whereas this discussion is based on statistical results that distinguish the influence of various factors more formally.

Here we will consider two approaches to analyzing premiums, each of which has similar results in terms of which liability rules are of consequence and in which direction. The results of the first approach, reported in the first column in Table 10.7, indicate the effect of each liability standard on premium levels separately. These effects are in addition to the separate effects that are exerted by the exposure level for the policy, the wage level in the state, the price level in the economy, and the riskiness of the insurance industry's investment portfolio. The second column of results also accounts for such influences but focuses instead on the change in the premium level.[29] In particular, how do liability rules alter the differences in premium levels over time?

In each case, the percentage effect of having the liability provision as compared with not having it are quite substantial. Moreover, in all instances the direction of the impacts are consistent across the two approaches, although the effects are much larger for the premium level results.

The provisions with the greatest negative impact on premiums are the state-of-the-art defense and statutes of limitation, which decrease the premium levels by 49 percent and 30 percent once other economic influences are taken into account. In contrast, damages provisions have a strong positive effect of 48 percent, which is consistent with the conclusion stated earlier in this chapter that such provisions are not necessarily damages caps but may boost premium levels. When the premium level in the previous year is taken into account, the effects are smaller, as one would expect, since much of the influence of liability rules will be on long-term trends in premiums rather than on year-to-year differences. The findings suggest that insurance differences over time continue to reinforce the long-run patterns. States with liability rules that lower premium levels also have diminishing premium levels over time.

These findings consequently suggest that the insurance premium adjustments to liability rules occur gradually over time. A long-term process is to be expected because claims and losses under a policy may occur long after the policy was written, and it may be difficult for insurers to discern what impact a new liability regime will have. What is important is that, as in the case of the loss ratio trends, the market is moving in the correct direction.

Overall, there is strong evidence that legal doctrines affect the insurance market for products liability. In four of the five cases considered, negative and statistically significant effects were observed. In addition, unlike the earlier results, these factors controlled for insurance exposure levels as well as a variety of other economic factors that are likely to influence insurance rates.

Conclusion

The influence of broad differences in state statutes pertaining to products liability is surprisingly great. One might have hypothesized that state laws simply formalize recent developments in common law and are not a binding constraint. Alternatively, one might expect only minor effects because the analysis did not include the recent wave of reforms that the liability crisis of the mid-1980s stimulated. But the performance of products liability insurance over the 1980–1984 period showed strong differences in the influence of state statutes.

Moreover, the direction of the influence followed the expected pattern.

The most persuasive of the state comparisons was the discrepancy in the growth of exposure levels in states with various products liability statutes. In every instance, the fraction of the market exhibiting an increase in the exposure amount was greater for states with products liability statutory provisions. To the extent that the products liability crisis has been reflected primarily in terms of denial of insurance coverage, this measure may be the most useful index of the success of the liability law provisions in preventing the emergence of a crisis.

The more detailed analysis of other measures of insurance performance reinforces this view. In particular, the main measure of insurance profitability—the loss ratio—tended to be considerably lower in states with statutory provisions pertaining to various aspects of products liability. Statistical analysis of premium levels, which distinguished the separate influence of each of these statutory provisions controlling for a variety of legal and economic factors that drive insurance premium rates, also showed the powerful influence of legal rules on insurance markets. Except in one case, there were strong negative influences of the statutory provisions on premiums.

All three kinds of evidence suggest a similar pattern of influence. In particular, statutory provisions relating to products liability have comparable effects whether one analyzes insurance availability, trends in loss ratios, or the effect on premium levels. Although these measures are not unrelated, they do offer three alternative perspectives on the performance of insurance markets, and by any standard of empirical analysis they present very robust evidence in support of the influence of the statutory provisions.

Differences in liability rules have clear-cut effects on both the profitability of insurance as well as its availability. To the extent that one uses an effective insurance market as the normative reference point, these changes enhance economic welfare by increasing the efficiency with which risks are spread in the economy.

These rules have important distributional effects as well, which may account for why more states have not adopted these provisions. No more than half of the states had adopted any of the statutory provisions considered. States with products liability statutes may differ in terms of their political constituencies. Improvements in the indices of insurance market performance may not be the objective of all parties within a state. Consumer groups and corporations, for example, have quite different objectives, and it should not be surprising that reforms that are desirable on only one criterion are not widely embraced. The plaintiff's bar and consumer organizations, for example, oppose limits on damages amounts. Another factor that may contribute to the absence of universal adoption of the measures discussed here is that states with such statutes may differ in some other fundamental way in their liability climate.

Perhaps the most surprising economic ramification of the results is that the influences across state groups were so apparent. If products liability statutes are effective in reducing costs, then these cost savings should ultimately be reflected in lower premiums. Thus, in the long run there should be no difference in the loss ratios across state groups, because the insurance industry should equalize the price of insurance, which is given by the inverse of the loss ratio.

Equalization of loss ratios is not a rapid process. There was evidence of substantial discrepancies across state groups. As predicted by economic theory, these differences are narrowing over time, but the pace of this change is slow. It would be an oversimplification to attribute this sluggishness solely to bureaucratic inertia and a lack of appropriate fine-tuning in the ratemaking procedure, although this may be a contributing factor. Rate making has a product orientation rather than a product-state focus. The premium structure is generally revised on the basis of the observed pattern of losses rather than on the basis of loss expectations subjectively formed according to possible changes in the liability law. Also, because the losses that can be linked to premiums in a given year may not be known for many years, shifts in the liability regime are not rapidly reflected in the insurance rates.

These results and the findings regarding the efficacy of statutory provisions enable us to make some predictions regarding the influence of the many reform efforts undertaken since the mid-1980s. If these efforts are in fact constraining and do not simply formalize prevailing doctrines, one would expect there to be a beneficial effect on the insurance market. These benefits in turn will be evidenced through lower prices for insurance, but they will tend to be apparent only in the long run. In the immediate period after introducing the reforms, the purchasers of insurance in the reforming states will not be able to fully internalize the savings that result, given the lagged response. The profits of insurance companies should consequently rise. Reform efforts that take place on a state basis rather than a national basis are particularly likely to be recognized slowly in the insurance rates charged.

These lags also suggest that one should be cautious in one's expectations and assessments of products liability reform efforts. Products liability laws are not well suited to providing a quick fix to temporary crises. Crises may stimulate interest in reforms, but the desirability of the actual proposals will hinge on their long-term impact rather than more immediate concerns. If the goal is to resolve difficulties in the long run, then a change in the statutory structure may make a difference. Similarly, one should be cautious in making evaluations of the impact of products liability reform efforts. It may take a long time to see the effect of reform on insurance market performance.

11

A Strategy for Principled Products Liability Reform

The surge in products liability costs and the escalation in products liability litigation do not necessarily imply that the law needs reform. Some shifting in the structure of liability may have been warranted, and the move to a more appropriate regime will necessarily be costly. Even after the dust has settled on the products liability insurance crisis of the 1980s, however, it remains clear that there are fundamental problems with the structure of products liability.

Three decades ago there may have been a stronger rationale for the expansion in products liability than there is today. In the past two decades private and social insurance efforts have increased. The government has also launched several risk regulation efforts. There should be a shifting of responsibilities to better exploit the comparative abilities of each of these different institutions. Indeed, as the social insurance and regulatory efforts continue to expand, reform may be needed well beyond what I have specified here.

Many of the most pronounced shortcomings of products liability stem from the overambitious allocation of insurance responsibilities to defendants. Strict liability emerged as a mechanism for imposing more broadly based insurance coverage on firms. Although this kind of insurance serves a valuable role within the context of manufacturing defects, for which insurance is usually feasible, within the realm of design defects the usual insurance analogies break down. The liability burden imposed by design defects is too great to be easily spread across all consumers. When those losses occur with a lag, the extent of the costs is unanticipated. There is no economic basis for assuming that future consumers will bear the burden of the insurance benefits paid to the consumers of the past. With shifting risks and responsibilities over time, this insurance structure will not be viable, as the experience of the private aircraft industry has demonstrated.

In effect, strict liability has established a myriad of social security programs throughout the United States economy. The federal Social Security program operates according to a pay-as-you-go financing scheme, the viability of which is periodically questioned. Private efforts operating with this same kind of Ponzi scheme without the financial resources of the federal government and the ability to require universal participation will not have favorable prospects of success.

The unworkability of the products liability insurance mechanism is most apparent in the case of toxic torts. The huge scope of liability coupled with a long time lag before the link between the firm's product safety decision and the liability burden occurs all but undermine any potential insurance function. In these cases, the funding of liability costs does not resemble so much an insurance market as it does a lump-sum tax. This tax then gets distributed to a group of plaintiffs who may or may not have been adversely affected by the producer's product.

Two other developments—the extension of strict liability to include design defects and the emergence of toxic torts—are inherently flawed in terms of their underlying economics. Moreover, the attractiveness of these policies is undermined even further by the increased prevalence of private and social insurance coverage.

Furthermore, we can relegate the brunt of the task of promoting safety to other institutions. The past two decades have witnessed the establishment of a series of regulatory agencies designed to promote product safety. In a world in which we have a Food and Drug Administration, a National Highway Traffic Safety Administration, and special-mission product safety agencies with substantial staff and expertise, it makes little sense to have juries making sweeping regulatory decisions by assessing design defect issues on the basis of the features of a particular case. When the responsibility for safety has already been assumed effectively by a regulatory agency, this overlap should be recognized and products liability should be used to augment these institutions, not to duplicate its functions.

The increased prominence of hazard warnings cases as a mechanism for demonstrating a design defect is another relatively new development that typifies the manner in which the courts have shifted the responsibility for safety. Whereas hazard warnings presumably should increase the responsibility of the product user to exercise care, in practice hazard warnings simply give plaintiffs another test that producers can fail. Meaningful liability reform will establish a national warnings policy that fosters a better allocation of responsibility.

Since damage awards are the price that must be paid for this increased liability, reformers' attention has focused on this component as well. For the most part, the increase in damages has largely been due to inflation rather than a change in the underlying concepts for setting damages. If courts generally adopt novel damages concepts, such as the deterrence value of life, the impact on products liability costs will dwarf that created by any of the usual items on the reform agenda. In one fell swoop, damages will increase by a factor of ten, transforming the role of products liability in our economy.

The soundest way to approach products liability reform in these areas is to consider it within the context of our two principal objectives, efficient incentives for controlling risks and efficient levels of insurance for the injured. Typical products liability reform discussions pay little attention to fostering consistent adherence to a principle but instead rely on a Chinese menu approach. From the liability doctrine area, reformers select abolition of strict liability; from the damages reform possibilities, they select damages caps; and so on. The only overriding purpose served by these choices is the reduction of liability costs. The apparent objective is not efficient deterrence or efficient insurance, but simply less cost. Undermining the products liability system is not tantamount to sound legal reform. If cost reduction were our sole objective, then we should abolish products liability altogether. Doing so is not sensible, since products liability serves a legitimate purpose. The approach that I will advocate below will not necessarily generate substantial cost relief, but it should lead to a sounder products liability structure.

Consider first the liability criteria. Not only is the current design defect test overly vague, but it also places an infeasibly large burden on producers, who simply do not have the ability to provide social insurance as courts seem to want them to do. I have proposed replacing strict liability for design defects by a reformulation of the risk-utility test in Chapter 4. In effect, this new test functions as a tightly specified negligence standard. The main distinction from the current approach is the recognition of competing merits of safety improvements for product designs in preference to including insurance as an independent objective of any design defect test. Even a reformulated design defect test will not be ideal, since the courts are not well suited to resolving product design questions. Answering these questions requires that greater attention be paid to government regulations, which ultimately should bear the brunt of this effort. If a product is in compliance with explicit government regulations mandating the safety attributes of the product, this compliance should be exculpatory. This defense will make the courts more effective, since courts will address manufacturing defects and those design problems that are not already being handled by institutions with greater expertise regarding the design.

It has often been remarked that a comprehensive risk-utility analysis is too difficult for judges and juries to undertake and that making societal benefit and cost decisions regarding product safety is beyond their competence. Such criticisms are not without foundation, but the solution is not to establish a simpler but less appropriate test for ascertaining product defects. Rather, we should recognize the limited competence of the courts and attempt to shift the task of promoting product safety to those institutions that are better equipped to handle the necessary societal tradeoffs. Courts should limit their focus to specific design changes not already addressed by government regulations. Broad assessments of whether a class of products are too risky to be marketed should be left to Congress and regulatory agencies. Moreover, compliance of specific design features with explicit government regulations should be exculpatory. These reforms constitute the second part of the reform approach I favor.

Third, the products liability system is in need of a risk-utility test for hazard warnings, a national warnings vocabulary, and increased reliance on scientific criteria for assessing warnings. These steps will foster a sounder treatment of warnings. What is most needed, however, is a general recognition that the consumer must play an active role in promoting product safety. The purpose of warnings is to engage the consumer's awareness of the risk so that proper caution can be taken by the consumer.

A sound legal policy toward hazard warnings will not simply create another area in which a product can fail a design defect test. Rather, its main impact should be to shift greater responsibility for safety to the consumer of a product so that the overall scope of liability will be diminished. Current warnings doctrines and the appalling treatment of warnings in the courts have resulted in the opposite effect.

All these measures will foster more targeted and effective risk reduction incentives. Safety incentives will not be created, however, unless firms ultimately pay some financial costs. At the present time, the price that firms pay after being found liable for an injury is appropriate from an insurance standpoint, but this cost is not an adequate incentive for safety in many instances. So long as firms can pay cutrate prices for the injuries their products inflict, tort liability will not fulfill its deterrence objective. If we wish to create appropriate incentives, the products liability system must rely on the same kinds of deterrence values for life and injury used in establishing government risk regulations. These values are not a matter of speculation but a result of highly developed and sound economic methods. Saying that an individual's life is worth $3 million or $5 million may be surprising, but if firms know that they will have to pay damages of this level for injuries caused by product defects they will have an incentive to reduce the risks posed by their products.

These deterrence values have two unambiguously desirable areas of applicability. First, they can be used in assessing liability. Did the firm provide the appropriate degree of product safety? These deterrence figures should be used to value injury costs when undertaking a risk-utility test. Second, in cases where juries now ponder appropriate values for punitive damages in personal injuries, these deterrence values provide much needed guidance. Adopting this approach will make it possible to eliminate punitive damages as they are currently set, since they will become superfluous.

Values based on the deterrence objective are not necessarily superior to the damages values now used, but at least there is a well-established methodology for establishing them. Before using these figures, however, one must determine that there is substantial inattention to product safety that will not be eliminated by the financial incentives created by current incentives generated by the courts.

If our objective is insurance, then we should rely on the more traditional compensation approaches now used by the courts, such as the present value of lost earnings. The difficulty is not with the underlying economics, which is clear-cut. Instead, the problem is with ascertaining the appropriate role of products liability. Do we want products liability to compensate victims appropriately and to send moderate safety signals in situations when it does come into play, or do we want it to assume a greater societal burden for promoting product safety? The shortcoming of the latter approach is that the penalties will be too high from an insurance standpoint. There is a tradeoff between promoting the efficient level of safety and providing the correct level of insurance. The current regime provides reasonably appropriate insurance, but often provides far too little deterrence, whereas the value-of-life numbers establish effective deterrence with excessive insurance.

To strike an appropriate balance between these competing concerns, the courts can utilize the value-of-life approach in selected extreme situations, such as when it is necessary to send a strong signal to a firm that its safety incentives are seriously deficient. The deterrence values will not be intended so much to punish firms as to convey to them the appropriate financial incentives for promoting safety. Instances of repeated patterns of injury or of flagrant underpricing of human life also would merit such treatment.

The Ford Pinto case exemplifies the importance of such incentives. Officials at the Ford Motor Company concluded that the design change for the gas tank location was not worthwhile because the prospective liability burden did not exceed the costs of the design change. Unfortunately, the prospective liability burden was underestimated since it only included lost earnings. Ford Motor Company in effect undervalued the lives that would be lost by a factor of ten. That is the main danger of not using appropriate deterrence values. We are sending firms price signals that in effect enable them to pay ten cents on the dollar for the economic value of the lives that will be lost as a result of product risks. If the courts wish to become a significant social institution for controlling risks, then changing the damages calculation procedure is essential.

Most reform proposals in the damages area focus not on these newly emerging concepts but instead on the role of pain and suffering and damages caps, which will reduce what little deterrent effect the courts now have. As the calculations in Chapter 5 indicated, damages caps will primarily penalize plaintiffs who have particularly high medical costs, such as brain damage victims. There is, however, a general need to rationalize pain and suffering damages, not necessarily because they are at the root of the products liability crisis, but because of their uncertainty and inequity. There has never been a sound or consistent conceptualization of how juries should take pain and suffering into account as they set awards. The scheduling approach that I suggested in Chapter 5 will guide juries in setting damages. The added discipline of this guidance should reduce the uncertainty with respect to pain and suffering compensation, but will not necessarily eliminate it.[1] Since it is generally understood that most plaintiffs use the pain and suffering component to pay their legal fees, further restrictions on pain and suffering awards might lead juries to augment other components of the award.

Although the rationale for these and other reform efforts is substantial, the greater danger is not that reforms will not be adopted immediately but rather that we will embark on an ill-conceived plan that will set back the long-run task of restructuring products liability. The federal regulatory reform efforts of the 1980s are instructive. Several critics interpreted regulatory reform as tantamount to deregulation. In the case of economic regulation, such as restrictions on airline schedules and flights, deregulation was sensible given the altered structure of markets in the latter part of the twentieth century. For social regulation of risks and environmental quality, the deregulation approach was misguided from the outset. There was a legitimate basis for government action that was never recognized by those implementing the reform efforts. What was needed for social regulation was a reform in the character of the policies, not a return to free markets.

The same is true of products liability. There is a legitimate need for products liability to foster improved product safety so long as direct government regulatory efforts remain incomplete. Tort liability also helps to ensure that appropriate compensation reaches accident victims. The solution is not to cap damages and to embrace every reform effort that will put plaintiffs at a disadvantage. Nor should we be content with the current regime, which places inappropriate insurance and design responsibilities on firms. The present system has adverse implications for product innovation and insurance market functioning, and it threatens to undermine the legitimate role that products liability has in our economy. What is needed is a balanced program of reform that recognizes the advantages of a vigorous liability system while at the same time coordinating these functions with other social institutions to better manage the risks in our lives.

Products Liability Costs
in Different Industries

Products liability costs vary substantially across industries. Table A.1 gives the 1980–1984 averages for the distribution of premiums among industry sectors. Although the popular view of products liability is in terms of consumer products subject to defects, in fact premiums are distributed among a much broader spectrum of the economy. Just under half of all bodily injury premiums are for manufacturing, and the great majority of these products—for example, fabricated metals and industrial machinery and equipment—are not consumer items. The leading category, miscellaneous manufacturing industries (Standard Industrial Classification no. 39), does include a large variety of risky consumer products, such as sporting goods, toys, lighters, matches, games, and Christmas trees, but products in this group are by no means responsible for the preponderance of all products liability premiums.

Perhaps the most surprising statistic in the table is the premium share attributed to the construction industry, which accounts for over 21 percent of premiums directly and an additional 2.6 percent through the building materials and garden supplies component of the retail trade category, or about one-fourth of all products liability premiums. In addition, many other categories have construction-related components. Producer goods also account for a prominent share of the products liability burden. Firms that are counted in categories such as durable goods and wholesale trade, industrial machinery, fabricated metals, electronic equipment, and transportation

Table A.1. Distribution of products liability premiums among industries, 1980–1984

Standard Industrial Classification number	Industry	Premium share, bodily injury (percent)	Premium share, property damage (percent)
	AGRICULTURE, FORESTRY, AND FISHING	5.17	5.11
1	Agricultural production—crops	0.28	0.34
2	Agricultural products—livestock	4.39	4.15
7	Agricultural services	0.50	0.62
	MINING	0.94	0.88
12	Coal mining	0.02	0.03
13	Oil and gas extraction	0.85	0.76
14	Nonmetallic minerals, except fuels	0.07	0.09
	CONSTRUCTION	21.13	35.64
15	General building contractors	5.80	9.08
16	Heavy construction except building	2.78	2.93
17	Special trade contractors	12.55	23.63
19	FIREARMS AND AMMUNITION	0.02	0.01
	MANUFACTURING	48.32	38.79
20	Food and kindred products	2.89	1.91
21	Tobacco products	0.02	0.00
22	Textile mill products	0.41	0.34
23	Apparel and other textile products	1.30	0.27
24	Lumber and wood products	0.84	1.16
25	Furniture and fixtures	1.60	0.31
26	Paper and allied products	0.45	0.57
28	Chemicals and allied products	2.32	2.59
29	Petroleum and coal products	0.11	0.25
30	Rubber and misc. plastics products	1.79	1.42
31	Leather and leather products	0.37	0.09
32	Stone, clay, and glass products	0.98	1.21
33	Primary metal industries	0.78	1.31
34	Fabricated metal products	6.77	6.00
35	Industrial machinery and equipment	5.25	3.71
36	Electronic and other electric equipment	2.54	3.20
37	Transportation equipment	2.06	1.17
38	Instruments and related products	1.33	0.68
39	Miscellaneous manufacturing industries	16.51	12.60

Table A.1. (continued)

Standard Industrial Classification number	Industry	Premium share, bodily injury (percent)	Premium share, property damage (percent)
	TRANSPORTATION AND PUBLIC UTILITIES	2.08	2.66
42	Trucking and warehousing	0.06	0.12
44	Water transportation	0.37	0.16
47	Transportation services	0.13	0.05
49	Electric, gas, and sanitary services	1.52	12.60
	WHOLESALE TRADE	5.33	4.83
50	Durable goods	4.06	4.38
51	Nondurable goods	1.27	0.45
	RETAIL TRADE	14.38	9.64
52	Building materials and garden supplies	2.55	2.60
53	General merchandise stores	0.39	0.20
54	Food stores	1.42	0.57
55	Automotive dealers and service stations	0.30	0.17
56	Apparel and accessory stores	0.40	0.16
57	Furniture and home furnishing stores	0.56	0.64
58	Eating and drinking places	5.19	1.89
59	Miscellaneous retail	3.57	3.41
	SERVICES	2.24	2.18
70	Hotels and other lodging places	0.34	0.11
72	Personal services	0.02	0.02
73	Business services	0.25	0.34
75	Auto repair, services, and parking	0.32	0.26
76	Miscellaneous repair services	0.20	0.37
79	Amusement and recreation services	0.00	0.00
80	Health services	0.06	0.03
86	Membership organizations	0.19	0.15
89	Services, not elsewhere classified	0.86	0.90
99	NONCLASSIFIABLE ESTABLISHMENTS	0.36	0.28

equipment are less visibly involved in the supply of consumer goods, but they are fully involved in the products liability system.

Premiums paid for insurance against property damage claims show an even greater concentration in construction and business-related categories. Although this difference between bodily injury and property damage is expected, the overall extent of the orientation away from retail consumer products and services is particularly striking.

In a competitive market, insurance firms should attempt to equalize the prices they charge for any given amount of coverage so that the loss ratios experienced in different industries will be equal. Equalization is difficult to achieve in practice because of the highly volatile nature of the losses that may be experienced under the policies. Despite the fact that the industry groups considered are fairly aggregative and the statistics have been averaged over 1980–1984, substantial variation in loss ratios can be seen in Table A.2. Many quite prominent industries have loss ratios in excess of 1.0, including miscellaneous manufacturing products, paper and allied products, and chemicals. At the other extreme, many industry groups have extremely low loss ratios, as is true throughout the construction industry and the mining industry (in the case of bodily injury coverage). Because these loss ratios may be highly volatile, one should not necessarily conclude that there are substantial inequities of insurance pricing. What these statistics do highlight is the considerable uncertainty in the insurance industry, given that the information that is presented in this table is the primary information used by the Insurance Services Office for ratemaking advice to the industry.

To assess the performance of the market for products liability insurance more precisely, it is helpful to examine in detail the critical measures of insurance industry operation for selected industries. Table A.3 presents such results on a year-by-year basis for six industry groups defined more narrowly than the groups in Tables A.1 and A.2. It is essential to utilize as refined a group as possible, because exposure units may vary and therefore not be effectively combined across industries. In addition, combining industries often masks many important changes taking place within a particular insurance market.

The largest share of premiums for both products liability and property damage is paid in the category miscellaneous services and manufacturing. Because of the substantial heterogeneity of this group, it has no meaningful exposure measure. The loss ratios are quite high, and premium growth was flat or negative in 1981 and 1982 and positive in the later years.

The more interesting set of results is for carpentry, for which more detailed information is available. The quantity of insurance purchased declined dramatically in 1982 and 1984 for both bodily injury and property damage coverage, as indicated by the drop in exposure levels in those years. This drop in turn was reflected at least to some extent in premiums, but the drop in premiums was not as great as the exposure decline because insurance prices rose; the measure of insurance price given by the premium per exposure rose during these years. One would expect in any economic market that as the price rises the quantity purchased will decline, and that is what in fact happened in the carpentry industry. It should be noted that the shifts in premium/exposure levels were accompanied by comparable movements in the loss/exposure levels. The price fluctuations therefore reflected the underlying risks generated by the particular firms receiving coverage.

Restaurants seem to have been undergoing drastic change in bodily injury coverage during the early 1980s. Exposure levels and premiums plummeted, but premiums per exposure level escalated. Higher insurance prices led to a shrinking market.

In some instances, both expansions and contractions in the market are observed. In the case of bodily injury coverage for general contracting—building construction, exposure levels and premiums dropped in 1981, but there was a resurgence of the market in the later years. In this market the decline followed a rise in the prices as reflected by the higher premium/exposure amount, and the expansion coincided with a decline and then a steadying of the price.

The industry displaying the most vigorous expansion throughout the period is the category of miscellaneous wholesalers—durable goods, which had increasing exposure and premium levels for both bodily injury and property damage coverage. In each case, the price of insurance as measured by the premium per exposure level remained steady. Relative to other rising prices in the economy, the real price of insurance actually declined, thus fostering a demand for additional coverage in an expanding economy.

The final pattern of interest here is that in the plumbing—pipe fitting category for property damage coverage. This industry characterizes a steadily declining market in which exposure and premium

Table A.2. Products liability insurance loss ratios by industry, 1980–1984

Standard Industrial Classification number	Industry	Bodily injury	Property damage
	AGRICULTURE, FORESTRY, AND FISHING	0.71	0.42
1	Agricultural production—crops	0.52	0.74
2	Agricultural products—livestock	0.77	0.36
7	Agricultural services	0.25	0.65
	MINING	0.39	0.38
12	Coal mining	0.09	0.24
13	Oil and gas extraction	0.40	0.34
14	Nonmetallic minerals, except fuels	0.43	0.82
	CONSTRUCTION	0.63	0.71
15	General building contractors	0.66	0.70
16	Heavy construction except building	0.50	0.44
17	Special trade contractors	0.64	0.74
19	FIREARMS AND AMMUNITION	7.02	5.94
	MANUFACTURING	1.19	0.76
20	Food and kindred products	0.76	0.85
21	Tobacco products	0.26	0.16
22	Textile mill products	0.92	0.48
23	Apparel and other textile products	0.52	0.33
24	Lumber and wood products	0.75	0.73
25	Furniture and fixtures	0.90	0.64
26	Paper and allied products	6.89	0.82
28	Chemicals and allied products	1.49	1.08
29	Petroleum and coal products	1.05	1.02
30	Rubber and misc. plastics products	0.81	1.07
31	Leather and leather products	0.61	0.26
32	Stone, clay, and glass products	1.38	0.97
33	Primary metal industries	0.75	0.30
34	Fabricated metal products	0.95	0.47
35	Industrial machinery and equipment	1.31	0.73
36	Electronic and other electric equipment	1.07	0.50
37	Transportation equipment	1.02	0.45
38	Instruments and related products	0.80	0.26
39	Miscellaneous manufacturing industries	1.36	0.97

Table A.2. (continued)

Standard Industrial Classification number	Industry	Bodily injury	Property damage
	TRANSPORTATION AND PUBLIC UTILITIES	0.71	0.57
42	Trucking and warehousing	0.19	0.36
44	Water transportation	0.17	0.52
47	Transportation services	0.10	0.09
49	Electric, gas, and sanitary services	0.91	0.60
	WHOLESALE TRADE	0.74	0.65
50	Durable goods	0.82	0.65
51	Nondurable goods	0.50	0.59
	RETAIL TRADE	0.56	0.43
52	Building materials and garden supplies	0.52	0.51
53	General merchandise stores	0.50	0.35
54	Food stores	0.83	0.30
55	Automotive dealers and service stations	0.53	0.28
56	Apparel and accessory stores	0.48	0.02
57	Furniture and home furnishing stores	0.58	0.40
58	Eating and drinking places	0.42	0.09
59	Miscellaneous retail	0.71	0.60
	SERVICES	0.79	0.50
70	Hotels and other lodging places	0.59	1.08
72	Personal services	1.04	0.13
73	Business services	0.84	0.68
75	Auto repair, services, and parking	0.84	1.06
76	Miscellaneous and repair services	0.38	0.23
79	Amusement and recreation services	0.57	0.04
80	Health services	0.26	0.05
86	Membership organizations	1.12	0.21
89	Services, not elsewhere classified	0.89	0.38
99	NONCLASSIFIABLE ESTABLISHMENTS	0.25	0.02

Table A.3. Changes in insurance coverage for industries with five largest premium shares in 1980

	1980	1981	1982	1983	1984
A. *Bodily injury coverage*					
MISC. SERVICES AND MANUFACTURING					
Percent change in exposure	N.A.	N.A.	N.A.	N.A.	N.A.
Percent change in premiums	N.A.	−4.64	−11.73	3.84	20.46
Premiums/exposure	N.A.	N.A.	N.A.	N.A.	N.A.
Loss/exposure	N.A.	N.A.	N.A.	N.A.	N.A.
Loss ratio	1.40	1.17	1.48	1.63	1.36
CARPENTRY FOR DETACHED RESIDENCES					
Percent change in exposure	N.A.	7.16	−57.86	18.86	−181.15
Percent change in premiums	N.A.	−17.92	−27.62	−5.75	11.71
Premiums/exposure	0.51	0.39	0.67	0.53	0.73
Loss/exposure	0.32	0.36	0.75	0.69	0.80
Loss ratio	0.63	0.92	1.13	1.31	1.10
RESTAURANTS					
Percentage change in exposure	N.A.	−98.37	−97.89	−53.24	−97.85
Percent change in premiums	N.A.	−24.55	−83.66	−68.98	98.68
Premiums/exposure	0.00	0.11	0.82	0.55	0.34
Loss/exposure	0.00	0.02	0.51	0.10	0.04
Loss ratio	0.27	0.22	0.62	0.19	0.11
GENERAL CONTRACTING, BUILDING CONSTRUCTION					
Percent change in exposure	N.A.	−37.59	16.12	6.61	29.24
Percent change in premiums	N.A.	−29.77	−11.32	4.30	29.14
Premiums/exposure	0.30	0.34	0.26	0.25	0.25
Loss/exposure	0.59	0.20	0.06	0.11	0.08
Loss ratio	1.96	0.58	0.23	0.45	0.32
MISC. WHOLESALERS, DURABLE GOODS					
Percent change in exposure	N.A.	2.79	1.80	13.82	17.61
Percent change in premiums	N.A.	−7.45	0.12	12.01	19.76
Premiums/exposure	0.34	0.30	0.30	0.30	0.30
Loss/exposure	0.12	0.15	0.22	0.16	0.18
Loss ratio	0.37	0.51	0.75	0.53	0.62

Table A.3. (continued)

	1980	1981	1982	1983	1984
B. Property damage coverage					
MISC. SERVICES AND MANUFACTURING					
Percent change in exposure	N.A.	N.A.	N.A.	N.A.	N.A.
Percent change in premiums	N.A.	0.16	−11.34	2.33	27.41
Premiums/exposure	N.A.	N.A.	N.A.	N.A.	N.A.
Loss/exposure	N.A.	N.A.	N.A.	N.A.	N.A.
Loss ratio	0.80	1.26	1.09	1.07	0.74
CARPENTRY FOR DETACHED RESIDENCES					
Percent change in exposure	N.A.	7.18	−57.39	23.73	−175.95
Percent change in premiums	N.A.	−14.40	−28.11	−3.83	−0.72
Premiums/exposure	0.30	0.24	0.41	0.32	0.42
Loss/exposure	0.07	0.09	0.27	0.16	0.12
Loss ratio	0.22	0.39	0.67	0.51	0.29
GENERAL CONTRACTING, BUILDING CONSTRUCTION					
Percent change in exposure	N.A.	−21.62	−1.49	6.64	35.67
Percent change in premiums	N.A.	−4.89	−1.91	−3.51	−0.67
Premiums/exposure	0.38	0.46	0.46	0.41	0.30
Loss/exposure	0.29	0.35	0.43	0.29	0.26
Loss ratio	0.69	0.83	1.01	0.72	0.72
MISC. WHOLESALERS, DURABLE GOODS					
Percent change in exposure	N.A.	6.53	1.60	15.19	17.07
Percent change in premiums	N.A.	7.04	2.58	7.89	6.72
Premiums/exposure	0.42	0.42	0.43	0.40	0.36
Loss/exposure	0.29	0.35	0.43	0.29	0.26
Loss ratio	0.69	0.83	1.01	0.72	0.72
PLUMBING, PIPE FITTING					
Percent change in exposure	N.A.	−42.37	−14.61	−7.18	−1.60
Percent change in premiums	N.A.	−6.98	−21.41	−13.74	−13.97
Premiums/exposure	0.81	1.30	1.20	1.11	0.97
Loss/exposure	0.26	0.59	0.87	1.10	1.12
Loss ratio	0.33	0.45	0.73	0.99	1.15

levels are dropping. Once again, the declines reflect the changing price structure for the coverage, as is evidenced by the premium/exposure level changes. Moreover, the rising prices have not fully reflected the change in the loss structure, as the loss/exposure levels escalated by an even greater amount.

What these patterns suggest is that there is indeed a crisis in insurance availability, but the character of the insurance industry does not appear to be that dissimilar from the functioning of other economic markets. In particular, as the prices of insurance rises, the quantity purchased will decline. Moreover, in situations in which the prices have escalated, the loss structure has changed similarly so that the relationship between premiums and losses has been maintained. Since the overall national statistics indicate high and in some cases increasing loss ratios in the 1980–1984 period in which insurance coverage dropped substantially, the price increases do not appear to be arbitrary but instead appear to have been generated at least in part through the influence of the changing legal structure for products liability insurance. Indeed, the very high loss ratios that were experienced were evidence of substantial price competition brought about by high interest rates. Price competition did not imply lower prices that would ensure a growing market for insurance, but it did lead to a situation where the overall premiums received often did not exceed the total value of the losses experienced.

The Litigation of Job-Related Claims

Factors Influencing the Disposition of a Claim

Table B.1 breaks down the characteristics of job-related claims in the 1977 ISO closed claims survey according to litigation status. This summary will provide a useful reference point for discussing the implications of more formal statistical analyses reported in detail elsewhere.[1] The table does not sort out the independent influence of each variable controlling for the other factors at work, but it is suggestive of the major operative influences.

A key determinant of the outcome of a claim is the magnitude of the financial loss, since this defines the stakes of the litigation. Claims with large financial losses are less likely to be dropped because the size of the anticipated court award is greater. This result is a direct implication of Chapter 3's litigation framework. In addition, some analysts of the litigation process hypothesize that there is a greater incentive to litigate large loss claims. The observed pattern of large loss claims being less likely to be dropped and more likely to be settled or litigated provides mutually consistent evidence of the impact of higher stakes.

A particularly intriguing influence is the negative effect of bodily injury losses on the plaintiff's propensity to win a court verdict. This result reflects the selection of cases that goes to court. Small-stakes cases that are litigated must offer a substantial probability of obtaining an award for the plaintiff to find it desirable to incur the litigation costs. In contrast, it will be financially worthwhile to pursue a case

Table B.1. Characteristics of job-related claims (means and standard deviations)

Variable	All job-related claims	Dropped claims	Settled claims	Court verdicts
Bodily injury loss ($)	51,800.43	27,755.38	53,815.04	109,165.73
	(232,961.11)	(83,882.06)	(269,588.61)	(195,729.09)
Bodily injury payment ($)	25,644.90	0.00	32,726.22	44,466.66
	(75,770.78)	(0.00)	(78,215.54)	(132,918.91)
Age (years)	36.00	35.62	36.28	34.72
	(12.68)	(11.46)	(13.24)	(11.25)
Sex (male = 1)	0.83	0.82	0.83	0.90
	(0.37)	(0.38)	(0.38)	(0.30)
Years of job experience	5.95	5.94	5.92	6.29
	(5.66)	(5.52)	(5.73)	(5.51)
Fatal injury (0–1)	0.11	0.10	0.09	0.25
	(0.31)	(0.30)	(0.29)	(0.43)
Violation of regulations other than OSHA (0–1)	0.26	0.15	0.29	0.32
	(0.44)	(0.36)	(0.45)	(0.47)
Violation of OSHA regulations (0–1)	0.17	0.10	0.19	0.18
	(0.37)	(0.31)	(0.39)	(0.38)

Subrogation by a workers' compensation carrier or employer instigated the claim (0–1)	0.23 (0.42)	0.34 (0.48)	0.20 (0.40)	0.15 (0.36)
Amount of lien against insured by workers' compensation carrier or employer ($)	9,795.83 (29,881.70)	4,508.55 (18,918.96)	10,615.48 (33,034.20)	15,310.69 (17,747.82)
Indemnification or contribution or subrogation sought by insurer against other parties (0–1)	0.24 (0.43)	0.05 (0.22)	0.31 (0.46)	0.24 (0.43)
Cross complaints involved in the case (0–1)	0.24 (0.43)	0.01 (0.12)	0.31 (0.46)	0.36 (0.48)
State whose law applies has sole remedy rule, and insured most likely would have sought compensation from the employer or workers' compensation carrier where possible (0–1)	0.46 (0.50)	0.47 (0.50)	0.45 (0.50)	0.53 (0.50)
Collateral benefits paid by government (0–1)	0.10 (0.31)	0.08 (0.27)	0.11 (0.31)	0.15 (0.36)
Collateral benefits paid by private source (0–1)	0.59 (0.49)	0.69 (0.46)	0.55 (0.50)	0.66 (0.48)
Theory of liability used in settlement or award is strict liability (0–1)	0.36 (0.48)	0.24 (0.43)	0.41 (0.49)	0.32 (0.47)
Theory of liability used in settlement or award is negligence (0–1)	0.32 (0.47)	0.25 (0.43)	0.36 (0.48)	0.17 (0.37)
Sample size	1447	354	979	114

with a very substantial reward even if the chance of a successful court verdict is slim. This inverse relationship between the loss level and the cutoff level of the required probability of success in court is consequently quite consistent with a rational case selection process.[2] This selection process in turn will generate an observed inverse relationship between losses and the propensity to win in court, as we also observed for all products claims.

The three variables that pertain to the victim capture a variety of factors relating to differing accident propensities and demographic-related litigation costs. Older claimants are less likely to win a court case, perhaps because of the greater role of contributory negligence among older claimants. On-the-job experience has the opposite effect on the claimant's prospects in court, as familiarity with the job tasks should enhance one's safety-related productivity. Sex plays no independent role whatsoever, in part because the bodily injury variable already captures sex-related differences in earnings loss.

Claims resulting from fatal injuries are more likely to be dropped, which in turn reduces the overall rate of out-of-court settlements for fatalities. Litigation costs may be greater in the case of fatal injuries, because the most immediate witness to the circumstances of the accident cannot testify regarding the causes of the accident. Differences in compensation rules for fatal and nonfatal injuries in terms of the treatment of pain and suffering and loss of consortium are also potentially instrumental.

Regulatory violations have a twofold effect: they increase the probability of plaintiff success, and they reduce the litigation costs by simplifying the task of demonstrating that the product is defective. These influences lead to a negative effect on dropping claims, which is coupled with an increase in the rate of out-of-court settlements and court verdicts. OSHA violations do have the expected positive effect on settlements, as do other types of regulatory violations.

Workers' compensation and its interactions with tort liability also affect the disposition of claims. If an insurance company defendant has launched a suit of its own, the claim is less likely to be dropped; the insurer's action in effect indicates a potentially legitimate claim, where the main issue is which party should be held liable. For indemnification actions to be successful, the worker's initial claim must be valid, and there must be a legitimate reason for the insurer to be filing a claim as well.

If there are cross complaints involved between the defendant and another party, the claim is less likely to be dropped and more likely to be litigated. Because of the high drop rate, such claims are more likely to be settled out of court, but conditional upon not being dropped these cases are less likely to be settled or are more likely to be litigated. The cross complaints variable seems to reflect a complex legal dispute that is difficult to resolve without litigation. On balance, plaintiffs have no particular advantage or disadvantage once these claims go to court, so there seems to be no evident bias in the mix of cases that is litigated.

In jurisdictions that have adopted a sole remedy rule, workers' compensation is the worker's exclusive remedy against the employer when the worker is eligible for benefits. Subrogation rules and other rights may also be restricted to some extent in sole remedy states. The sole remedy variable has the expected positive effect on dropping claims.

For much the same reason, collateral payments are also of interest. They may be a signal that other institutional mechanisms may have been a more appropriate source of compensation than a tort liability suit. The receipt of privately provided compensation, such as employer-provided sick leave or disability pay, increases the likelihood that the claim will be dropped and decreases both the settlement and litigation rates, but governmental benefits have no significant effect. Publicly provided social insurance does not imply the same degree of private responsibility for the accident, which may account for the different influence of collateral government payments.

The final set of variables pertains to the liability doctrine that was pertinent to the claim. Strict liability provides the stronger basis for claims since strict liability claims are less likely to be dropped, which is consistent with a higher perceived chance of plaintiff success.

The Determinants of Compensation Levels

Table B.2 gives data on losses and compensation for the nineteen injury diagnoses reported. The injury groups eliciting the most frequent job claims are fractures, amputations, lacerations, and burns, which together account for over half of all claims. Products injuries unrelated to employment have a similar relative frequency in many cases but appear to be less heavily concentrated in the injury groups with large losses, such as brain damage and paraplegia. The third and fourth columns of data report the average loss and payment

Table B.2. Compensation amounts by injury type for job-related products liability claims

Injury diagnosis	Percent of job claims	Percent of job claims/ percent of non-job claims	Average bodily injury loss ($)	Average bodily injury payment ($)	Results for claims with non-zero payments	
					Average bodily injury payment ($)	Average replacement rate
Amputation	16.0	14.5	44,932	35,714	55,100	1.016
Asphyxiation	1.2	1.2	117,862	45,517	110,543	0.598
Brain damage	2.1	3.0	280,982	123,695	161,341	0.496
Bruise-abrasion	5.0	1.1	8,984	1,336	2,829	1.448
Burn	11.4	1.4	44,015	16,002	26,404	1.451
Cancer	1.2	12.0	54,225	48,944	64,003	2.417
Concussion	2.4	3.0	49,971	26,672	40,588	0.652
Dermatitis	1.2	0.5	1,736	1,132	1,750	1.515
Dislocation	0.8	2.0	23,521	23,667	47,333	2.638
Disease	0.4	0.4	87,968	13,428	20,142	10.596
Electrical shock	0.9	3.0	175,551	16,991	27,610	0.148
Fracture	20.5	1.2	32,181	22,488	33,064	1.041
Laceration	11.7	1.2	42,337	7,270	11,999	0.179
Paraplegia	0.5	5.0	769,545	35,935	125,773	0.371
Poison	2.4	0.2	9,520	833	1,535	0.771
Quadriplegia	0.2	1.0	360,000	0	N.A.	N.A.
Respiratory	2.6	5.2	53,394	37,062	50,788	1.045
Sprain/strain	7.0	1.7	10,586	29,056	39,516	3.211
Other	8.8	0.3	84,901	40,898	67,454	0.886

values for all claims, regardless of whether they received any compensation. Although payment levels are below loss levels for almost all injuries, in many cases payments take on a zero value because the claim was dropped or lost in court.

The most meaningful statistics are those reported in the final two columns, which give the average payment levels and the loss replacement rates (that is, payments/losses) for claims receiving some positive amount of compensation. The seriousness of the claimed financial losses varies widely. For several injury groups—bruise-abrasion, dermatitis, and poisoning—the loss levels are under $3,000. At the high end of the spectrum are several injury groups with losses in excess of $100,000: asphyxiation, brain damage, and paraplegia. The large-loss claims typically involve substantial medical expenses.

The general pattern displayed is that the loss replacement rates are generally about 1.0, with an average of 0.794. Overall, there is less than full replacement for financial losses. Diseases are the greatest exception, as they have a replacement rate in excess of 10.0, but this injury group is so small that its performance may not be reliable.

The existence of loss replacement levels in excess of 1.0 for ten of the diagnosis groups does not indicate an irrational outcome. Compensation for pain and suffering and nonmonetary losses, such as loss of consortium for the surviving spouse, are legitimate and important concerns not captured in the financial loss measure.

The considerable degree of replacement for job-related claims is similar to the average performance of products liability claims. The evidence presented in Chapter 3 for all claims indicated an average loss replacement rate of 1.0 for cases settled out of court and 1.7 for successful court verdicts. The frequency of overcompensation of losses is somewhat lower for job-related claims.

Statistical analysis of the factors influencing payment levels indicates the same patterns for job-related claims as for claims more generally.[3] For cases settled out of court, increases in the level of losses raise the compensation amount on roughly a one-for-one basis. The somewhat higher responsiveness of payments to losses for job-related claims may be due to the mix of claims that are picked up in the sample. The job-related claims include only losses that pass a minimal threshold because of the presence of workers' compensation. The very small losses with the highest replacement rates, which contribute to the large drop-off in the replacement rate for all products liability claims as claim size increases, do not appear in the job-related claims sample.

Workers' compensation is a strong influence on the level of compensation. Claims that are the result of subrogation actions with a low claims amount are associated with low payments, but if the dollar amount of the lien is substantial, then the bodily injury payment amount is increased.

Cross complaints have a significant positive effect on payments. Given the fact that a payment has been made, the existence of cross complaints may indicate that the potential stakes were sufficiently large that both parties were willing to incur substantial costs in an effort to shift the liability burden.

Cases that are the result of subrogation actions against the insured tend to be settled for lower amounts, since presumably the insurer or employer who initially assumed the claim bears some of the liability. Thus, both the plaintiff's maximum asking amount and the defendant's maximum offering amount will be less. In contrast, if the insurer has initiated a subrogation or indemnification action against another party, then its offering amount will be greater because of the prospect of recouping some of its losses in subsequent actions. The plaintiff's asking amount will not be reduced, which means that the expected amount of the out-of-court settlement will rise.

It is noteworthy that in many cases workers have already obtained some other type of compensation. In 10 percent of the cases, collateral governmental benefits have been received, and in 59 percent of the cases workers have received private collateral payments. Collateral benefits do not necessarily imply that there will be multiple recoveries, since many of the claims in the sample are the result of subrogation actions by insurers and employers.

Notes

1. Diagnosing the Liability Crisis

1. *New York Times*, July 30, 1988, I, 7:2, from Associated Press. Dr. Glassman's injury was incurred when he fell off a rented horse while trying to hit a polo ball. His suit claimed that his saddle had loosened because of a defective strap. See *Los Angeles Times*, July 28, 1988.
2. *Moran v. Fabergé*, 273 Md. 538, 552–553, 332 A.2d 11, 20 (1975).
3. Fisse and Braithwaite (1983) provide an extensive review of the Pinto case, which will be discussed in greater detail in Chapter 5.
4. *New York Times*, February 9, 1987, p. 25. The subsequent easing of the insurance crisis was accompanied by the introduction of several new roller coasters, including the world's fastest and tallest—the Viper, at Six Flags Magic Mountain in California. See *USA Today*, May 14, 1990, p. 9E.
5. See Posner (1986), Polinsky (1989), and Shavell (1987).
6. *New York Times*, April 28, 1990, p. A1. Fraudulent and exaggerated personal injury claims have contributed to this situation. Many of the hundreds of claimants who emerge following major accidents do not even recall the fundamental aspects of the accident in which they claim to have been involved, such as the time of the accident or the direction in which the train was traveling.
7. *Wall Street Journal*, August 10, 1990, p. B1.
8. See Stimpson (1988) for statistics on the aircraft industry. Since, however, the product liability cost represents the cost for *all* planes ever produced and the number of planes currently produced is low, the liability cost per plane estimate is misleadingly high. Nevertheless, it is clear that this industry has borne substantial costs.
9. See Moore and Viscusi (1989).

10. Liability costs for Colorado ski resorts already constituted 3 percent of their total costs and were escalating, leading ski resorts to seek greater control of these costs. *Wall Street Journal*, January 23, 1990, p. B8.

2. The Dimensions of the Liability Crisis

1. See Tort Policy Working Group, U.S. Department of Justice, *Report on the Causes, Extent, and Policy Implications of the Current Crisis in Insurance Availability and Affordability* (1986); Report of the ABA Action Commission to Improve the Tort Liability System (1987); and the American Law Institute, *Compensation and Liability for Product and Process Inquiries*, Final Report, Preliminary Draft No. 2 (1990).

2. These explanations are articulated in the excellent assessment of the crisis by Abraham (1988). Other assessments appear in Abraham (1987), Priest (1987b), Winter (1988), Trebilcock (1987), and Harrington (1988). These concerns raise more generally the issue of product liability as an insurance market. See Epstein (1985).

3. Insurance Information Institute (1988).

4. See U.S. General Accounting Office (1988) for an assessment of the state court trends.

5. Filing counts in the annual reports of the Administrative Office of the U.S. Courts overstate the actual number of suits that are commenced, since a case is counted every time it is transferred from one district or level to another. See Dungworth (1988) for adjusted case counts for 1974–1986 that reflect similar growth trends.

6. Available data from the Administrative Office of the U.S. Courts since 1984 and estimated shares of asbestos cases in earlier years from Dungworth (1988) indicate that asbestos suits rose from just over 1 percent in 1975 to over 5 percent of all civil litigation by 1987.

7. See data from the Administrative Office of the U.S. Courts.

8. National Safety Council (1988). Also see Viscusi (1984) for a detailed assessment of the trends.

9. National Safety Council (1988), pp. 70–71. Mileage alone accounts for most of the higher accident rates.

10. Ibid., p. 10.

11. The stringency of current asbestos regulations is reflected in the high cost per life saved. See Morrall (1986), p. 30. Moreover, asbestos was recently banned by the Environmental Protection Agency except for very specialized uses.

12. The history of the emergence of social regulation is chronicled in MacAvoy (1979).

13. The asbestos-share statistics for 1984–1990 are based on actual data reported in the *Annual Report of the Director of the Administrative Office of the U.S. Courts*. Figures for asbestos litigation before the statistical year 1984 are estimated values. In particular, the number of asbestos cases commenced is estimated as 0.9598 multiplied by the number of asbestos suits filed, which is the ratio of commenced to filed suits for asbestos for

1984–1986. The share of nonasbestos cases is simply the total number of cases commenced minus the actual or estimated number of asbestos cases.

As impressive as the asbestos statistics are, they may represent but a small part of the total amount of litigation that could arise from occupational disease.

14. See Henderson and Eisenberg (1990).
15. Henderson and Eisenberg (1990).
16. Ibid., p. 572.
17. For example, the self-insurance share for "other liability coverage" was 0.30 in 1983, 0.32 in 1986, 0.31 in 1987, and 0.31 in 1988. Calculations were based on data in Conning and Co. (1987a,b).
18. Conning and Co. (1987a), p. 11.
19. *Wall Street Journal*, May 12, 1986, p. 14.
20. See Insurance Information Institute (1988), p. 34.
21. This estimate for 1985 was prepared by Kakalik and Pace (1986), p. 66.
22. *Henningsen v. Bloomfield Motors, Inc.*, 32 N.J. 358, 161 A.2d 69 (1960).
23. For the history of the development of product liability law, see Epstein (1988), Priest (1985), and Shapo (1987).
24. Insurance Information Institute (1983), p. 6.
25. *Economic Report of the President* (1989), p. 390.
26. Insurance Information Institute (1985), p. 6.
27. Differences in accounting procedures and in the character of industries make the base used to calculate rates of return (i.e., net income) different. In addition, the time pattern for recording losses experienced under policies is an important concern in interpreting insurance returns. In the long run, however, all losses ultimately will be reflected in the rates of return.
28. Insurance Information Institute (1983). Also, see Abraham (1988).
29. The 20 percent figure is based on results for the workers' compensation insurance program, which may represent a best-case scenario.
30. *Economic Report of the President* (1989), p. 308.
31. *New York Times*, March 15, 1990, pp. C1 and C16.
32. *Wall Street Journal*, November 7, 1989, p. A3.

3. The Litigation Process

1. See, among other, Posner (1986), Landes and Posner (1987), Shavell (1987), and Polinsky (1989).
2. For an overview of the data, see Insurance Services Office (1977), which is a survey volume of the data generated by this extensive study by the New York ISO office.
3. There is reason to believe that litigation in mass torts will not assume the same pattern as it does in individual cases. Once a basic pattern of liability is established, as has happened in the asbestos cases, the other cases should start to fall into line, and the variation in the settlement levels should be expected to shrink. But even after this caveat is noted,

the broad scope of the ISO sample contains many different kinds of products liability claims. Although some distinctions proved desirable, there was no evidence of such widely varying behavior as to make examination of the entire sample uninstructive. For the most part, features common to all accident categories determined behavior. The size of the financial loss greatly influenced payment levels, and these financial losses, coupled with the particular legal criteria, largely determined other aspects of behavior. Even for the class of claims that might be thought to be most distinctive—cases of cancer that occur with a substantial lag after exposure to the product hazard—there was no evidence of divergent behavior.

4. This tally of claims pertains to each injured party–defendant combination. A single injury associated with several products would, as a consequence, be reflected in multiple claims.

5. See the 1975 and 1978 issues of *Reports of the Proceedings of the Judicial Conference of the United States.*

6. For a comparison of the ISO data with 1979 data from the Alliance of American Insurers (1980), which involved a much smaller sample of large loss claims only, see Viscusi (1983a).

7. For further discussion of status violations, see Keeton et al. (1984), pp. 220–233.

8. Keeton et al. (1984), pp. 692–694; and American Law Institute (1965), §§ 402A and B. Also see Epstein (1980), for discussion of the evolution and foundations of modern products liability law; and Shavell (1980), for a theoretical analysis.

9. American Law Institute (1965), § 402A.

10. Keeton et al. (1984), p. 684. For a discussion of the economic implications of negligence and strict liability, see Shavell (1980) and Polinsky (1983).

11. See Shapo (1987).

12. Supporting data for medical malpractice claims are presented in Danzon and Lillard (1983).

13. Some of this difference may arise because records which are missing data but which otherwise appear valid have been excluded from my products liability sample. If these are included, the disposition of cases is a bit closer to the medical malpractice results: 32 percent dropped, 64 percent of all claims settled (94 percent of claims not dropped were settled), 3.8 percent of all claims leading to a court decision (with claimants winning 36 percent of all cases). The court verdict success rate for plaintiffs is affected very little, but the number of dropped cases is much greater where cases with missing data are included.

14. According to Priest and Klein (1984), the fifty-fifty split will result under even less restrictive assumptions; in particular, the main requirement is that the parties have symmetric payoffs in court. As I will indicate below, this symmetry in payoffs is not the case.

15. In addition, statistical analysis of the determinants of plaintiff success rates also indicates that some substantive variables, such as strict liability,

have a differential effect. This result also contradicts the predictions of a symmetric case selection model.

16. A more recent study by the U.S. General Accounting Office (1989) of 305 verdicts in five states indicated a somewhat higher plaintiff success rate of 45 percent. Since the plaintiff success rate varied from 33 percent in Massachusetts to 75 percent in North Dakota, the need for a large national sample is apparent.

17. These statistics are a bit overoptimistic in terms of the plaintiffs' prospects since they reflect only those records for which there is complete information. The claims for which there were missing data for many of the key variables consisted disproportionately of claims that were dropped. If one does not exclude such claims, for the overall sample 32.3 percent of the claims were dropped, 63.9 percent of all claims and 94.4 percent of all claims not dropped were settled, 2.4 percent of total claims and 63.9 percent of court decisions involved claimants losing in court, and 1.4 percent of total claims and 36.1 percent of court decisions involve claimants winning in court. These more detailed statistics are reported in Lillard and Viscusi (1989).

18. Viscusi (1986b), pp. 321–346.

19. This and all the remaining discussion of claimant success rates will be based on the estimates presented in Viscusi (1986b) and in Lillard and Viscusi (1990).

20. For similar reasons, large loss claims will be more likely to lead to lawsuits against multiple parties. Since the data reflect only payments by one individual defendant instead of all defendants as a group, the award figures may understate the total payments received by any particular injured claimant.

21. See Lillard and Viscusi (1990).

22. See Viscusi (1988e).

23. This result has been borne out in a formal analysis in Lillard and Viscusi (1990).

24. See Neely (1988), p. 1.

25. See Lillard and Viscusi (1990).

26. Administrative and litigation costs will also tend to follow this pattern if they do not increase proportionally with the size of the loss.

27. It should be noted that this impact on the expected award may be complex. For example, when companies are assessing the expected payoff in court they must also take into account the impact on related products liability actions as well.

4. The Design Defect Test

1. See Fischhoff et al. (1981), Viscusi (1985a), and Viscusi and Magat (1987).

2. Viscusi (1990a).

3. See Viscusi (1988c). Indeed, in this case, warning about low levels of

cancer risks in food produces risk estimates several orders of magnitude larger than the actual risk level.

4. *Wall Street Journal*, "Vaccine Bill Is Bad Medicine" [Editorial], October 24, 1986, p. A12.

5. Specifically, the FDA proposed a package insert noting that "it is not possible to prove that any drug . . . is totally free of risk, or absolutely safe, if taken during pregnancy." Moreover, it concluded that Bendectin had been "the most carefully studied" drug of its type and that there was "no evidence that any drug is safer" for treating morning sickness. The cautious, perhaps even legalistic nature of the FDA's wording is noteworthy. See *Federal Register*, vol. 45, no. 236, December 5, 1980, pp. 80740–80743.

6. Merrell Dow terminated all production of the drug thirteen days after a jury awarded $750,000 to a deformed girl whose mother had taken Bendectin while pregnant. See *New York Times*, June 10, 1983, p. A16.

7. Bureau of National Affairs, *Product Safety and Liability Reporter*, August 12, 1988, p. 768.

8. Further discussion of these data is provided in Viscusi and Moore (1991). The products liability statistics are based on the ISO files discussed in Chapter 2, and the sales data are from the U.S. Department of Commerce. Information on the significance of product and process patents is drawn from the Profit Impact of Marketing Strategies (PIMS) data base developed by the Harvard Business School. The computerized data bases for innovation and products liability were merged by the authors so that the results reported in this table represent an average of firm-specific effects.

9. See Epstein (1980).

10. See Wade (1973). See also O'Reilly (1987).

11. In addition to Wade (1973), see Keeton (1979), and Keeton (1980).

12. *Byrns v. Riddell, Inc.*, 113 Ariz. 264 (1976).

13. See O'Reilly (1987).

14. See Larsen (1984).

15. For an alternative critique of risk-utility analysis, see Priest (1987b).

16. See Schwartz (1988).

17. See, for example, *Cepeda v. Cumberland Engineering Co., Inc.*, 76 N.J. at 174, 386 A.2d 816; and *Gomulka v. Yavapai Machine and Auto Parts, Inc.*, Ariz. Ct. App. Div. 1, No. 1 CA-CIV 9043.

18. See *O'Brien v. Muskin Corp.*, 94 N.J. 169, 463 A.2d 298 (1983).

19. *Comacho v. Honda Motor Co.*, Colo. Sup. Ct., No. 85SC112.

20. *Ortho Pharmaceutical Corp. v. Health*, Colo. Sup. Ct., No. 835A293.

21. *Barker v. Lull Engineering Co.*, 20 Cal. 2d 413.

22. Shapo (1987).

23. See Schwartz and Viscusi (1990a) for further discussion of this example. An excellent discussion of the various defect tests can be found in Schwartz (1988).

24. See Wade (1973), pp. 837–838.

25. Stigler (1987), pp. 70–72.

26. *Beshada v. Johns-Manville Products Corp.*, 90 N.J. 191, 205–206 (1982). More generally, see Epstein (1985).
27. *O'Brien v. Muskin Corp.*, 94 N.J. 169, 179–180 (1983).
28. Priest (1987c).
29. See Kakalik and Pace (1986), pp. 40–41.
30. Ibid., p. 68.
31. Viscusi (1984a).
32. U.S. Bureau of the Census (1988), p. 92.
33. Eisner and Strotz (1961).
34. The schedule for this maximum willingness-to-pay value is given by the demand curve for the product, which has been estimated for many products.
35. The risk-utility measure is positive if the consumer's surplus that is reaped by the purchasers of the product exceeds the unexpected injury costs inflicted by it. When applying this criterion, all deferred impacts should be weighted accordingly—a process known as discounting. Discounting often is undertaken in court cases when the present value of lost earnings for accident victims is ascertained. The reason for discounting is that one must recognize the fact that a dollar today has a higher value than a dollar in the future even if we exclude inflation. In terms of the risk-utility measure, any unexpected injury costs tend to be more remote in time than the benefits. In the case of deferred health risks, this time lag must be taken into account when establishing the appropriate values. If, for example, one were to use a 2 percent real rate of interest when assessing the value of a dollar thirty years hence, one would find that the present value of this dollar in today's money is only 55 cents. Unanticipated future injury costs would consequently be reduced by 45 percent because of discounting.
36. In the economics literature, the profit component is often referred to as the "producer's surplus"—a concept that has been a fundamental part of economic analysis for most of the century.
37. *Dart v. Wiebe Mfg., Inc.*, Ariz. Sup. Ct., No. 17766-PR. Also, see Wade (1973), p. 850.
38. See Larsen (1984).
39. Bureau of National Affairs (1988).
40. See Wade (1973), p. 842.
41. *Patterson v. Rohm Gesellschaft*, 608 F.Supp. 1206 (N.D. Texas 1985).
42. American Law Institute (1965), § 402A, comment i.
43. For a broader discussion of these issues, see Crist and Majoras (1987). Also see Viscusi (1990c).
44. American Law Institute, § 402A, comment k.
45. See Wade (1973), pp. 838–841.

5. The Explosive Mathematics of Damages

1. *New York Times*, March 8, 1988, pp. 1 and 12.
2. Jury Verdict Research (1989), p. 35.

3. For supporting details, see the *New York Times*, May 24, 1990, p. C1, and the *Wall Street Journal*, June 5, 1990, p. B1.
4. See Shavell (1980) and Polinsky (1983).
5. Health impacts also have an important temporal dimension that is not shared in the case of property losses. The welfare losses imposed by temporary financial impacts of accidents often can be ameliorated by drawing upon one's financial resources until compensation is paid. The subsequent compensation through the courts can offset the losses from the resources that were drawn down in order to meet the financial costs imposed by the accident. For health impacts, it is less feasible to transfer resources across time to maintain one's well-being. An accident may inflect substantial pain and suffering. The courts provide future compensation, and there is no mechanism to trade off health losses now for financial rewards.
6. Similarly, the idea of a *hedonic* value of life derives from the statistical procedures used to disentangle compensation that individuals receive for risk from other quality components of the product or job imposing the risk. The early economic literature in this area focused on hedonic price indexes for automobiles, which were simply quality-adjusted estimates of the price of autos that took into account changes in the various attributes of different automobile models.
7. In particular, the insurance amount is based on the level of compensation that would be selected if the individual fully understood the risk and if there were actuarially fair insurance available; in other words, the price of the insurance corresponds to the person's specific risk, and there are no administrative costs.
8. Viscusi and Evans (1990).
9. The figures below are based on joint research with Professor Jerome Culp of Duke Law School using Westlaw and Lexis computer searches. The sample of cases for which amounts actually paid are known is under half the total number of cases and under half the total punitive damages awarded by the courts.
10. Jury Verdict Research (1990), p. 20.
11. See the study prepared for the Association of Trial Lawyers of America by Broder (1986).
12. This calculation ignores discounting for the sake of simplicity. If losses were increasing at a value equal to the rate of interest, the assumption of equal dollars lost per year would be correct.
13. Calculations using information in *Economic Report of the President* (1989), p. 373.
14. Stanley and Peterson (1987), pp. vii–viii, document a 29 percent posttrial adjustment. Moreover, they indicate that in 80 percent of all cases there is no adjustment. Their study focused chiefly on Cook County and San Francisco, California.
15. The slow rate of wage growth in recent years is due in part to the influx of many new classes of workers into the economy, notably women and

black males, each of whom have had less previous labor market experience and consequently will be paid less than the earlier mix of workers.

16. There are good economic reasons for not extrapolating over a thirty-year period on the basis of a single year's statistics. Moreover, these national statistics reflect changes in the worker mix, not simply changes in wages of a particular worker. Even given these caveats, these calculations correctly indicate the pressures that are being exerted on awards levels. In the case of earnings losses, the pressure is clearly downward.

17. Another factor affecting average verdicts is that the mix of cases also may have become more severe over time. The increasing number of asbestos-related cases has altered the case mix toward a more severe class of injuries involving cancer and death. Overall, there is little evidence that increases in awards levels reflect increased generosity by juries. Medical price inflation, not runaway juries, is the principal source of the escalation.

18. American Law Institute (1965), §903, comment a.

19. Ibid.

20. For discussion of this point, see Harper, James, and Gray (1986).

21. Ibid.

22. For discussion of the Belli speech and its use in court, see Harper, James, and Gray (1986), pp. 565–569, and Epstein, Gregory, and Kalven (1984).

23. *Williams v. AirLingus Irish Airlines*, D.C.S.N.Y., No. 85 Civ. 1935. This case was decided in the U.S. District Court for Southern New York in 1987.

24. *Bailes v. Toro Co.*, Minn. Dist. Ct., Hennepin Cty., No. 84-12534.

25. *Newsweek*, August 7, 1989, p. 27. *Blum v. Airport Terminal Services*, 762 S.W.2d 67(Mo., 1988), provided an award of $1.5 million for the fear of a crash and subsequent pain and suffering.

26. See *King v. Eastern Airlines*, 536 So. 2d 1023 (Fla., 1987). The case involved a free fall that took place over the Atlantic Ocean.

27. *New York Times*, August 31, 1990, p. B9. The case involved a park tramway ride in Palm Springs, California.

28. U.S. Department of Justice Tort Policy Working Group (February 1986). See, in particular, recommendation no. 4. Similar issues are discussed within the context of products liability by Schwartz (1988), and for medical malpractice by Danzon (1985) and Weiler (1987).

29. Insurance Services Office (1977).

30. This calculation utilized the Consumer Price Index, where the base year was a simple average of the 1976 and 1977 price levels. For supporting data, see the *Economic Report of the President* (1989), p. 373.

31. The first component of this calculation is the dollar value of the bodily injury payment. From this amount one must subtract the dollar value of the bodily injury loss, which is comprised of three components: medical expenses, wage loss, and other dollar losses. Thus, I define pain and suffering as the gap between dollar payments and dollar loss, when

this amount is positive. This procedure equates pain and suffering with noneconomic losses. In particular, I define

$$PS_i = \text{Financial payment}_i - \text{Financial loss}_i,$$

for claimant i. For awards where PS_i is negative, I set the pain and suffering amount as zero, so that we have

$$[\text{Pain and suffering}]_i = \begin{cases} PS_i & \text{if } PS_i > 0 \\ 0 & \text{if } PS_i \le 0 \end{cases}$$

32. The excess financial payment above the loss may take into account factors other than pain and suffering. More generally, financial payments are influenced by a number of factors, particularly for out-of-court settlements. Bargaining power of the parties and prospects in court also affect payment levels. For example, there may be compensation to the spouse of a fatally injured accident victim for loss of consortium. Another possible financial component is compensation for the victim's loss of ability to enjoy life or a parent's loss of enjoyment of life due to an injury to a child. Aggregating such values with pain and suffering does not involve a substantial simplification, since this compensation is also for nonmonetary health losses. A different class of difficulties arises with respect to financial losses. The loss figures used here are reported losses, not actual losses. The amount of the loss is recorded in the data set by the insurance company. To the extent that this variable reflects the insurance company's loss estimate, the financial loss will be understated. However, if the data set primarily reflects the loss level reported by the claimants, who will have a tendency to overstate their true losses, then pain and suffering will be understated.

    Not only is the net direction of bias unknown, but the bias may also vary with the loss level. Very large loss claims with substantial long-term medical costs may have a very wide possible variance, which means that the propensity for underestimation by the insurance company and overestimation by the claimant will be especially great.

33. For discussion of this cap, see the U.S. Department of Justice (February 1986).

34. This figure is based on regression estimates presented in Viscusi (1988b), table 3. These findings are for nonfatal injuries.

35. The term *hedonic* has also arisen in court cases with respect to compensation for the pleasures of life. Although hazard pay is sometimes specified in labor market contracts, often it is not, and in general one must utilize statistical techniques to disentangle the relationship.

36. A more comprehensive review of the entire literature appears in Moore and Viscusi (1990). By focusing on my studies alone, I avoid discussions regarding differences in methodologies.

37. See Viscusi (1983b).

38. In particular, the estimates were generated using information from the National Traumatic Occupational Fatality Survey of the National Institute of Occupational Safety and Health. This survey consisted of a de-

tailed census of all job-related fatalities in the early 1980s, whereas other measures of death risks were based on Bureau of Labor Statistics surveys that constituted a partial assessment of all death risks.

39. Insurance Services Office (1977), p. 113.

40. See Viscusi and Moore (1987).

41. Although this variation of the deterrence values with income may be somewhat different for worker populations different from those considered, the values provide a general index of the extent of the relationship with income, which appears to be similar to that of other economic damage components.

42. The reason for this less than full replacement is that disabling job injuries diminish the welfare benefits one can derive from insurance. If workers were forced to pay for this insurance themselves in an otherwise perfectly functioning insurance market they would obtain somewhat less than full coverage.

43. U.S. Office of Management and Budget (1989).

44. The components of this calculation as well as Ford's assessment of the values are based on an internal Ford Motor Company document from 1973 by E. F. Grush and C. S. Saunby, *Fatalities Associated with Crash-Induced Fires and Fuel Leakages*, which is cited in Fisse and Braithwaite (1983).

45. Although the $5 million number is an appropriate estimate for this time period, according to the results in Moore and Viscusi (1990), this estimate takes advantage of more recently available data. It should be pointed out, however, that estimates for the 1970s reported in Viscusi (1979) also indicate a value of life in the $3 million to $6 million range, which is comparable to the unit deterrence values used in the table.

46. See Viscusi, Magat, and Huber (1990).

47. Further discussion of an attorney's fee proposal appears in the report of the American Law Institute (1990).

48. An intriguing proposal for addressing the problem of minor injuries is to have pain and suffering floors to eliminate the overcompensation of small claims and to limit pain and suffering to truly serious injuries. See Weiler (1989). This approach would limit court awards for pain and suffering and would eliminate their feedback effects on settlements. What it would not do is eliminate the pain and suffering payments generated by the high litigation costs faced by the defendant. The prospect of such costs makes the firm willing to settle a claim out of court for more than the expected economic damages, and plaintiffs use this extra amount to pay for attorney's fees.

6. Regulation of Product Safety

1. The CPSC bases many of its actions on its injury surveillance system data. See Viscusi (1984a), pp. 48–54, and Viscusi (1985b).

2. See, e.g., Clean Air Act, 42 U.S.C. § 7604(a) (1982); Calif. Health & Safety Code § 25249.7 (West. Supp. 1988).

3. Administrative Procedure Act, 5 U.S.C. § 553 (1982). The process is even more complex than indicated by the Act because agencies' regulatory agendas must be approved annually before they can proceed. See Executive Order No. 12,498, 50 *Fed. Reg.* 1036 (1985), reprinted in 5 U.S.C. § 601 (supp. IV, 1986).
4. Federal Food, Drug, and Cosmetic Act, 21 U.S.C. § 355 (1982 & supp. IV, 1986); see also Grabowski and Vernon (1983), pp. 14–28.
5. 15 U.S.C. § 1392 (1982); 49 C.F.R. §§ 571.209–.210 (1988).
6. 15 U.S.C. § 1472 (1982); 16 C.F.R. § 1700.15 (1988).
7. For an analysis of compliance rates for these standards, see Magat and Viscusi (1990).
8. The average facility covered by OSHA regulations will be inspected once every 34 years at the current rate of enforcement activity. Currently the total annual penalties levied by OSHA are under $10,000,000. Viscusi (1986a), pp. 254–258. For a recent assessment of the effect of OSHA enforcement and a discussion of the data presented in Table 6.3, see Viscusi (1986a).
9. See, for example, the statement by then CPSC commissioner Sam Zagoria, *Washington Post*, November 14, 1983, p. A15.
10. Viscusi (1984c), pp. 324–327.
11. Viscusi (1985b), pp. 527–553.
12. National Academy of Sciences (1990), p. 3.
13. These results are also borne out in regression analysis as well. See Viscusi (1988d).
14. The effect of regulatory violations on out-of-court settlements depends on whether it boosts the amounts defendants offer by more than the increase in the claimant's reservation settlement amount. With symmetric payoffs, there will be no effect. Payoff asymmetry may be introduced if firms will face additional lawsuits involving the product if there is a successful court case against it. Firms will also have relatively higher payoff levels to the extent that claimant risk aversion reduces the certainty equivalent of an expected court award. See Viscusi (1986b, 1988d, 1988e).

7. Hazard Warnings

1. 15 U.S.C. § 1331–1431 (1982).
2. The Saccharin Study and Labeling Act (November 1977).
3. Emergency Regulations, Art. 6, § 12601 (b) (4) (A), to be codified at Calif. Admin. Code Tit. 22, § 12601 (b) (4) (A).
4. Viscusi (1988c).
5. Alameda County Complex Asbestos Litigation, Calif. Ct. App. 1st Dist., Nos. A037335 and A037462, 9/20/88.
6. See, for example, the report prepared for the Office of Policy Analysis, National Institute on Alcohol Abuse and Alcoholism by Macro Systems, Inc. (1987). This influential report, which formed the basis for the congressional imposition of mandatory labeling of alcoholic beverages, mistakenly equates labeling impact with efficacy.

7. Viscusi and Magat (1987).
8. Individuals, for example, greatly overestimate the risks of death from highly publicized events such as earthquakes and tornadoes, but consistently underassess much more consequential risks such as the chance of dying from heart disease or stroke. See Fischhoff et al. (1981).
9. Calif. Admin. Code Tit. 22, § 12601 (b) (4) (A).
10. For supporting discussion with respect to these and other impacts of Proposition 65 discussed in the paragraphs above, see Viscusi (1988c), pp. 283–307.
11. This lifetime risk level of saccharin appears in Travis et al. (1987), pp. 415–420.
12. See Viscusi (1988c).
13. Although such studies have been undertaken for Proposition 65 warnings and for a variety of consumer products such as household chemicals and pesticides, few regulatory agencies or firms have done so. In the face of substantial uncertainties regarding the nature of individual response to warnings, there should be an effort to acquire information on the impact these policies will have before we launch efforts that will have fundamental effects on risk-taking behavior. Put somewhat differently, there should be an effort to devote the same kind of pre-testing and prior assessment of the impact of hazard warnings as is devoted to the test marketing with respect to other attributes of products.
14. Magat, Viscusi, and Huber (1988), pp. 201–232.
15. This discussion is based on the 1986 case, *Uptain v. Huntington Lab, Inc.*, Colo. Sup. Ct., No. 84SC136.
16. Viscusi and O'Connor (1984), pp. 942–956.
17. *Marchant v. Dayton Tire & Rubber Co.*, CA 1, Nos. 87-1487 and 87-1634. Also see *Firestone Tire & Rubber Co. v. Battle*, Texas Ct. App. 1st Dist.,No. 01-87-00241-CV.
18. The risk arises from the greater size and mass of softballs as well as their new poly-core composition. A Michigan head injury case claiming inadequate warnings (*Carol E. Reinhart v. U.S. Slo-Pitch Softball Association, Steeles Sports Co., Liberty Park of America, and Michael Carzos*) led to a settlement in excess of $1 million.
19. *Collins v. Hyster*, Ill. App. Ct., 3rd Dist., No. 3-87-0785, 9130188.
20. *Schilling v. Blount Inc.*, Wis. Ct. App. Dist.I, No. 89-0085.
21. *Argubright v. Beech Aircraft Corp.*, CA 5, No. 88-2177, 3/28/89.
22. *Thorp v. James B. Beam Distilling Co.*, C87-1527-R, D.C. Wash., verdict rendered 5/18/89. Wholly apart from potential fetal alcohol syndrome risks, malnutrition is a possible result of a high alcohol component in one's diet.
23. *Connelly v. General Motors Corp.*, Ill. App. Ct. 1st Dist. 1st Div., No. 1-88-1081. The blowout occurred after a Buick Opel was given an 860-pound load.
24. The court ruled that it would be speculative for the jury to assume that the risks of underinflated tires was common knowledge. See *Leonard v. Uniroyal, Inc.*, CA 6,No. 84-5507.

25. *Jaramillo v. Riddell Inc.*, Calif. Sup. Ct. (San Bernadino Cty.), No. OCV31309. The victim's share of negligence was found to be only 7.5 percent.

26. *Kroger Co. Sav-On Store v. Presnell,* Ind. Ct. App. 4th Dist., No. 4-885A232.

27. *Swayze v. McNeil Laboratories, Inc.*, CA 5, No. 85-1894. A similar principle holds for medical equipment as well. See the ruling of the Missouri Supreme Court in *Kirsch v. Picker International, Inc.*, CA 8, No. 83-2550; *Schrammel v. G. D. Searle & Co.*, CA 3, No. 88-1901; and *Dublin v. Prime,* N.Y. Sys. Ct. 2nd Jud.Dist. Kings Cty., No. 15731/-81.

28. *Smith v. Walter C. Best, Inc.*, D.C.W.Pa., No. 85-2366, 1/18/90.

29. *Tasca v. GTE Products, Inc.*, Mich. Ct. App., No. 98599.

30. Barret et al. (1986), pp. 598–602.

31. One such study of saccharin warnings is that of Schucker et al. (1983), pp. 46–56.

32. For a review of this evidence, see Ippolito, Murphy, and Sant (1979).

33. In particular, for chloroacetophenone, the implicit value of an injury is $23,988 = 1,919/(.18 - .10)$. Similarly, for asbestos, the implicit value of injury is $17,624 = 2,996/(.26 - .09)$. In each case, the implicit value of an injury equals the amount required to accept the risk divided by the magnitude of the risk increase.

34. Moreover, only 11 percent of the workers exposed to asbestos indicated that they would take the job again if there were no wage increase. These workers for the most part were already in high-risk jobs, indicating that this willingness does not represent a breakdown in market functioning.

35. *Moore v. Kimberly-Clark Corp.*, CA 5, No. 88-4008, 3/8/89.

36. *Physicians' Desk Reference*, 1988 ed. (Oradell, N.J.: Medical Economics Co. of Litton Industries, 1988), p. 2066.

37. *Miller v. Upjohn Co.*, La. Ct. App. 1st Cir., Nos. 83 CA 1355–1356, 465 So.2d 42. The Louisiana intermediate appellate court upheld these verdicts in 1985.

38. See, in particular, the comparison of Clorox and Kroger-Bright brand of bleach in Viscusi and Magat (1987).

39. One should demonstrate for each particular instance that the format and structure adopted adheres to the kind of vocabulary one would reasonably expect to be effective in that context. Comparisons within a class of products approved by this regulatory agency will often be instructive in this regard, since it will be indicative of the extent to which the warning departs from what has been achieved by other firms operating within a similar product context subject to identical regulatory constraints. However, compliance with regulatory guidelines that permit substantial variability should not necessarily be exculpatory since one cannot always be assured that these warnings are as desirable on a risk-utility basis as other approaches that could have been adopted.

40. *Ferebee v. Chevron Chemical Co.*, 736 F.2d 1529 (CA D.C., 1984).

41. The genesis of this proposal is the hazard warnings section of the American Law Institute report prepared by Alan Schwartz and myself (1990b).

8. Environmental and Mass Toxic Torts

1. See, for example, Viscusi (1985c) for a summary of the debate over the health effects of cotton dust exposure.
2. See Bureau of Labor Statistics (1989). The shortcomings of these data collection methods are discussed in U.S. Department of Labor (1980).
3. U.S. Department of Labor (1980). The Bureau of Labor Statistics bases its statistics on employers' reports to the Occupational Safety and Health Administration (OSHA) on workplace ailments. These reports may miss chronic illnesses caused by workplace exposures if the illness appears after the worker has changed jobs.
4. Mesothelioma, for example, has been closely linked to asbestos exposure; Selikoff, Churg, and Hammond (1965). Mesothelioma is a form of cancer that originates in the lining of the lung or abdominal wall and has been principally linked to asbestos.
5. By one estimate, potential asbestos industry liability, expressed in current dollars, is $38.2 billion. The net worth of the asbestos industry is approximately $25.6 billion. The combined net worth of the insurance companies that have been involved in asbestos claims so far is $11.5 billion. See MacAvoy, Karr, and Wilson (1982), pp. 76–78. The tremendous scientific uncertainties and difficulties involved in demonstrating causality create a substantial potential variance of the true cost around these estimates.
6. See *American Law Institute* (1965), § 402A.
7. See Wade (1965).
8. *American Law Institute* (1965) § 402A, comment j.
9. See, e.g., *Borel v. Fibreboard Paper Products Corp.*, 493 F.2d 1076, 1089 (5th Cir. 1973), *cert. denied*, 419 U.S. 869 (1974).
10. Keeton et al. (1984). See, e.g., *Borel v. Fibreboard Paper Products Corp.*, ibid. But cf. *Beshada v. Johns-Manville Products Corp.*, 90 N.J. 191, 202–204, 447 A.2d 539, 545–546 (1982) (under strict liability theory, knowledge of a product's hazards is not a valid defense for failure to give adequate warnings).
11. *American Law Institute* (1965), § 523; see also id., § 402A, comment n. Manufacturers of hazardous products can reduce their potential future liability by informing product users of the risks they face.
12. *American Law Institute* (1965), §§ 431, 433. Under strict liability theory, proximate cause is established when the product is shown to be a substantial factor in bringing about the disease.
13. Keeton et al. (1984), p. 713.
14. See Senate Committee on Environment and Public Works (1982), pp. 56–62; Epstein (1982), p. 16. Even if the plaintiff can identify all the suppliers, join them as defendants, and convince the jury that they caused his disease, the court must still decide how to allocate liability among the various defendants. In addition, a producer that is held liable may be faced with its own set of liability allocation issues. Its liability may need to be allocated among several insurance companies, which in turn

may have sold off much of the policy to excess carriers or reinsurance companies. See *Keene Corp. v. Insurance Co. of N. Am.*, 667 F.2d 1034, 1044–47 (D.C. Cir., 1981), *cert. denied*, 102 S.Ct. 1644 (1982). The terms of policies written decades ago may not make clear which party is responsible for occupational diseases that were unanticipated at the time.

Assignment of liability becomes particularly difficult when the worker has been exposed to hazards at a series of workplaces or when a single employer has been covered by a series of insurers. In such situations, the critical problem is determining which point in the exposure-latency-manifestation chain triggers liability. Under an exposure theory, the insurer at the time of the hazardous exposure is liable. Under a manifestation theory, the insurer at the time the worker became ill is liable. See *Keene Corp.*, id., at 1047 (holding that both exposure and manifestation trigger insurance policy coverage). Cf. *Eagle-Pitcher Indus., Inc. v. Liberty Mut. Ins. Co.*, 682 F.2d 12 (1st Cir. 1982) (favoring the manifestation theory), *cert. denied*, 103 S.Ct. 1279, 1280 (1983); *Insurance Co. of N. Am. v. Forty-Eight Insulations, Inc.*, 633 F.2d 1212 (6th Cir. 1980), *aff'd on rehearing*, 657 F.2d 814 (1981) (applying exposure theory under Illinois and New Jersey laws); *Porter v. American Optical Corp.*, 641 F.2d 1128 (5th Cir. 1981) (endorsing the exposure theory).

15. See Viscusi (1984b). The time limits contained in the statutes vary, but they typically run from one to six years after the date of injury in negligence and strict liability lawsuits. The effect of these statutes of limitations is especially onerous in those states where the time period begins on the date of exposure to the hazard. See "The Fairness and Constitutionality of Statutes of Limitations for Toxic Tort Suits," 96 *Harvard Law Review* 1683 (1983).

    Some states have tried to ease the harshness of these time limits by passing laws that toll the statute of limitations until a disease has manifested itself. Other states have gone further and passed laws which toll the running of the statute until the time when the individual has ascertained or reasonably could have ascertained the connection between exposure to the workplace hazard and the illness.

16. Manville Corp., one of the world's leading producers of asbestos, filed for Chapter 11 protection in August 1982 because of products liability suits arising from asbestos production; *Wall Street Journal*, Aug. 27, 1982, p. 1, col. 6. Two other asbestos producers, UNR Industries, Inc. and Amatex Corp., have filed Chapter 11 petitions largely because of asbestos suits. Note, "The Manville Bankruptcy: Treating Mass Tort Claims in Chapter 11 Proceedings," 96 *Harvard Law Review* 1121 (1983).

17. See MacAvoy, Karr, and Wilson (1982), p. 76.

18. See Larson (1952).

19. This result and the data in the rest of the paragraph are drawn from Kakalik et al. (1983), except when noted otherwise.

20. See Kakalik et al. (1984).

21. Schuck (1986).

22. Ibid.

23. The dates for the events in Table 8.1 not reported in the *Wall Street Journal* are based on the chronology in Schuck (1986).
24. Bureau of National Affairs, *Product Safety and Liability Reporter*, December 9, 1988, pp. 1194–1195.
25. Bureau of National Affairs, *Product Safety and Liability Reporter*, September 15, 1989, pp. 901–902. The other statistics in this paragraph are also based on this article.
26. *New York Times*, March 5, 1990, p. C2.
27. *Product Safety and Liability Reporter*, June 8, 1990, p. 644.
28. *New York Times*, June 2, 1990, p. A1.
29. *Wall Street Journal*, September 10, 1990, p. B12. Also see *New York Times*, July 8, 1990, sec. 3, p. 1; *Washington Post*, July 10, 1990, p. D1; and *Wall Street Journal*, July 10, 1990, p. A3.
30. *New York Times*, March 5, 1990, p. C2. In response to these high fees, Judge Weinstein imposed a 20 percent cap on attorney's fees for some cases in 1990. See the *Wall Street Journal*, August 22, 1990, p. B5.
31. The statistics in this paragraph are from Bureau of National Affairs, *Product Safety and Liability Reporter*, November 10, 1989, pp. 115–116.
32. *Wall Street Journal*, March 19, 1990, p. B8.
33. *Wall Street Journal*, November 7, 1989, p. A3.
34. *New York Times*, November 10, 1987, p. 36.
35. *Washington Post*, March 22, 1990, p. E5.
36. Ibid.
37. Makdisi (1989) provides an excellent assessment of the proportional liability concept and its application in tort cases.
38. See Brennan (1989).
39. H.R. 3175, 98th Congress, 1st Session (1983), reprinted in "The Occupational Disease Compensation Act of 1983"; hearings on H.R. 3175 before the Subcommittee on Labor Standards of the House Committee on Education and Labor, 98th Congress, 1st Session 1983.
40. See Viscusi (1984b).
41. Ibid.
42. Ibid.
43. *New York Times*, July 7, 1989. In 1990 OSHA proposed cutting its already strict asbestos exposure level in half. See the *Wall Street Journal*, July 18, 1990, p. B1.
44. The company's extensive testing of the product was generally favorable, but it included one set of results indicating that the product caused cancer in mice. *New York Times*, May 19, 1990, p. 16. Vice President Quayle concluded, as did many other observers, that the product was a "new, safe, and inexpensive substitute for asbestos." See Quayle (1990).

9. Workers' Compensation

1. For a review of the history of workers' compensation, see Darling-Hammond and Kniesner (1980) and Weiler (1986).
2. See Weiler (1986) for a superb discussion of the legal issues raised in

this paragraph as well as the general characterization of the different compensation systems.

3. This shift from a negligence to a strict liability regime is discussed in Chelius (1976).

4. See Viscusi (1984b, 1988a). Weiler (1986) cites statistics showing that workers' compensation compensates only 250 cancer cases per year, as compared with the expected job contribution of thousands of cancer fatalities annually.

5. See the monograph by Weiler (1986) prepared for the American Law Institute Project.

6. Indeed, the issue of who actually pays the tax is an economic illusion that is largely propagated by legislators who earmark workers' compensation taxes as being paid by employers rather than employees. Workers' net take-home pay will be the same irrespective of the labeling of the taxes as an employer or employee contribution.

7. *Chicago Tribune*, August 7, 1988, sec. 2, pp. 1–2.

8. See Moore and Viscusi (1989, 1990).

9. This estimate is based on Moore and Viscusi (1989) and on data from the National Institute for Occupation Safety and Health that 6,901 workers were killed every year in job-related accidents over the 1980–1984 period.

10. Evidence of the impact of OSHA is based on Viscusi (1986c), pp. 567–580.

11. In 1987, for example, workers' compensation premiums were $23.4 billion. See the Insurance Information Institute (1988).

12. See Moore and Viscusi (1990).

13. The size of the wage offset suggests that workers view the level of workers' compensation benefits as adequate from an insurance standpoint. Workers are now valuing increases in benefits at less than the additional premium cost.

14. Some litigation analyses predict that there will be a greater propensity to litigate high-stakes claims, as is borne out in the comparison of job-related and other products claims. See, for example, the discussions in Posner (1973) and Danzon and Lillard (1983).

15. See Weiler (1986), Abraham (1986), and Keeton (1971) for discussions of subrogation provisions. The liens against the insured average just under $10,000. Since only 23 percent of all claims are the subject of subrogation actions, this average includes three-fourths of the observations in which the value of liens is zero. The resulting average lien figure is in keeping with the sample's average loss levels.

16. See Weiler (1986).

10. Will Products Liability Reform Matter?

1. For perspectives on the liability crisis, see Abraham (1987, 1988), Priest (1987b), Winter (1988), Schwartz (1988), Trebilcock (1987).

2. The multivariate analysis in Viscusi (1990b) does, however, take into account the different magnitudes; both approaches yield similar results.

3. *Economic Report of the President* (1989).

4. Although standard errors of the estimates are not reported, all reported differences are statistically significant, given the immense sample size.

5. The Insurance Services Office's rating procedures, described in Webb et al. (1984), place little weight on state differences in tort law: "For other lines the varying loss potential in different geographical areas has been, to a degree, influenced by the particular tort environment in the area. The same considerations do not hold true for many product classes."

6. Complications could arise if states added or repealed their products liability statutes during the period under study. For the most part, however, the groupings changed very little. From a statistical standpoint, one can view the liability doctrine categories as being predetermined rather than as simultaneously determined factors. Of the twenty-five states with products liability definitions, twenty-two states did not have any changes in the statutes from 1980 to 1984. Of the three states with changes, one involved the addition of one subsection to the existing definitions in 1980 and two states (Washington and Kansas) added a set of product liability definition provisions in 1981. Overall, there was very little change in the mix of states with product liability definitions or in the nature of these definitions from 1980 to 1984. Moreover, from 1981 to 1984 there were no changes whatsoever.

7. If refined data were available on the temporal distribution of the losses, it would be the present value of the losses plus the administrative costs that should not exceed the premiums plus any return on the premiums if a policy is to earn a profit. Because of these complications, the discussion below focuses primarily on differences and changes in loss ratios rather than in their level.

8. These projections are obtained using the loss projection factors developed by the Insurance Services Office on the basis of past claims histories. The second insurance component in Table 10.2—premium levels—involves no such projection.

9. *Journal of Product Liability* (1985) is the source of the state-by-state categorizations of the state-of-the-art defense provisions.

10. As in the case of liability definitions, the set of states with state-of-the-art defenses was very stable. Only one of the fourteen states with statutory provisions including state-of-the-art defenses introduced these provisions in the 1980–1984 period. That state, Washington, did so in 1981. One other state made a minor modification—a change in one subsection. Overall, the set of state-of-the-art provisions and the states having them was completely unchanged from 1982 to 1984 and exhibited very little change in 1980–1981. The ISO data consequently allow us to compare two fairly stable sets of legal regimes.

11. Model Uniform Products Liability Act 107, 44 *Fed. Reg.* 62714, 62728-9

(1979). Indeed, the Model Uniform Products Liability Act notes the ambiguity of the state-of-the-art concept and only clarifies it to the extent that it states that it implies that "all post-manufacturing change is excluded from evidence."

12. Ind. Code Ann. (Burns Cum. Supp., 1987) 33-1-1.5-4 and Ky. Rev. Stat. Ann. (Cum. Supp., 1986) 411.310(2).

13. Tenn. Code Ann. (1980) 29-28-105(b) and Wash. Rev. Code Ann. (West Cum. Supp., 1987) 7.72.050(1).

14. *Forum* (1981) is the source of the statutes of limitation breakdown. The set of states with statutes of limitation specified in product liability statutes remained almost invariant over the 1980–1984 period. One state introduced such a provision in 1980, but otherwise there was substantial stability.

15. U.S. Department of Commerce, Draft Uniform Products Liability Law, 44 *Fed. Reg.* 2996, 3008 (1979). The difficulties posed by older products have long been noted, and the United States Department of Commerce has long viewed this as a major area in need of liability reform.

16. Ala. Code (Supp., 1979) 6-5-502.

17. Idaho Code (1980) 6-1303.

18. Conn. Gen. Stat. Ann. (West Supp., 1980) 52-577(a).

19. Ind. Code Ann. (Burns Cum. Supp., 1987) 33-1-1.5-5.

20. The source of the state breakdowns for collateral source rules and damages is the National Conference on State Legislatures (1988).

21. None of the seven states with collateral source statutory provisions in their products liability codes experienced a change in the provisions from 1980 to 1984.

22. Of the fifteen states with damages provisions, two underwent some change in the 1980–1984 period. Damages limitations were introduced in Idaho in 1980 and in Illinois in 1982. For the most part these changes do not affect the composition of the statutory reference group samples.

23. Ala. Code (Supp., 1979) 6-5-520.

24. Ibid.

25. Ibid.

26. Colo. Rev. Stat. (Supp., 1981) 13-21-406.

27. Two states adopted damages limits in the early 1980s, and others did so in the 1970s, but there may be a lag before their full impact can be generated.

28. See Viscusi (1990b).

29. More specifically, the regression analysis included the lagged premium level as an explanatory variable.

11. A Strategy for Principled Products Liability Reform

1. In many instances it should be recognized that the appropriate level of pain and suffering insurance may be zero. Nevertheless, from a deterrence standpoint positive pain and suffering awards are often sensible.

Appendix B. The Litigation of Job-Related Claims

1. The results in this section are based on the more formal statistical analysis presented in Viscusi (1989a).
2. For discussion of this particular selection issue, see Viscusi (1986b).
3. See Viscusi (1989a) for these results.

Bibliography

Abraham, K. 1986. *Distributing Risk: Insurance, Legal Theory, and Public Policy.* New Haven: Yale University Press.

—— 1987. Making Sense of the Liability Crisis. *Ohio State Law Journal* 48:399–411.

—— 1988. The Causes of the Insurance Crisis. *New Direction in Liability Law: Proceedings of the Academy of Political Science* 37(1):54–66.

Ackerman, B., and R. B. Stewart. 1985. Reforming Environmental Law. *Stanford Law Review* 37:1333–65.

Alliance of American Insurers. 1980. *Highlights of Large-Loss Product Liability Claims.* Chicago: Alliance of American Insurers.

American Law Institute. 1965. *Restatement (Second) of Torts.* St. Paul: American Law Institute.

—— 1990. *Compensation and Liability for Product and Process Inquiries.* Final Report, Preliminary Draft No. 2. St. Paul: American Law Institute.

Arrow, K. 1971. *Essays in the Theory of Risk-Bearing.* Chicago: Markham.

Barrett, M. J., et al. 1986. Changing Epidemiology of Reyes Syndrome in the United States. *Pediatrics* 77(4):598–602.

Brennan, T. 1988. Causal Chains and Statistical Links: The Role of Scientific Uncertainty in Hazardous-Substance Litigation. *Cornell Law Review* 73:469–533.

—— 1989. Helping Courts with Toxic Torts. *University of Pittsburgh Law Review* 51(1):1–71.

Broder, I. 1986. *An Analysis of Million Dollar Verdicts.* Washington: Association of Trial Lawyers of America.

Bureau of Labor Statistics. 1983. *Occupational Injuries and Illnesses in the United States by Industry, 1981.* BLS Bulletin 2164. Washington, D.C.: Government Printing Office.

—— 1989. *Occupational Injuries and Illnesses in the United States by Industry,*

1987. BLS Bulletin 2328. Washington, D.C.: Government Printing Office.

Bureau of National Affairs. 1988. *Product Liability and Safety Reporter*, March 4.

Calabresi, G. 1970. *The Costs of Accidents.* New Haven: Yale University Press.

Chelius, J. R. 1976. Liability for Industrial Accidents: A Comparison of Negligence and Strict Liability Systems. *Journal of Legal Studies* 5:293–309.

Conference Board. 1987. *Product Liability: The Corporate Response.* Report #893. New York: The Conference Board.

——— 1988. *The Impact of Product Liability.* Report #908. New York: The Conference Board.

Congressional Budget Office. 1982. *Disability Compensation: Current Issues and Options for Change.* Washington, D.C.: Government Printing Office.

Conning and Co. 1987a. *Alternative Commercial Lines Insurance Mechanisms.* Hartford: Conning and Co.

——— 1987b. *Alternative Markets Update.* Hartford: Conning and Co.

Cooter, R. D. 1990. Economic Theories of Legal Liability. *Journal of Economic Perspectives Conference.*

Crandall, R. W. 1983. *Controlling Industrial Pollution: The Economics and Politics of Clean Air.* Washington, D.C.: The Brookings Institution.

Crandall, R. W., and J. Graham. 1984. Automobile Safety Regulation and Offsetting Behavior: Some New Empirical Estimates. *American Economic Review Papers & Proceedings* 74:328–331.

Crist, P. G., and J. M. Majoras. 1987. The "New" Wave in Smoking and Health Litigation—Is Anything Really So New? *Tennessee Law Review* 54:551–604.

Danzon, P. M. 1985. *Medical Malpractice.* Cambridge: Harvard University Press.

Danzon, P. M., and L. A. Lillard. 1982. *The Resolution of Medical Malpractice Claims: Research Results and Policy Implications.* RAND Corporation Institute for Civil Justice, R-2793-ICJ. Santa Monica: RAND Corporation.

——— 1983. Settlement Out of Court: The Disposition of Medical Malpractice Claims. *Journal of Legal Studies* 12:345–377.

Darling-Hammond, L., and T. J. Kniesner. 1980. *The Law and Economics of Workers' Compensation.* RAND Corporation Institute of Civil Justice, R-2716-ICJ. Santa Monica: RAND Corporation.

Dewees, D. N. 1986. Economic Incentives for Controlling Industrial Disease: The Asbestos Case. *Journal of Legal Studies* 15:289–320.

Dewees, D. N., and R. Daniels. 1988. Prevention and Compensation of Industrial Disease. *International Review of Law and Economics* 8:51–72.

Dungworth, T. 1988. *Product Liability and the Business Sector: Litigation Trends in Federal Courts.* RAND Corporation Institute for Civil Justice, R-3668-ICJ. Santa Monica: RAND Corporation.

Economic Report of the President. 1989. Washington, D.C.: Government Printing Office.

Eisner, R., and R. Strotz. 1961. Flight Insurance and the Theory of Choice. *Journal of Political Economy* 69:355–368.

Epstein, R. 1980. *Modern Products Liability Law: A Legal Revolution*. Westport: Quorum Books.

———— 1985. Products Liability as an Insurance Market. *Journal of Legal Studies* 14(3):645–670.

Epstein, R., C. Gregory, and H. Kalven. 1984. *Cases and Materials on Torts*. Boston: Little, Brown.

Fischer, D. A. 1974. Products Liability—The Meaning of Defect. *Missouri Law Review* 39:339–362.

Fischhoff, B., et al. 1981. *Acceptable Risk*. Cambridge: Cambridge University Press.

Fisse, B., and J. Braithwaite. 1983. *The Impact of Publicity on Corporate Offenders*. Albany: State University of New York Press.

Government Research Corp. 1983. *Victim Compensation: The Policy Debate*.

Grabowski, H., and J. Vernon. 1983. *The Regulation of Pharmaceuticals*. Washington, D.C.: American Enterprise Institute.

Hammond, E. C., and J. Churg. 1968. Asbestos Exposure, Smoking and Neoplasia. *Journal of the American Medical Association* April:106–110.

Harper, F. V., F. James, and O. S. Gray. 1986. *The Law of Torts*. 2d ed. Boston: Little, Brown.

Harrington, S. 1988. Prices and Profits in the Liability Insurance Market. In R. Litan and C. Winston, eds., *Liability: Perspectives and Policy*. Washington, D.C.: Brookings Institution.

Henderson, J., and T. Eisenberg. 1990. The Quiet Revolution in Products Liability: An Empirical Study of Legal Change. *UCLA Law Review* 37:479–553.

Huber, P. 1988. *Liability: The Legal Revolution and Its Consequences*. New York: Basic Books.

Insurance Information Institute. 1983. *Insurance Facts: 1983–1984 Property/ Casualty Fact Book*. New York: Insurance Information Institute.

———— 1984. *Insurance Facts: 1984–1985 Property/Casualty Fact Book*. New York: Insurance Information Institute.

———— 1985. *Insurance Facts: 1985–1986 Property/Casualty Fact Book*. New York: Insurance Information Institute.

———— 1988. *Insurance Facts: 1988–1989 Property/Casualty Fact Book*. New York: Insurance Information Institute.

———— 1990. *Insurance Facts: 1990 Property/Casualty Insurance Facts*. New York: Insurance Information Institute.

Insurance Services Office. 1977. *Product Liability Closed Claims Survey*. New York: Insurance Services Office.

Ippolito, R. R., D. P. Murphy, and D. Sant. 1979. *FTC Consumer Responses to Cigarette Health Information*. Washington, D.C.: FTC Bureau of Economics.

Jury Verdict Research. 1989. *Current Award Trends in Personal Injury*.

———— 1990. *Current Award Trends in Personal Injury*.

Kakalik, J. S., et al. 1983. *Costs of Asbestos Litigation*. RAND Corporation Institute for Civil Justice, R-3042-ICJ. Santa Monica: RAND Corporation.

———— 1984. *Variation in Asbestos Litigation Compensation and Expenses*. RAND

Institute for Civil Justice, R-3132-ICJ. Santa Monica: RAND Corporation.

Kakalik, J. S., and N. M. Pace. 1986. *Costs and Compensation Paid in Tort Litigation*. RAND Institute for Civil Justice, R-3391-ICJ. Santa Monica: RAND Corporation.

Keeton, R. E. 1971. *Basic Text on Insurance Law*. St. Paul: West Publishing Co.

Keeton, W. P. 1961. Products Liability—Current Developments. *Texas Law Review* 40:193–210.

———— 1979. Products Liability—Design Hazards and the Meaning of Defect. *Cumberland Law Review* 10:293–316.

———— 1980. The Meaning of Defect in Products Liability Law—A Review of Basic Principles. *Missouri Law Journal* 45:579–596.

Keeton, W. P., et al. 1984. *Prosser and Keeton on the Law of Torts*. 5th ed. St. Paul: West Publishing Co.

Landes, W. M., and R. A. Posner. 1984. Tort Law as a Regulatory Regime for Catastrophic Personal Injuries. *Journal of Legal Studies* 13:417–34.

———— 1985. A Positive Economic Analysis of Products Liability. *Journal of Legal Studies* 14:535.

———— 1987. *The Economic Structure of Tort Law*. Cambridge: Harvard University Press.

Larsen, K. 1984. Strict Products Liability and the Risk-Utility Test for Design Defect: An Economic Analysis. *Columbia Law Review* 84:2045–2067.

Larson, A. 1952. *The Law of Workmen's Compensation*. New York: Matthew Bender.

Lave, L. B. 1981. *The Strategy of Social Regulation: Decision Frameworks for Policy*. Washington, D.C.: Brookings Institution.

Lillard, L., and W.K. Viscusi. 1990. The Bargaining Structure of the Litigation Process. RAND Corporation and Duke University working paper.

MacAvoy, P. 1979. *The Regulated Industries and the Economy*. New York: Norton.

MacAvoy, P., J. Karr, and P. Wilson. 1982. The Economic Consequences of Asbestos-Related Disease. New Haven: Yale School of Organization and Management, Working Paper No. 27.

Magat, W. A. 1979. The Effects of Environmental Regulation on Innovation. *Law & Contemporary Problems* Winter–Spring:4–25.

Magat, W. A., and W. K. Viscusi. 1990. The Effectiveness of EPA's Regulatory Enforcement: The Case of Industrial Effluent Standards. *Journal of Law and Economics* 23:331–360.

Magat, W. A., W. K. Viscusi, and J. Huber. 1988. Consumer Processing of Hazard Warning Information. *Journal of Risk and Uncertainty* 1:201–232.

Makdisi, J. 1989. Proportional Liability: A Comprehensive Rule to Apportion Tort Damages Based on Probability. *North Carolina Law Review* 67(5):1063–1101.

Menell, P. S. 1990. Environmental Liability Systems in the United States: The Limitations of Legal Institutions. *Journal of Economic Perspectives Conference*.

Montgomery, J. E., and D. G. Owen. 1976. Reflections on the Theory and

Administration of Strict Tort Liability for Defective Products. *Southern California Law Review.*

Moore, M. J., and W. K. Viscusi. 1989. Promoting Safety through Workers Compensation: The Efficacy and Net Wage Costs of Injury Insurance. *RAND Journal of Economics* 20(4):499–515.

———— 1990. *Compensation Mechanisms for Job Risks: Wages, Workers' Compensation, and Product Liability.* Princeton: Princeton University Press.

Morrall, J., III. 1986. A Review of the Record. *Regulation* 10(2):25–34.

Nader, R. 1988. The Assault on Injured Victims' Rights. *Denver University Law Review* 64:625.

National Academy of Sciences. 1990. *Developing New Contraceptives: Obstacles and Opportunities.* Washington, D.C.: National Academy Press.

National Conference of State Legislatures. 1987. *Summary of State Statutes on Products Liability.* Denver: National Conference of State Legislatures.

National Highway Traffic Safety Administration, U.S. Department of Transportation. 1986. *Effect of Car Size on Fatality and Injury Risk in Single-Vehicle Crashes.* Washington, D.C.: National Highway Traffic Safety Administration.

National Safety Council. 1988. *Accident Facts.* Chicago: National Safety Council.

National Traumatic Occupational Fatality Survey of the National Institute of Occupational Safety and Health.

Neely, R. 1988. *The Product Liability Mess: How Business Can Be Rescued from the Politics of State Courts.* New York: Free Press.

Office of Policy Analysis, National Institute on Alcohol Abuse and Alcoholism. 1987. *Review of the Research Literature on the Effects of Health Warning Labeling* (by Macro Systems, Inc.).

O'Reilly, J. 1987. *Product Defects and Hazards: Litigation and Regulatory Strategies.* New York: Wiley.

Pauly, M. 1968. The Economics of Moral Hazard: Comment. *American Economic Review* 58:531–535.

Peltzman, S. 1975. The Effects of Automobile Safety Regulations. *Journal of Political Economy* 83:677–725.

———— 1987. The Health Effects of Mandatory Prescriptions. *Journal of Law and Economics* 30:207–238.

Peterson, M. A. 1987. *Civil Juries in the 1980's: Trends in Jury Trials and Verdicts in California and Cook County, IL.* RAND Institute for Civil Justice, R-3466-ICJ. Santa Monica: RAND Corporation.

Polinsky, A. M. 1989. *An Introduction to Law and Economics.* 2d ed. Boston: Little, Brown.

Posner, R. A. 1973. An Economic Approach to Legal Procedure and Judicial Administration. *Journal of Legal Studies* 2:399–458.

———— 1986. *Economic Analysis of Law.* 3d ed. Boston: Little, Brown.

Priest, G. L. 1985. The Invention of Enterprise Liability: A Criticial History of the Intellectual Foundations of Modern Tort Law. *Journal of Legal Studies* 14(3):461–528.

———— 1987a. Measuring Legal Change. *Journal of Law, Economics, and Organization* 3:193–225.

———— 1987b. Modern Tort Law and Its Reform. *Valparaiso University Law Review* 22(1):1–38.

———— 1987c. The Current Insurance Crisis and Modern Tort Law. *Yale Law Journal* 96:1521–1590.

———— 1990. The Modern Expansion of Tort Liability: Its Source, Its Effect, and Its Reform. *Journal of Economic Perspectives.*

Priest, G. L., and B. Klein. 1984. The Selection of Disputes for Litigation. *Journal of Legal Studies* 13(1):1–55.

Quayle, D. 1990. Now Is the Time for Product Liability Reform. *Product Safety and Liability Reporter.* 23(March):306–309.

Rabin, R. 1987. Environmental Liability and the Tort System. *Houston Law Review* 24:27–52.

Rheingold, P. D. 1990. Appendix E. In American Bar Association Commission on Mass Torts, *Report to the House of Delegates.*

Rosenberg, D. 1984. The Causal Connection in Mass Exposure Cases: A "Public Law" Vision of the Tort System. *Harvard Law Review* 97: 849–929.

Schuck, P. 1986. *Agent Orange on Trial: Mass Toxic Disasters in the Courts.* Cambridge: Harvard University Press.

———— 1988. The New Judicial Ideology of Tort Law. *Proceedings of the Academy of Political Science* 37:4–17.

Schucker, R. E., et al. 1983. The Impact of the Saccharin Warning Label on Sales of Diet Soft Drinks in Supermarkets. *Journal of Public Policy and Marketing* 2:46–56.

Schwartz, A. 1985. Products Liability, Corporate Structure, and Bankruptcy: Toxic Substances and the Remote Risk Relationship. *Journal of Legal Studies* 14:689–736.

———— 1987. Products Liability Reform: A Theoretical Review. In American Law Institute Project on Compensation and Liability for Product and Process Injuries.

———— 1988. Proposals for Products Liability Reform: A Theoretical Synthesis. *Yale Law Journal* 97:357–419.

———— 1989. Views of Addiction and the Duty to Warn. *Virginia Law Review* 75:509–560.

Schwartz, A., and W. K. Viscusi, 1990a. *Defects and Defect Rules.* Philadelphia: American Law Institute.

———— 1990b. *Product Warnings.* Philadelphia: American Law Institute.

Selikoff, I. J., J. Churg, and E. C. Hammond. 1964. Asbestos Exposure and Neoplasia. *Journal of the American Medical Association* 6(April):22.

———— 1965. Relation between Exposure to Asbestos and Mesothelioma. *New England Journal of Medicine* 272:560–565.

Selikoff, I. J., et al. 1967. Asbestosis and Neoplasia. *American Journal of Medicine* 42:487–496.

Senate Committee on Environment and Public Works, 97th Congress, 2d Session. 1982. *Injuries and Damages from Hazardous Wastes—Analysis and*

Improvement of Legal Remedies, pt. 1, pp. 52–62. Washington, D.C.: Government Printing Office.

Shapo, M. 1974. A Representational Theory of Consumer Protection: Doctrine, Function and Legal Liability for Product Disappointment. *Virginia Law Review* 60:1109–1388.

———— 1987. *The Law of Products Liability*. Boston: Warren, Gorham, Lamont.

Shavell, S. 1980. Strict Liability vs. Negligence. *Journal of Legal Studies* 9:1–25.

———— 1987. *Economic Analysis of Accident Law*. Cambridge: Harvard University Press.

Spence, M. 1977. Consumer Misperceptions, Product Failure and Product Liability. *Review of Economic Studies* 44:561–572.

Stanley, M. G., and M. A. Peterson. 1987. *Posttrial Adjustments to Jury Awards*. RAND Corporation Institute for Civil Justice, R-3511-ICJ. Santa Monica: RAND Corporation.

Stewart, R. 1987a. *Compensation and Liability for Product and Process Injuries: Fall 1987 Progress Report*. St. Paul: American Law Institute.

———— 1987b. Crisis in Tort Law? The Institutional Perspective. *University of Chicago Law Review* 54:184–199.

———— 1987c. The Roles of Liability and Regulation in Controlling Enterprise Risks. In American Law Institute Project on Compensation and Liability for Product and Process Injuries.

Stigler, J. G. 1987. *The Theory of Price*. New York: Macmillan.

Stimpson, E. W. 1988. Product Liability: A Root Cause of the Aviation Industry's Decline. *Legal Backgrounder* (Washington, D.C.: Washington Legal Foundation).

Travis, C., et al. 1987. Cancer Risk Management: A Review of 132 Federal Regulatory Decisions. *Environmental Science and Technology* 21:415–420.

Trebilcock, M. 1987. The Social Insurance–Deterrence Dilemma of Modern North American Tort Law: A Canadian Perspective on the Product Liability Insurance Crisis. *San Diego Law Review* 24:929–1002.

U.S. Bureau of the Census. 1988. *Statistical Abstract of the United States*. Washington, D.C.: Government Printing Office.

U.S. Chamber of Commerce. 1976. *Analysis of Workers' Compensation Laws*. Washington, D.C.: Government Printing Office.

U.S. Department of Justice, Tort Policy Working Group. 1986. *Report on the Causes, Extent, and Policy Implications of the Current Crisis in Insurance Availability and Affordability*. Washington, D.C.: Government Printing Office.

U.S. Department of Labor. 1980. *An Interim Report to Congress on Occupational Diseases*. Washington, D.C.: Government Printing Office.

U.S. General Accounting Office. 1988. *Product Liability: Extent of "Litigation Explosion" in Federal Courts Questioned*. Washington, D.C.: U.S. General Accounting Office.

———— 1989. *Product Liability: Verdicts and Case Resolution in Five States*. Report HRD-89-99. Washington, D.C.: U.S. General Accounting Office.

U.S. Office of Management and Budget. 1989. *Regulatory Program of the United States*. Washington, D.C.: Government Printing Office.

Viscusi, W.K. 1979. *Employment Hazards: An Investigation of Market Performance.* Harvard Economic Studies No. 148. Cambridge: Harvard University Press.

—— 1981. Occupational Safety and Health Regulation: Its Impact and Policy Alternatives. In J. Crecine, *Research in Public Policy Analysis and Management* 2:281–299. Greenwich: JAI Press.

—— 1983a. Alternative Approaches to Valuing the Health Impacts of Accidents: Liability Law and Prospective Evaluations. *Law and Contemporary Problems* 46:49–68.

—— 1983b. *Risk by Choice: Regulating Health and Safety in the Workplace.* Cambridge: Harvard University Press.

—— 1984a. *Regulating Consumer Product Safety.* Washington, D.C.: American Enterprise Institute.

—— 1984b. Structuring an Effective Occupational Disease Policy: Victim Compensation and Risk Regulation. *Yale Journal on Regulation* 2:53–81.

—— 1984c. The Lulling Effect: The Impact of Child-Resistant Packaging on Aspirin and Analgesic Ingestions. *American Economic Review* 74: 324–327.

—— 1985a. Are Individuals Bayesian Decision Makers? *American Economic Review* 75(2):381–385.

—— 1985b. Consumer Behavior and the Safety Effects of Product Safety Regulation. *Journal of Law & Economics* 28(2):527–554.

—— 1985c. Cotton Dust Regulation: An OSHA Success Story? *Journal of Policy Analysis and Management* 4(3):325–343.

—— 1985d. Market Incentives for Safety. *Harvard Business Review* 63(4): 133–138.

—— 1986a. Reforming OSHA Regulation of Workplace Risks. In L. Weiss and M. Klass, eds., *Regulatory Reform: What Actually Happened.* Boston: Little, Brown.

—— 1986b. The Determinants of the Disposition of Product Liability Claims and Compensation for Bodily Injury. *Journal of Legal Studies* 15(2):321–346.

—— 1986c. The Impact of Occupational Safety and Health Regulation, 1973–1983. *RAND Journal of Economics* 17(4):567–580.

—— 1988a. Liability for Occupational Accidents and Illnesses. In R. Litan and C. Winston, eds., *Liability: Perspectives and Policy.* Washington, D.C.: Brookings Institution.

—— 1988b. Pain and Suffering in Product Liability Cases: Systematic Compensation or Capricious Awards? *International Review of Law and Economics* 8(2):203–220.

—— 1988c. Predicting the Effects of Food Cancer Risk Warnings on Consumers. *Food Drug Cosmetic Law Journal* 43(2):283–307.

—— 1988d. Product Liability and Regulation: Establishing the Appropriate Institutional Division of Labor. *American Economic Review* 77(2): 300–304.

—— 1988e. Product Liability Litigation with Risk Aversion. *Journal of Legal Studies* 17(1):101–121.

——— 1989a. The Interaction between Product Liability and Workers' Compensation as Ex Post Remedies for Workplace Injuries. *Journal of Law, Economics, and Organization* 5(1):185–210.

——— 1989b. Toward a Diminished Role of Tort Liability: Social Insurance, Government Regulation, and Contemporary Risks to Health and Safety. *Yale Journal on Regulation* 6:65–107.

——— 1990a. Do Smokers Underestimate Risks? *Journal of Political Economy* 98:6.

——— 1990b. The Performance of Liability Insurance in States with Different Products Liability Statutes. *Journal of Legal Studies* 19, in press.

——— 1990c. Wading through the Muddle of Risk-Utility Analysis. *American University Law Review* 39(3):573–614.

——— 1991. The Dimensions of the Liability Crisis. *Journal of Legal Studies* 20:1, in press.

Viscusi, W. K., and W. Evans. 1990. Utility Functions That Depend on Health Status: Estimates and Economic Implications. *American Economic Review* 80(3):353–374.

Viscusi, W. K., and J. Hersch. 1990. The Market Response to Product Safety Litigation. *Journal of Regulatory Economics* 2:2, in press.

Viscusi, W. K., and W. A. Magat. 1987. *Learning about Risk: Consumer and Worker Responses to Hazard Information.* Cambridge: Harvard University Press.

Viscusi, W. K., and M. J. Moore. 1987. Workers' Compensation: Wage Effects, Benefit Inadequacies, and the Value of Health Losses. *Review of Economics and Statistics* 69(2):249–261.

——— 1991. Rationalizing the Relationship between Product Liability and Innovation. In Peter Schuck, ed., *Tort Law and the Public Intent: Competition, Innovation, and Consumer Welfare.* New York: Norton.

Viscusi, W. K., and C. J. O'Connor. 1984. Adaptive Responses to Chemical Labeling: Are Workers Bayesian Decision Makers? *American Economic Review* 74:942–956.

Viscusi, W. K., W. A. Magat, and J. Huber. 1991. Pricing Environmental Health Risks: Survey Assessments of Risk-Risk and Risk-Dollar Trade-offs for Chronic Bronchitis. *Journal of Environmental Economics and Management,* vol. 20, forthcoming.

Wade, J. W. 1965. Strict Tort Liability of Manufacturers. *Southwestern Law Journal* 19:5–25.

Wade, J. 1973. On the Nature of Strict Tort Liability for Products. *Mississippi Law Journal* 44:825–851.

Webb, B., et al. 1984. *Insurance Industry Operations,* vol. II. Malvern: American Institute for Property and Liability Underwriters.

Weiler, P. 1986. *Legal Policy for Workplace Injuries.* Philadelphia: American Law Institute Project on Compensation and Liability for Product and Process Injuries.

——— 1987. *Legal Policy for Medical Injuries: The Issues, the Options, and the Evidence.* Philadelphia: American Law Institute Project on Compensation and Liability for Product and Process Inquiries.

—— 1989. Workers' Compensation and Product Liability: The Interaction of a Tort and Non-Tort Regime. *Ohio State Law Journal* 50:825–854.

Winter, R. A. 1988. The Liability Crisis and the Dynamics of Competitive Insurance Markets. *Yale Journal on Regulation* 5:455–499.

—— 1990. The Liability Insurance Market. Stanford Conference on "The Law and Economics of Liability."

Index